THE FATHERS OF THE CHURCH

A NEW TRANSLATION

VOLUME 140

THE FATHERS OF THE CHURCH

A NEW TRANSLATION

ST. AMBROSE

TREATISES ON NOAH AND DAVID

Translated by

BRIAN P. DUNKLE, SJ
Boston College School of Theology and Ministry

THE CATHOLIC UNIVERSITY OF AMERICA PRESS
Washington, D.C.

Printed in the United States of America
The paper used in this publication meets the minimum requirements of the American National Standards for Information Science—Permanence of Paper for Printed Library Materials, ANSI Z39.48 - 1984.
∞
Library of Congress Cataloging-in-Publication Data is available from the Library of Congress.
ISBN 978-0-8132-3239-3

In Memory of Matthew Dunkle

CONTENTS

ACKNOWLEDGMENTS

This volume began in Fall 2015, when I proposed a Latin translation project to the members of my seminar "Ambrose of Milan" as a supplement to the course readings. A group of students, including Mark Daniel, Deepan Rajaratnam, Juan Carlos Rivera, SJ, and Kathleen Schmitz, worked with me through the opening sections of *On Noah,* which I knew was unavailable in English. Another member of the group, Jason LaLonde, SJ, supplied a careful translation of a section of the treatise for his final paper, which I have consulted. I am grateful to them all. In particular, I owe a great debt to another member of the class, Richard Nichols, SJ, who read through the complete translation and caught quite a few oversights and blunders. My parents, John and Margaret Dunkle, served yet again as careful proofreaders, and I thank Michael Magree, SJ, and Aaron Pidel, SJ, for advice on some details of translation. Carole Monica Burnett at Catholic University of America Press has been a tremendous help in the editing and production of the volume.

I finished revisions to the translations at the beginning of my time as the Patricia H. Imbesi Fellow at Villanova University's Augustinian Institute. Allan Fitzgerald, OSA, the Institute's director, and Anna Misticoni offered me a warm welcome and generous hospitality during the privileged semester of Spring 2018. I thank the members of the St. Joseph's University Jesuit community for their friendship and conversation while I resided in Philadelphia. My colleagues at the Boston College School of Theology and Ministry, especially the dean, Thomas Stegman, SJ, have been vital supports to my research and teaching, above all by shielding me from the demands of committee work in my initial years on the faculty. I also thank my rectors, James Gartland, SJ, and Michael Boughton, SJ, as well as the members of St. Peter Faber Jesuit community, especially those I have lived with in St. Francis Xavier House. They have all been very kind to me.

ABBREVIATIONS

Ambrose of Milan

Apol. alt.	*Apologia altera*
Apol. Dau.	*De apologia prophetae Dauid*
Ep.	*Epistulae*
Ep. ext. coll.	*Epistulae extra collectionem*
Eu. sec. Lucam	*Expositio euangelii secundum Lucam*
Fid.	*De fide (ad Gratianum Augustum)*
Noe	*De Noe*

Other Authors

QG	Philo of Alexandria, *Quaestiones et solutiones in Genesim*

General Abbreviations

CSEL	Corpus Scriptorum Ecclesiasticorum Latinorum (Prague, Vienna, Leipzig)
LXX	Septuagint
SAEMO	Sancti Ambrosii Episcopi Mediolanensis Opera (Milan)
SC	Sources Chrétiennes (Paris)

SELECT BIBLIOGRAPHY

Sources

Ambrose of Milan. *Apologia prophetae David ad Theodosium Augustum*. Edited by Pierre Hadot. SC 239. Paris: Cerf, 1977.

———. *De Iacob, De Ioseph, De patriarchis, De fuga saeculi, De interpellatione Iob et David, De apologia prophetae David, De Helia, De Nabuthae, De Tobia*. Edited by Karl Schenkl. CSEL 32/2. Prague, Vienna, Leipzig, 1897.

———. *Exameron, De paradiso, De Cain, De Noe, De Abraham, De Isaac, De bono mortis*. Edited by Karl Schenkl. CSEL 32/1. Prague, Vienna, Leipzig, 1896.

———. *Opere esegetiche II/I: Il paradiso terrestre; Caino e Abele; Noè*. Introduction, translation, and notes for *Il paradiso terrestre* and *Caino e Abele* by Paolo Siniscalco; for *Noè* by Agostino Pastorino. SAEMO 2.1. Milan: Biblioteca Ambrosiana, 1984.

———. *Opere esegetiche V: Le due apologie di David*. Introduction, translation, and notes by Filippo Lucidi. SAEMO 5. Milan: Biblioteca Ambrosiana, 1981.

Philo of Alexandria. *Questions and Answers on Genesis*. English translation of the Armenian by Ralph Marcus. Cambridge, MA: Harvard University Press, 1953.

Literature

Bonato, Antonio. "Il tema della giustizia nel pensiero di Ambrogio." In *Giustizia—Giustificazione nei Padri della Chiesa,* edited by Antonio Bonato, 225–73. Rome: Borla, 2001.

Brown, Peter. *Power and Persuasion in Late Antiquity: Towards a Christian Empire*. Madison: University of Wisconsin Press, 1992.

Claus, Felix. "La datation de l''Apologia prophetae David' et de l''Apologia David altera'; Deux oeuvres authentiques de Saint Ambroise." In *Ambrosius Episcopus,* edited by Giuseppe Lazzati, 168–93. Milan: Vita e Pensiero, 1976.

Colish, Marcia. *Ambrose's Patriarchs: Ethics for the Common Man*. Notre Dame, IN: University of Notre Dame Press, 2005.

Connolly, Richard Hugh. "Some Disputed Works of St. Ambrose." *Downside Review* 65 (1947): 7–20 and 121–30.

Dassmann, Ernst. *Frömmigkeit des Kirchenvaters Ambrosius von Mailand: Quellen und Entfaltung.* Münster: Aschendorffsche, 1965.

De Capitani, Franco. "Analogie fra una opera ambrosiana discussa ed alcuni scritti antimanichei di sant'Agostino." *Rivista di Filosofia Neoscolastica* 66 (1974): 59–88.

Dunkle, SJ, Brian. *Enchantment and Creed in the Hymns of Ambrose of Milan.* Oxford: Oxford University Press, 2016.

———. "Sin, Mercy, and David's *Felix Culpa*," for *Studia Patristica: Papers Presented at the Eighteenth International Conference on Patristic Studies Held in Oxford, 2019.* Forthcoming.

Frede, Hermann Josef. "Problem des ambrosianischen Bibeltextes." In *Ambrosius Episcopus,* edited by Giuseppe Lazzati, 365–92. Milan: Vita e Pensiero, 1976.

Graumann, Thomas. *Christus Interpres: Die Einheit von Auslegung und Verkündigung in der Lukaserklärung des Ambrosius von Mailand.* Berlin: de Gruyter, 1994.

Hadot, Pierre. "Une source de l'*Apologia David* d'Ambroise: Les commentaires de Didyme et d'Origène sur le psaume 50." *Revue des sciences philosophiques et théologiques* 60 (1976): 205–25.

Lazzati, Giuseppe. *Il valore letterario della esegesi ambrosiana.* Milan: Archivio Ambrosiano, 1960.

Leppin, Hartmut. "Das Alte Testament und der Erfahrungsraum der Christen. Davids Buße in den Apologien des Ambrosius." In *Die Bibel als politisches Argument. Voraussetzungen und Folgen biblizistischer Herrschaftslegitimation in der Vormoderne,* edited by Andreas Pečar and Kai Trampedach, 119–33. Munich: R. Oldenbourg, 2007.

———. "Zum politischen Denken des Ambrosius: Das Kaisertum als pastorales Problem." In *Die Christlich-philosophischen Diskurse in der Spätantike: Texte, Personen, Institutionen,* edited by Therese Fuhrer, 33–49. Stuttgart: Franz Steiner, 2008.

Madec, Goulven. *Saint Ambroise et la philosophie.* Paris: Études Augustiniennes, 1974.

Markschies, Christoph. "Ambrosius und Origenes: Bemerkungen zur exegetischen Hermeneutik zweier Kirchenväter." In *Origeniana Septima: Origenes in den Auseinandersetzungen des 4. Jahrhunderts,* edited by Wolfgang A. Bienert and Uwe Kühneweg, 545–70. Leuven: Leuven University Press, 1999.

McCarthy, Michael C. "Divine Wrath and Human Anger: Embarrassment Ancient and New." *Theological Studies* 70 (2009): 845–74.

McLynn, Neil. *Ambrose of Milan: Church and Court in a Christian Capital.* Berkeley: University of California Press, 1994.

Nauroy, Gérard. *Exégèse et création littéraire chez Ambroise de Milan: L'exemple du* De Ioseph patriarcha. Paris: Études Augustiniennes, 2007.

———. "L'Écriture dans la pastorale d'Ambroise de Milan." In *Le monde latin antique et la Bible,* edited by Jacques Fontaine and Charles Pietri, 371–408. Paris: Beauchesne, 1985.

Nazzaro, Antonio Vincenzo. "Ambrogio vescovo di Milano e l'imperatore Teodosio I il Grande." In *Atti del convegno nazionale di studi «Intellettuali e potere nel mondo antico», Torino, 22–23–24 aprile 2002*, edited by Renato Uglione, 259–301. Turin: Edizioni dell'Orso, 2003.

Pasini, Cesare. *Ambrogio di Milano: Azione e pensiero di un vescovo.* Milan: San Paolo, 1996.

Petit, Madeleine. "Le rencontre de David et Bersabée (II Sam. 11, 2–5. 26–27): Les interprétations des Pères des premiers siècles." In *Selon les Septante: Trente études sur la Bible grecque des Septante en hommage à Marguerite Harl*, edited by Gilles Dorival and Olivier Munnich, 473–81. Paris: Cerf, 1995.

Pizzolato, Luigi. *La dottrina esegetica di sant'Ambrogio.* Milan: Vita e pensiero, 1978.

———. "La Sacra Scrittura fondamento del metodo esegetico di sant'Ambrogio." In *Ambrosius Episcopus: Atti del Congresso internazionale di studi ambrosiani nel XVI centenario della elevazione di sant'Ambrogio alla cattedra episcopale, Milano, 2–7 dicembre 1974*, edited by Giuseppe Lazzati, 393–426. Milan: Vita e pensiero, 1976.

Ramsey, Boniface. *Ambrose.* New York: Routledge, 1997.

Roques, Martine. "L'authenticité de l'*Apologia David altera:* Historique et progrès d'une controverse (I)–(II)." *Augustinianum* 36 (1996): 53–92, 423–58.

———. "La tradition manuscrite de l'*Apologia Dauid altera* attribuée à Ambroise." *Recherches augustiniennes et patristiques* 34 (2005): 239–97.

Runia, David. *Philo in Early Christian Literature: A Survey.* Minneapolis: Fortress, 1993.

Savon, Hervé. "Doit-on attribuer à saint Ambroise l'*Apologia David altera?*" *Latomus* 63 (2004): 930–62.

———. "Maniérisme et allégorie dans l'oeuvre d'Ambroise de Milan." *Revue des Études Latines* 55 (1977): 203–21.

———. *Saint Ambroise devant l'exégèse de Philon d'Alexandrie.* 2 vols. Paris: Études Augustiniennes, 1977.

Schubert, Christoph. "'. . . nihil difficilius quam hominis interiora comprehendere': Zu einem bisher nicht identifizierten Zitat bei Ambrosius, *Noe* 1,1." *Zeitschrift für antikes Christentum* 7 (2003): 338–42.

Smith, J. Warren. *Christian Grace and Pagan Virtue: The Theological Foundation of Ambrose's Ethics.* New York: Oxford University Press, 2011.

Trisoglio, Francesco. "Legittimità e desacralizzazione del potere politico in S. Ambrogio." *Il pensiero politico* 43 (2010): 307–17.

Visonà, Giuseppe. "Ambrogio Teodosio Davide: Note sull'*Apologia prophetae David* e sull'*Apologia David altera* di sant'Ambrogio." *Annali di Scienze Religiose* 2 (1997): 257–99.

Zahnd, Ueli. "Novus David–νέος Δάυιδ. Zur Frage nach byzantinischen Vorläufern eines abendländisches Topos." *Frühmittelalterliche Studien* 42 (2008): 71–87.

INTRODUCTION

INTRODUCTION

Ambrose and the Three Treatises

Ambrose of Milan (340–397 AD) has long been recognized as one of the first great church politicians, a bishop who negotiated the ascendance of the Christian community in a major imperial see against challenges from civic and religious rivals.[1] Recent scholarship has prompted renewed interest in his achievements in other areas: as a theologian he helped to clarify the status and articulation of Nicene orthodoxy in the Roman West;[2] he is one of the first composers of Latin Christian hymnody, and certainly the most influential;[3] and his reputation as an effective pastor, made famous through Augustine's account of Ambrose's role in his return to the Christian faith, has inspired a range of studies on his preaching and catechesis.[4] The three works included in this volume, *On Noah* and two *Defens-*

1. The classic treatment of Ambrose's involvement in matters of "church and state" is Hans von Campenhausen, *Ambrosius von Mailand als Kirchenpolitiker* (Berlin: de Gruyter, 1929); most recently see Michael Stuart Williams, *The Politics of Heresy in Ambrose of Milan: Community and Consensus in Late Antique Christianity* (Cambridge: Cambridge University Press, 2017). For a sympathetic overview of his life, see Cesare Pasini, *Ambrogio di Milano: Azione e pensiero di un vescovo* (Milan: San Paolo, 1996).

2. For extensive engagement with his ethics and theology, see J. Warren Smith, *Christian Grace and Pagan Virtue: The Theological Foundation of Ambrose's Ethics* (Oxford: Oxford University Press, 2010); somewhat more historical is Christoph Markschies, *Ambrosius von Mailand und die Trinitätstheologie: Kirchen- und theologiegeschichtliche Studien zu Antiarianismus und Neunizänismus bei Ambrosius und im lateinischen Westen (364–381 N.Chr.)* (Tübingen: J. C. B. Mohr Siebeck, 1995).

3. Brian Dunkle, SJ, *Enchantment and Creed in the Hymns of Ambrose of Milan* (Oxford: Oxford University Press, 2016).

4. Augustine, *Confessions,* 6.1.1–6.4.6; on Ambrose's preaching and catechesis, see Christoph Jacob, *"Arkandisziplin", Allegorese, Mystagogie: Ein neuer Zugang zur Theologie des Ambrosius von Mailand* (Frankfurt: Hain, 1990).

es of David, previously unavailable in English, shed light on the breadth of Ambrose's varied career: in particular, they relate to his engagement with secular politics while offering representative samples of his broader, biblically-founded pastoral program.

Ambrose's writings have often elicited mixed judgments. The recent interest in Ambrose's thought and writings is in part a reaction to earlier dismissals of the bishop's work as derivative and unoriginal. The charge is an old one: Ambrose's contemporary rival Jerome accused him of plagiarizing from Greek sources.[5] Labeled a mere translator, Ambrose has often been ignored by scholars who look for innovation in early Christianity.[6] Ambrose, they conclude, remained little more than a transmitter of the voices of the tradition.

Yet Ambrose has long impressed readers by his good sense in drawing the very best from that tradition, as well as for his powers of persuasion. Even though Ambrose's views on spiritual allegorical exegesis depend heavily on Origen and Philo, Augustine himself records that it was Ambrose's preaching on the Old Testament that allowed him to see the treasures hidden beneath the literal meaning of the text.[7] Likewise, many today find Ambrose's striking, if derivative, spiritual readings of familiar biblical accounts and characters illuminating and fresh.[8] On these accounts, Ambrose's excellence is precisely his gift for adapting the wisdom he inherited to his congregation.

Recent scholarship has treated the tension between these divergent views of Ambrose's theology with care and subtlety. As an expert reader of Greek, Ambrose had access to the insights of the East and could make the thought of Philo, Origen,

5. Prologue to his translation of Didymus the Blind, *On the Holy Spirit.*

6. On Ambrose the "unscrupulous plagiarist," see Harald Hagendahl, *Latin Fathers and the Classics* (Göteberg: Göteberg Elanders, 1958), 372. Many have responded to charges of "plagiarism"; see Luigi Pizzolato, *La dottrina esegetica di sant'Ambrogio* (Milan: Vita e Pensiero, 1978), 5–7.

7. Augustine, *Confessions,* 5.8.24.

8. For a summary of recent reconsiderations of Ambrose's exegesis, see Thomas Graumann, *Christus Interpres: Die Einheit von Auslegung und Verkündigung in der Lukaserklärung des Ambrosius von Mailand* (Berlin: de Gruyter, 1994); also Gérard Nauroy, *Exégèse et création littéraire chez Ambroise de Milan: L'exemple du* De Ioseph patriarcha (Paris: Études Augustiniennes, 2007), esp. 75–107.

Hippolytus, Basil, and Didymus, among others, available to his Western, Latin-speaking audience.[9] We understand better that Ambrose drew deeply from both Greek and Latin authorities, a practice that, in turn, influenced the tradition of Western biblical interpretation. At the same time, Ambrose often adapted the insights he culled to speak to the pressing social and political issues of his day.[10] As a preacher famous for his stands against political powers, Ambrose offers biblical models to civic leaders in Milan, the main imperial residence of his day, to instruct them as they attempt to balance their Christian commitments with the demands of their public office. Thus *On Noah* and the *Defenses of David* show Ambrose as a conduit, a biblical commentator, and moral guide, especially for Christians involved in "secular" or "temporal" affairs.

The three treatises represent distinctive phases in Ambrose's theological and pastoral development, when Ambrose employed the figure of the biblical patriarchs to speak directly to the empire in the language and imagery of Scripture. *On Noah* dates most likely to the late 370s, a period that marked the new bishop's dependence on Greek learning; perhaps to compensate for his limited training in Scripture, Ambrose drew extensively from the writings of Philo the Jew, among others, to develop his thought.[11] The *Defenses of David* date most likely to the late 380s. At this point in his career Ambrose had established himself as a leading Christian intellectual and major player in church politics, especially in his dealings with the emperor Theodosius (r. 379–395). Thus familiarity with these writings allows us to compare the thought of Ambrose early in his career with his mature thought.

9. On Philo and *De Noe*, see Hervé Savon, *Saint Ambroise devant l'exégèse de Philon d'Alexandrie* (Paris: Études Augustiniennes, 1977); on *Apol. David* and Didymus and Origen, see Pierre Hadot, "Une source de l'*Apologia David* d'Ambroise: Les commentaires de Didyme et d'Origène sur le psaume 50," *Revue des sciences philosophiques et theologiques* 60 (1976): 205–25.

10. See especially J. H. W. G. Liebeschuetz, *Ambrose and John Chrysostom: Clerics between Desert and Empire* (Oxford: Oxford University, 2011), 77–84.

11. See Savon, *Saint Ambroise devant l'exégèse,* 105–6.

Ambrose on Scripture: Allegory and Catechesis

As their titles indicate, the three works center on episodes from the lives of Noah and King David. Modern readers are often surprised at Ambrose's enduring interest in Old Testament figures, whom he treats at greater length than any of his contemporaries. As Marcia Colish, among others, has shown, Ambrose was drawn to treat the biblical patriarchs as models for Christian virtue as well as types of Christ for ethical and theological reasons.[12] Even the seemingly trivial details of the lives of Abraham, Isaac, Jacob, and Joseph foreshadow the career of Jesus, the Son of God, and offer instruction for the many catechumens who were receiving sacramental initiation in Ambrose's Church.

For Ambrose, the biblical patriarchs could fulfill the exemplary function that the classical heroes, such as Aeneas, had served for the non-Christian Romans.[13] Ancient ethical theory understood *imitatio* or imitation as the basis for moral improvement: to achieve excellence one tried to emulate the virtues that characterized the greats of the past as well as to avoid the vices that they overcame. Ambrose was one of the Church's first bishops to realize the potential of this approach for catechumens: he saw that through a program of ethical pedagogy, a Christian congregation, like a Roman citizenry, could be formed into a cohesive and honorable polity. To this end Ambrose presents Noah and David as models for the influx of Christians into the Church at this period.[14]

While Ambrose's congregation would have comprised Christians from a range of social classes, his focus on David and Noah as "leaders" would have had special resonance for the elite, who might be inclined to excuse their own vices on the basis of their

12. Marcia Colish, *Ambrose's Patriarchs: Ethics for the Common Man* (Notre Dame, IN: University of Notre Dame Press, 2005).

13. On the use of exempla in Roman moral training, see Teresa Morgan, *Popular Morality in the Early Roman Empire* (Cambridge: Cambridge University Press, 2007), 122–59; on Ambrose and exempla see Goulven Madec, *Saint Ambroise et la philosophie* (Paris: Études Augustiniennes, 1974), 179–86.

14. Craig Satterlee, *Ambrose's Method of Mystagogical Preaching* (Collegeville, MN: Liturgical Press, 2004), includes a lengthy treatment of the profile of new Christians in this period.

social status; indeed, especially in treating David, Ambrose reminds his congregation that David's greatest virtue is humility: his feats are especially impressive when we consider that he could have abused his power with little consequence.[15] At the same time, in presenting David and Noah as models for virtue, Ambrose tends to downplay the obvious faults in their careers; Noah is excused for his drunkenness (Gn 9.20–23), while many of David's "minor" sins, such as calling for the census (2 Sm 24.1–17), are mostly ignored. Ambrose, then, is not offering biographies of these biblical figures but rather framing their careers in terms that encourage his audience to Christian virtue, especially justice and humility.

And yet, for Ambrose, Old Testament figures were more than models for imitation or mirrors of the elite: by their actions and in their very nature they participated in the life and work of Jesus Christ. Ambrose shared with all early Christian readers of Scripture the principle that the Bible was a single book centered on the Incarnation.[16] Hence, close study of the careers of the patriarchs could illuminate the Christian understanding of the Lord's *mysteria* or "mysteries," a term that Ambrose uses throughout his preaching to refer to the shadows and images that give a glimpse of God's nature and plan revealed through Jesus Christ, God the Word.[17] Through their specific traits and deeds, Noah the "just" man and David the "anointed" point to the Incarnate Christ. David, in particular, anticipates Christ in his humility and even his "condescension" to a level of sinful-

15. See *Apol. Dauid* 4.15. On David in particular in Ambrose's exemplary ethics, see Hartmut Leppin, "Das Alte Testament und der Erfahrungsraum der Christen: Davids Buße in den Apologien des Ambrosius," in *Die Bibel als politisches Argument: Voraussetzungen und Folgen biblizistischer Herrschaftslegitimation*, ed. Andreas Pecar and Kai Trampedach (Munich: Oldenbourg, 2007), 119–34.

16. For a recent, expansive treatment of the theme, see Hans Boersma, *Scripture as Real Presence: Sacramental Exegesis in the Early Church* (Grand Rapids: Baker Academic, 2017); Graumann, *Christus Interpres,* 255–76, treats the method in Ambrose's *Exposition of the Gospel of St. Luke.*

17. For an exhaustive treatment of Ambrose's vocabulary for biblical and sacramental mystery, especially the terms *figura, mysterium,* and *sacramentum,* which appear often in these treatises, see Giampietro Francesconi, *Storia e simbolo: "Mysterium in figura": La simbolica storico-sacramentale nel linguaggio e nella teologia di Ambrogio di Milano* (Brescia: Morcelliana, 1981).

ness, as he takes on the state of human weakness while somehow remaining unstained by the sin itself.[18] Thus Ambrose's treatments of Noah and David reflect and inform his developing thoughts on Christ's nature and function.

On Noah

The first treatise in the volume, *On Noah* (*De Noe*), is an early work that, like much of Ambrose's mature catechetical preaching, combines a Stoic moral pedagogy with spiritualizing biblical exegesis.[19] In the treatise Ambrose offers a detailed analysis of the events and personalities of the Genesis flood narrative, beginning with the name and character of Noah and concluding with a brief reference to Nimrod (Gn 6.1–9.29). In Ambrose's account Noah embodies both a philosophical ideal and a prefiguring, or "type," of Christ. The patriarch Noah, along with his Ark, is a model of the just one (*iustus*) and the wise person (*sapiens*), terms that would have resonated both biblically and philosophically for a learned audience. As Ambrose himself notes, *iustitia* ("justice") is fundamental to Scripture: it is one of Christ's characteristic virtues as well as the major theme of David's laments in the Psalms.[20] At the same time, the *sapiens* is the ideal Stoic saint, one who exhibits an "indifference" or *apatheia* amid the trials and sufferings of life.[21] Thus Noah is the model for both pagan and Christian virtue, enduring the "rough seas" and guiding his household to safety (and salvation) through his prudence and fortitude.

The prominence of Stoic themes in the treatise reflects, in part, Ambrose's profound debt to Philo of Alexandria (c.25 BC–50 AD). Early in his career Ambrose turned often to Phi-

18. See Leppin, "Das Alte Testament," 123–24.

19. On the method, see Colish, *Ambrose's Patriarchs,* 40–46.

20. *De Noe* 3.7b; on *iustitia* in Ambrose see Antonio Bonato, "Il tema della giustizia nel pensiero di Ambrogio," in *Giustizia—Giustificazione nei Padri della Chiesa,* ed. Antonio Bonato (Rome: Borla, 2001), 225–73.

21. See Richard Sorabji, *Emotion and Peace of Mind: From Stoic Agitation to Christian Temptation* (Oxford: Oxford University Press, 2000), 385–99, on the Christian reception of Stoic ideas of *apatheia;* on qualifications to *apatheia* in Ambrose's preaching on Joseph, see Colish, *Ambrose's Patriarchs,* 139–40.

lo, a Hellenistic Jew whose exegesis and philosophical treatises, heavily influenced by Platonic and Stoic thought, were a major source for Christian theologians, especially Origen and other Alexandrian theologians.[22] In a series of five "Philonian" writings—*On Paradise, On Cain and Abel, On Abraham II, On the Flight from the World,* and *On Noah*—Ambrose quotes and paraphrases his (unnamed) source at length.[23] Of these treatises, Hervé Savon classifies *On Noah* as the most "Philonian."[24]

The source for the structure and philological content of *On Noah* is Philo's *Questions and Answers on Genesis.*[25] Philo's original, composed in Greek but extant only in Armenian, takes the form of a series of investigations that expound the text of Genesis, beginning from the creation of Adam (Gn 2.4) and ending with Abraham's circumcision of foreigners (Gn 17.27). The format determines the approach, biblical verse by verse: for example, a reader might wonder why the measurements of the Ark are mentioned in the scriptural text, and Philo responds in turn, often with extended and surprising explanations in which numerology abounds. Ambrose removes Philo's question-and-answer framework but incorporates much of his content.

Ambrose's debt to Philo in *On Noah* appears not only in adopting Stoic and Platonic ethics, but especially in presenting the cosmos and the soul in philosophical terms.[26] Via Philo, Ambrose applies the Stoic concept of natural law and the immanence of cosmic rationality in the form and structure of

22. David Runia, *Philo in Early Christianity: A Survey* (Minneapolis: Fortress, 1993), offers a thorough review of Philo's presence in patristic sources.

23. On Ambrose as *Philo Christianus,* see the editor of the Armenian recension of Philo's text, J. B. Aucher, *Philonis Judaei Paralipomena Armena* (Venice: I. Lazarus, 1826).

24. Savon, *Saint Ambroise devant l'exégèse,* 1.87; the other works are *De paradiso, De Cain, De Abraham II,* and *De fuga saeculi.*

25. Indeed, Ambrose follows Philo so closely that his Latin has been used to establish the Greek text of the lost original. Philo's text is available through the English translation of the Armenian by Ralph Marcus, *Questions and Answers on Genesis* (Cambridge, MA: Harvard University Press, 1953); for parallels see Enzo Lucchesi, *L'usage de Philon dans l'oeuvre exégétique de saint Ambroise* (Leiden: Brill, 1977).

26. The classic study of Ambrose's debt to philosophical ideals is Madec, *Saint Ambroise et la philosophie;* on Ambrose and Platonism see 109–32.

the human body and soul. The Stoic background informs Ambrose's extended treatment of the parallels between the details of the Ark's construction and the features of the human body. It also explains the recurring references to the distinction between "goods," "evils," and "indifferents" and to the place of "disturbances" and "movements" in generating "affections" in the soul.[27] For Stoics, certain objects, such as the virtues, are good in themselves and should be pursued, while other objects, such as the vices, are to be avoided. A third category of objects, including wealth, health, and strength, are "indifferent"; they are good or evil only insofar as they help us to pursue goods and avoid evils. As for psychic "disturbances," the Stoics maintained that the soul was subject to various forces that could prompt the individual "governing faculty" (*principale* in Latin) to temptation or repulsion.[28] The wise person learned to control rather than be controlled by the influences of those movements.

While his adoption of so many philosophical positions directly from Philo might suggest that Ambrose lacks original thought, the method can benefit modern scholars. It is precisely because Ambrose's text generally follows Philo so closely that the bishop of Milan's unique contributions stand out: in those moments where Ambrose diverges from or otherwise alters his source, we spot a creative thinker at work. Raffaele Passarella, for instance, has demonstrated Ambrose's impressive medical learning by examining Ambrose's studied selection of Latin equivalents for Philo's biological terms.[29] *On Noah,* then, can serve as a test case for Ambrosian experimentation.

Moreover, Ambrose Christianizes Philo's Jewish and philosophical claims. As Savon shows through a rigorous comparison of Ambrose's and Philo's texts, Ambrose consistently modifies Philo's positions for his Milanese congregation. Ambrose follows Philo, for instance, in noting that the destruction of the first

27. On Stoic psychology and indifferents in Ambrose, see Colish, *Ambrose's Patriarchs,* 98–99.

28. On the *principale* (*hēgemonikon* in Greek) see Julia Annas, *Hellenistic Philosophy of Mind* (Berkeley: University of California Press, 1992), 55–61.

29. Raffaele Passarella, "Medicina in allegoria: Ambrogio, Filone e l'arca di Noè," in *Tra IV e V secolo: Studi sulla cultura latina tardoantica,* ed. I. Gualandri (Bologna: Cisalpino Monduzzi, 2002), 189–252.

tables of the Law indicates the superiority of the inner, spiritual law over any outward, material actions, but he proceeds to argue that the act also signifies the superiority of the Christian dispensation over the Old Testament.[30] Ambrose frequently criticizes "Jewish" errors;[31] indeed, the only time anywhere in his corpus that Ambrose identifies Philo by name, he faults his source for the limits of his "Jewish sensibility" (*iudaicus affectus*).[32] Ambrose also tempers Philo's enthusiasm for Plato and philosophy.[33]

At the same time, Ambrose supplements Philo's exegesis by inserting Christian catechetical details that are central to his pastoral project.[34] In particular, Ambrose introduces themes and language from the Christian creeds to emphasize the Son's union with God the Father.[35] He also regularly introduces texts from the Gospels and Pauline literature to supplant Philo's Old Testament authorities.[36] When Ambrose alters Philo's text, he most often quotes Scripture directly; while Philo relies on Platonic and philosophical terms, Ambrose, as Gérard Nauroy puts it, "speaks the Bible."[37] In *On Noah* Ambrose is no mere translator.

Indeed, Ambrose begins *On Noah* by applying his exposition to his congregation's context: he refers to the chaotic times that society confronts, alluding, it seems, to the situation in northern Italy after the Roman Empire's defeat in 378 by Gothic forces at

30. *Noe* 13.46.

31. E.g., *Noe* 13.45. On Ambrose and Jewish interpretation, see Maria Doerfler, "Ambrose's Jews: The Creation of Judaism and Heterodox Christianity in Ambrose of Milan's 'Expositio Evangelii Secundum Lucam,'" *Church History* 80 (2011): 749–72; Wilhelm Wilbrand, "Ambrosius von Mailand und sein Verhältnis zum Judentum," in *Veritati: Eine Sammlung geistesgeschichtlicher, philosophischer, und theologischer Abhandlungen, als Festgabe für Johannes Hessen zu seinem 60. Geburtstag,* ed. Willy Falkenhahn (Munich: Reinhardt, 1940), 156–61.

32. See *De paradiso* 4.25; see Savon, *Saint Ambroise devant l'exégèse,* 97–98.

33. See Savon, *Saint Ambroise devant l'exégèse,* 125–26.

34. E.g., *Noe* 13.47.

35. Savon, *Saint Ambroise devant l'exégèse,* 87–139.

36. See, for instance, *Noe* 8.26 and 29.11. On occasion he inserts a reference to a classical Latin authority; see, for instance, Cicero at 7.17.

37. Gérard Nauroy, "L'Écriture dans la pastorale d'Ambroise de Milan," in *Le monde antique et la bible,* ed. Jacques Fontaine and Charles Pietri (Paris: Beauchesne, 1985), 402.

Adrianople (modern-day Edirne, Turkey).[38] The name "Noah" signifies "rest" (one of the etymologies in the text that is accurate according to modern analysis) and should therefore signify the tranquility that is offered when one lives justly, no matter the circumstances. Noah's life, times, and family indicate precisely how the just life offers Christians a model of "indifference" in the face of their own northern Italian trials and suffering.

To make his case, Ambrose analyzes not merely the basic plot of the flood account but also every phrase and word in the scriptural text. His procedure leads him not only to examine details in language and imagery that would appear extraneous to most modern readers but also to uncover spiritual meanings buried beneath the surface of the text.

Ambrose and Spiritual Interpretation in *On Noah*

One of the most striking features of Ambrose's debt to Philo is his frequent, explicit distinction between the "literal" meaning (*ad litteram*) of the text and the "higher sense" (*sensus altior*), especially in the latter chapters of the treatise.[39] The method, familiar to any reader of patristic literature, draws on ancient approaches that first identified the plain or even bodily sense of the narrative before uncovering a spiritual meaning.[40] In *On Noah* his meaning is often linked to the contemplative ascent of the soul in light of the work and mission of Christ, the true "just man." In other passages, the higher meaning pertains to the contrast between the "literal" Jewish nation and the "spiritual" Christian people.[41]

Many readers will find Ambrose's interpretations stretched, if not absurd. Even the literal readings that Ambrose offers seem to twist any plain sense of the text: the pitch that seals the Ark,

38. For a succinct historical account of the war see Michael Kulikowski, *Rome's Gothic Wars: From the Third Century to Alaric* (New York: Cambridge University Press, 2007), 123–43.

39. Ambrose employs many terms for the distinction, including *secundum seriem* and *simplicior* (*Noe* 15.53 and 15.55) for the literal sense, and *allegoria* (15.54) and *altior* (11.38) for the higher or spiritual sense.

40. See, among many others, Boersma, *Scripture as Real Presence,* esp. 27–55.

41. *Noe* 8.26.

for instance, refers to the earwax that protects the human head and buffers sounds entering the ear canal.[42] We must recall, however, that many of these interpretations are drawn directly from Philo, perhaps in moments when Ambrose is aiming simply to make the Alexandrian's original available to his readers. At the same time, these idiosyncratic interpretations reflect Ambrose's own conviction that the literal meaning of the text is very often related to the "body" or the material universe. While modern readers might presume that a "literal" description of the construction of the Ark refers simply to its physical dimensions, for Ambrose even those details, insofar as they are physical and not spiritual, relate to other physical facts, such as the human body itself.[43]

Ambrose generally relates the "higher" sense to the spiritual nature of the human being. Thus when Genesis 6.7 notes that God destroyed all the other creatures along with humanity in the flood, the higher meaning holds that once the ruling faculty in humanity is destroyed, the entire system of human sensation and health collapses; for the human capacity for self-direction, the *principale,* is what accounts for and sustains all other human functions. In developing the spiritual or allegorical interpretation of the flood narrative, Ambrose, following Philo, applies the text to the individual's moral and spiritual well-being.

After many chapters that pair the literal and the spiritual sense of the account, the treatise concludes abruptly, with a brief treatment of the aftermath of the flood, including Noah's drunkenness and the names included in the genealogy at the beginning of Genesis 10. There is, then, no rhetorical recapitulation, moralizing conclusion, or final doxology. Rather, despite occasional direct address to a congregation, *On Noah* hews closely to the commentary layout of Philo's original; Ambrose simply leaves off at a particular point in the text. He will reprise his project in another Philonian treatise, *On Abraham II.*[44]

42. *Noe* 7.19.

43. *Noe* 6.13.

44. Ambrose, *De Abraham,* composed as two books around 380.

Date and Setting of *On Noah*

On Noah is one of Ambrose's earliest exegetical writings and, according to Agostino Pastorino, the first of his treatments of the patriarchs.[45] If the treatise's opening descriptions of the chaos indeed refer to the aftermath of the Battle of Adrianople in 378, then we can safely date the text to around 380.[46] While later dates have been suggested, they have not gained wide acceptance. Most scholars agree that the treatise's straightforward method of borrowing directly from Philo reflects Ambrose's relative immaturity.[47]

The circumstances of the composition are less certain. While certain features suggest an oral delivery, the treatise is much longer than most of Ambrose's sermons, and, as noted above, it lacks the final doxology typical of Ambrose's preaching.[48] Moreover, the text's extended treatment of obscure details of anatomy, medicine, and allegory seem poorly suited for a broad congregation.[49] Indeed, Ambrose's scholarly devotion to his source also suggests that the treatise was composed more for a learned than for a pastoral setting. Perhaps the text originated as a sermon on Noah, which Ambrose subsequently adapted for publication by incorporating the extended Philonian sections.[50] Such an origin would account for the lengthy passages that reflect academic rather than pastoral interests, a process of development that has been proposed for the bishop's *Defense of David,* which I discuss now.

45. Agostino Pastorino, *Sant'Ambrogio: Opere esegetiche II/I: Noè* (Milan: Biblioteca Ambrosiana, 1984), 317; for a brief summary of issues related to dating, see Giuseppe Visonà, *Cronologia Ambrosiana/Bibliografia Ambrosiana (1900–2000)* (Milan: Biblioteca Ambrosiana, 2004), 125–26. Augustine cites the work as *De arca Noe;* see *Contra duas epistulas Pelagianorum* 4.2.29 and *Contra Iulianum Pelagianum* 2.2.4.

46. On the reactions to the battle, see Noel Lenski, "*Initium mali Romano imperio:* Contemporary Reactions to the Battle of Adrianople," *Transactions of the American Philological Association* 127 (1997): 129–68.

47. Pastorino, *Noè,* 313–17.

48. For oral elements, cf. *Noe* 20.70.

49. We find few parallels in other treatises on patriarchs, for instance.

50. Indeed, most of Ambrose's patriarchal treatises began as homilies, and structural parallels between them and *On Noah* suggest a similar origin.

The *Defenses of David*

This volume also includes two "defenses" (*apologiae*) for David, which were often transmitted as a single work in the medieval manuscript tradition: the first is typically entitled *De apologia prophetae Dauid ad Theodosium Augustum* (*Defense of the Prophet David to Theodosius Augustus*), while the second, once it became identified as a distinct sermon, was labeled *Apologia Dauid altera* (*Second Defense of David*).[51] The first, addressed to the emperor Theodosius, is attributed with certainty to Ambrose, while the second has long been considered inauthentic by many scholars, including the editor of the standard critical edition, Karl Schenkl, primarily on the basis of manuscript evidence and stylistic peculiarities.[52]

During the twentieth century, however, a series of scholars defended the authenticity of the *Second Defense* both by challenging stylistic objections and by explaining the rationale behind the distinctive features of the work's composition. In a pair of articles, Hugh Connolly offered an extended list of the parallels between the *Second Defense* and Ambrose's corpus, while subsequent scholars, including Giuseppe Visonà and the translator of the Italian version of the text, Filippo Lucidi, have proposed explanations for the peculiarities of the text's style and composition.[53] According to Visonà, once we consider that the *Second Defense* may have been delivered directly to a congregation, the compositional oddities may be taken to reflect Ambrose's "oral style."[54] These scholars argue that the manuscripts combining

51. Or *quae uulgo uocatur altera* ("which is generally called 'the second'"); on the background, see Roques, "La tradition manuscrite de l'*Apologia Dauid altera,*" esp. 262–65.

52. Karl Schenkl, *Sancti Ambrosii Opera* 2 (Vienna: Tempsky, 1897), vii–xi.

53. Hugh Connolly, "Some Disputed Works of St. Ambrose," *Downside Review* 65 (1947): 7–20 and 121–30; Giuseppe Visonà, "Ambrogio Teodosio Davide: Note sull' 'Apologia prophetae David' e sull' 'Apologia David altera' di sant-Ambrogio," *Annali di Scienze Religiose* 2 (1997): 257–99; see also Felix Claus, "La datation de l''Apologia prophetae David' et de l''Apologia David altera'; Deux oeuvres authentiques de Saint Ambroise," in *Ambrosius Episcopus,* ed. Giuseppe Lazzati (Milan: Vita e Pensiero, 1976), 168–93. Martine Roques, "L'authenticité de l'*Apologia David altera,*" *Augustinianum* 36 (1996): 53–92.

54. Visonà, "Ambrogio Teodosio Davide," 279–82.

the two works reflect the genuine Ambrosian origin of both treatises. In addition, in preparation for a forthcoming critical edition of the *Second Defense* in the Sources Chrétiennes collection, Martine Roques has identified a ninth-century source for the text's manuscript tradition, an important response to the standard objection to the work's authenticity on the basis of external criteria.[55] To be sure, Savon has offered an extended response to attempts to defend the authenticity of the *Second Defense.* The strongest aspect of his case, however—the absence of the work in the earliest manuscript tradition—has been challenged by Roques's findings; his other arguments, which focus on the inconsistency in the interpretations of the figure of Bathsheba in the *Second Defense,* are less compelling.[56] I am inclined to accept the authenticity of the *Second Defense,* although it will require Roques's updated critical edition to settle the matter.[57]

The debate on the *Second Defense*'s authenticity raises questions about the sequence of the "first" and "second" defenses. Some evidence suggests that the *Second Defense* predates the *Defense of David* and that copyists later combined them into a single work. Lucidi, among others, has argued that the traditional sequence of these two works is an inversion of the chronological sequence.[58] His case rests on the somewhat broad and generic character of the *Second Defense,* especially its division into three classes that would concern a newly catechized Milanese congregation. Thus the close textual parallels between the two

55. Martine Roques, "La tradition manuscrite de l'*Apologia Dauid altera* attribuée à Ambroise," 262–65.

56. Savon, "Doit-on attribuer à saint Ambroise?" 930–62: in *Defense of David* Bathsheba is generally presented as a victim, while in *Second Defense* she is a seductress, a dangerous woman in light of Prv 6 and 7. Savon also argues that the *Second Defense* is not cited by any ancient authorities, but see Franco De Capitani, "Analogie fra una opera ambrosiana discussa ed alcuni scritti antimanichei di sant'Agostino," *Rivista di Filosofia Neoscolastica* 66 (1974): 59–88, for parallels with Augustine.

57. So it is disappointing that a 2014 update on the Sources Chrétiennes website indicates that Martine Roques had completed the edition but that she was awaiting the assistance of another Ambrosian scholar to complete the introduction and notes.

58. Lucidi, *Le due apologie,* 32–33; see also Visonà, "Ambrogio Teodosio Davide," 258.

defenses, which had been used to argue for the *Second Defense*'s dependence on the *Defense of David,* in fact suggest that the *Second Defense* provided Ambrose with the raw material from which he could construct his sermon addressed to Theodosius at a later date. At this later point Ambrose would have supplemented his original draft with learned materials, especially the extensive borrowings from Didymus and Origen (which I discuss below), better suited for an educated audience than for a broadly diverse congregation. In any case, the overview of the content and aims of the two *Defenses* must remain somewhat provisional, since our interpretation of both *Defenses* depends to some extent on the authenticity of the second treatise and the chronology of both.

Both treatises look like sermons. Compositional elements suggest they were delivered over a number of days in a liturgical setting.[59] The *Defense of David* refers regularly to the readings, especially Ps 51(50) and the passage from John on the woman caught in adultery (Jn 8.3–11), clarifying for the congregation "what you have just heard."[60] Even if the texts originated as sermons, they were probably revised for publication.

Throughout both *Defenses* David is presented not simply as a king but also as a holy man, a prophet (note the extended title of the *Defense of David*), and the author of the Psalms. Ambrose emphasizes David's humility, especially in accepting the rebuke from Shimei (2 Sm 16.7–12) and correction from Nathan (2 Sm 12).[61] Primarily through his authorship of the Psalms, David reveals the coming of the Word in Christ, and Ambrose often quotes the psalm text as spoken directly by David.[62] David is an *alter Christus.*

59. See Lucidi, *Opere esegetiche V: Le due apologie di David,* SAEMO 5 (Milan: Biblioteca Ambrosiana, 1981), 25–26; these elements could be literary artifice, of course.

60. Lucidi, *Le due apologie,* 36, suggests that Psalm 94 (93) and the Song of Songs were also read before the *Apol. alt.*

61. Cf. *Apol. Dauid* 6.31 and *Apol. alt.* 11.56.

62. Occasionally Ambrose makes a parallel connection, familiar in ancient Christianity, between Solomon and biblical wisdom literature, especially the Song of Songs.

A Defense of the Prophet David to the Emperor Theodosius

The first of the two sermons is inscribed to the emperor Theodosius, offering a defense and rationale for the behavior of King David after the death of Uriah and his subsequent marriage to Bathsheba.[63] The text has two parts. The first (1.1–7.40) recounts and explains David's major sins, while the second (8.41–18.85) includes a line-by-line exegesis of Psalm 51(50), traditionally identified as David's lament after the killing of Uriah the Hittite. Both parts exhibit many of the traits of Ambrose's typological exegesis and moral preaching that we have discussed in *On Noah:* the bishop consistently presents King David as a model for ethical behavior and a type of Christ even to the point of exonerating him of responsibility for many of his wicked actions. As in *On Noah,* "literal" readings of certain events are paired with "spiritual" interpretations.[64] Thus the life of David guides the audience to Christ and to the virtues of courage and repentance.

Pierre Hadot has argued that the defense itself, especially the first part, takes the form of a classical Roman *concessio,* a rhetorical genre that Ambrose would have learned during his training for a career in civil government.[65] In the *concessio* the defense "concedes" the charge brought against his client, but then proceeds to highlight extenuating circumstances as well as the defendant's virtues to excuse or even justify his behavior.[66] In the case of David, then, Ambrose begins the sermon by acknowledging that David had committed adultery with Bathsheba and murdered Uriah. But the burden of the first part of the sermon is to show that the crime was not as bad as it seems, in part because David was otherwise entirely virtuous and in part because the crime itself served better to establish David as a model for fallen humanity; David's adultery and participation in Uriah's death are "covered over" by his repentance and meritorious ac-

63. Often named *Bersabee* in Ambrose's text.

64. Cf. *Apol. David* 4.18.

65. Pierre Hadot, Introduction to Ambrose of Milan, *Apologie de David,* SC 239 (Paris: Cerf, 1977), 8–9; see Cicero, *De inuentione* 1.11.15.

66. Hadot, Introduction, *Apologie de David,* 7–9.

tions.[67] Moreover, even David's sin contains a mystery: his condescension to take up the lowly Bathsheba foreshadows Christ coming to the church of the gentiles.[68] According to Hadot, the original *concessio* was later combined with an independent text of the Psalm 51 commentary.[69]

Date and Setting of the *Defense of the Prophet David*

On account of a reference to the *Defense of David* in Ambrose's *Commentary on the Gospel of Luke,* scholars can date the *Defense* before 390. A probable allusion in the text to the assassination of the emperor Gratian in 383 allows us to establish the *terminus a quo.* Hadot reads certain portions of the *Defense* to refer to military events around 388, and hence dates the *Defense* to the late 380s or, perhaps, early in 390.

At the same time, the defense's dedication to Theodosius has long prompted scholars to relate the text to Ambrose's famous encounters with Roman imperial authority.[70] During the 380s Ambrose grew self-confident in confronting the major political players of his day. In part because of his background and training in political affairs and in part because of the status of his see (Milan had been used as an imperial residence for de-

67. *Apol. Dauid* 3.9.

68. *Apol. Dauid* 3.14–3.20. On patristic accounts of the adultery, see Madeleine Petit, "Le rencontre de David et Bersabée (II Sam. 11, 2–5. 26–27): Les interprétations des Pères des premiers siècles," in *Selon les Septante: Trente études sur la Bible grecque des Septante en hommage à Marguerite Harl,* ed. Gilles Dorival and Olivier Munnich (Paris: Cerf, 1995), 473–81.

69. Hadot, Introduction, *Apologie de David,* 33–40.

70. Ambrose's frequent engagements with power have earned him the reputation of a consummate "Kirchenpolitiker," a church-politician eager to accrue power and influence for the expanding Christian community; the label stems from von Campenhausen, *Ambrosius von Mailand als Kirchenpolitiker.* On Ambrose's interactions with imperial power in his preaching, see Hartmut Leppin, "Zum politischen Denken des Ambrosius: Das Kaisertum als pastorales Problem," in *Die Christlich-philosophischen Diskurse in der Spätantike: Texte, Personen, Institutionen,* ed. Therese Fuhrer (Stuttgart: Franz Steiner, 2008), 33–49; also, Marta Sordi, "I rapporti di Ambrogio con gli imperatori del suo tempo," in *"Nec timeo mori": Atti del Congresso internazionale di studi ambrosiani nel XVI centenario della morte di sant'Ambrogio; Milano, 4–11 Aprile 1997,* ed. Luigi F. Pizzolato and Marco Rizzi (Milan: Vita e Pensiero, 1998), 107–18.

cades), Ambrose began to engage and challenge civil powers to a greater extent than any of his contemporaries did. Starting with the famous controversy over the Altar of Victory in 384, when Ambrose helped convince the emperor Valentinian II not to restore a pagan statue to the Roman Senate, Ambrose offered the imperial authorities counsel and even rebuke, which could be effective in altering state policy.

Two events in particular are possible occasions for the *Defense*'s address to Theodosius. In 388 Ambrose confronted the emperor about his handling of an affair in Callinicum (modern-day Raqqa in Syria), when Theodosius proposed to rebuild a synagogue that a group of unruly monks, with the encouragement of their local bishop, had burned down. According to Ambrose, while the arson was regrettable, there was no good reason to contribute to the restoration of the Jewish worship site nor to fine the instigators.[71]

In the second incident, in 390, Ambrose rebuked Theodosius for his role in the massacre of citizens at Thessalonica.[72] While the details of the affair are disputed, Theodosius seems to have ordered the attack in response to a riot that had killed a local general. The subsequent bloodshed shocked even sympathetic observers, prompting Ambrose to demand that the emperor publicly repent his crime before he could be granted readmission to the Eucharist. The famous stand-off, celebrated in artwork and literature through the centuries, ended when Theodosius capitulated. It has been interpreted as a symbolic triumph of Ambrose as representative of the Church over secular powers.

Reports of the confrontations over the affair at Callinicum and the massacre of Thessalonica, including Ambrose's own accounts, often depict the bishop's challenge to Theodosius in terms drawn from the life of David.[73] Like David in his murder

71. See Neil McLynn, *Ambrose of Milan: Church and Court in a Christian Capital* (Berkeley: University of California Press, 1994), 298–302.

72. See McLynn, *Ambrose of Milan,* 315–29; also Peter Brown, *Power and Persuasion in Late Antiquity: Towards a Christian Empire* (Madison: University of Wisconsin Press, 1992), 111–13.

73. See Paulinus of Milan, *Vita Ambrosii* 39.5; see Ambrose, *Ep.* 10.74.22, for the aftermath of the Callinicum affair, and *Ep. extra coll.* 11.8 regarding Thessalonica. On Ambrose's "Davidization" of the emperor, see Ueli Zahnd, "Novus David–

and adultery, Theodosius sinned by ordering the massacre or by failing to uphold the faith; like David, Theodosius would have to honor divine authority and to repent publicly. Furthermore, if Theodosius is the new David, then Ambrose is identified with the prophet Nathan.[74] Through Ambrose's exegesis, 2 Samuel provides the framework for interpreting contemporary events.[75]

Given this framework, then, the *Defense of David*'s frequent references to David's humility and repentance take on a new resonance. Ambrose hopes to inspire the emperor to interpret his own crimes and subsequent remorse in light of the biblical exemplar. The lament at the heart of Psalm 51 (50) can function as Theodosius's prayer as much as it was David's. Moreover, Ambrose hopes to lead the emperor to view his own legacy in terms of the Christian life rather than in terms of his secular achievements.[76] To be sure, Ambrose's exhortation to humility and repentance extends well beyond Theodosius to speak to Christians of all backgrounds;[77] nevertheless, the dramatic historical context lends a certain urgency to the sermon's tone.

After presenting David's repentance as a model for imperial virtue, Ambrose includes an extended commentary on Psalm 51 (50). As noted, Ambrose develops this section of the treatise by drawing on Origen of Alexandria (c.184–253 AD) and, especially, Didymus the Blind (313–398 AD).[78] Both authors composed

---

νέος Δάυιδ. Zur Frage nach byzantinischen Vorläufern eines abendländisches Topos," *Frühmittelalterliche Studien* 42 (2008): 76–78.

74. See 2 Sm 12.1–14.

75. For a challenge to this approach, however, see Leppin, "Das Alte Testament," 126–28, who emphasizes the lack of any explicit reference to a public act of penance at Milan in the text; Visonà, "Ambrogio Teodosio Davide," 290, rejects the link to Thessalonica, preferring Callinicum.

76. Compare Augustine's treatment of Theodosius's humility in *City of God* 5.26.

77. On the limits of an exclusively political reading of the sermon, see my forthcoming article, "Sin, Mercy, and David's *Felix Culpa*," for *Studia Patristica: Papers Presented at the Eighteenth International Conference on Patristic Studies Held in Oxford, 2019*.

78. On Origen, see Christoph Markschies, "Ambrosius und Origenes: Bemerkungen zur exegetischen Hermeneutik zweier Kirchenväter," in *Origeniana Septima: Origenes in den Auseinandersetzungen des 4. Jahrhunderts*, ed. Wolfgang A. Bienert and Uwe Kühneweg (Leuven: Leuven University, 1999), 545–70.

commentaries on this Psalm, fragments of which survive in Greek collections of *catenae* on the Psalter.[79] Ambrose had long relied on Didymus and Origen to furnish him with spiritual and allegorical readings of Old Testament texts; indeed, Ambrose's dependence on Didymus, in particular in his treatise *On the Holy Spirit,* prompted Jerome's first charge of plagiarism.

Hadot conjectures a complex origin for the final composition. The *Defense of David* would have begun as an exposition of Psalm 51 (50), to which Ambrose then added the citations from Origen and Didymus.[80] He would have then inserted this commentary into a sermon on David's sin and confession, which was addressed at some point to the emperor Theodosius, perhaps in response to the massacre at Thessalonica in 390. The surviving *Defense of David,* then, would comprise three relatively independent sources: Ambrose's note on Psalm 51 (50), material from Origen and Didymus, and a sermon on David's sin and repentance.[81] Despite the multiplicity of its sources, however, the *Defense* shows a remarkable thematic consistency, emphasizing the potential for shared human sinfulness to yield to God's abundant mercy.[82]

The Second Defense of David

While the third work included in this collection, the *Second Defense of David,* shows signs of composition from distinctive literary units, it also seems to reflect an original, single delivery.[83] Sharing many of the themes and emphases of the *Defense of David,* including a treatment of Psalm 51 (50),[84] the method of presentation, which includes abrupt and digressive transitions, resembles many of Ambrose's other preached sermons;[85]

79. See Hadot, "Une source de l'*Apologia Dauid* d'Ambroise," 205–25.

80. Ibid., 224.

81. For a similar process of composition, compare *De Isaac uel anima,* which combines an exegesis of Isaac and Rebecca in Genesis 24 with an Origenian exegesis of the *Song of Songs.*

82. Dunkle, "Sin, Mercy, and David's *Felix Culpa,*" forthcoming.

83. See Visonà, "Ambrogio Teodosio Davide," 261.

84. *Apol. alt.* 12.62–75.

85. Visonà, "Ambrogio Teodosio Davide," 262.

indeed, some have argued that the text originated as a stenographer's transcription.[86] The surviving text can seem untidy, yet it remains adaptable to a broad and diverse congregation.

The *Second Defense* is divided into three parts comprising a schema that is made explicit at different points in the address: the first addresses the gentiles, the second the Jews and other religious rivals, and the third fellow members of the Church.[87] Each part of the sermon speaks to an audience with distinctive concerns about David's life. Gentiles, for instance, might believe that David's crimes compromise the viability of the Church, for, they claim, Christians would be following a sinful model; Jews, on the other hand, might maintain that David is, in fact, the Messiah. Last, the Church would want to find deeper meaning in David's corrupt deeds.

This framework, however, most likely does not match Ambrose's historical context. Scholars maintain, for instance, that Ambrose had little real contact with the Jewish community of Milan; other readers are skeptical about the presence of organized heretical factions in Milan during this period.[88] Still, the rhetorical structure allows Ambrose to develop a comprehensive reading of these episodes from David's life in relation to a range of christological and ethical concerns. Moreover, as Ambrose proceeds through these three potential audiences, he would progress through three levels of engagement with Scripture: a "gentile" reading that might cause offense in the audience by its report of certain vices, a "Jewish" or "heretical" reading that would fall into christological errors by misunderstanding Christ's presence in scripture as fully divine and fully human, and, last, an ecclesial reading that explores the mysterious relevance of the history of David's fall and pardon for a vision of the Church.[89] Hence, the *Second Defense* offers more than an exoneration for the historical King of Israel: it provides a guide for

86. Lucidi, *Due apologie,* 42–43.

87. See *Apol. alt.* 3.5 and 4.21; Savon, "Doit-on attribuer?" 930, claims this "souci presque maniaque" is "un trait bien peu ambrosien," dismissing the parallel at *De fide* 2 prol.

88. Doerfler, "Ambrose's Jews," 751; Williams, *Politics of Heresy,* esp. 1–10.

89. Leppin, "Das Alte Testament," 120; see also Nauroy, "L'Écriture dans la pastorale," 371–408.

Christian readers seeking deeper insights into the spiritual and sacramental meaning of the Old Testament.

Text and Translation

The Latin text is that of Karl Schenkl for the Corpus Scriptorum Ecclesiasticorum Latinorum series.[90] For the *Defense of David* I follow also the Sources Chrétiennes text, edited by Pierre Hadot, which expressly supplements rather than revises Schenkl's version.[91] Lacunae and other difficulties in the manuscripts are noted in the translation. Although these works have not been translated into English, Italian versions, along with scholarly introductions and notes, appear in the series Sancti Ambrosii Episcopi Mediolanensis Opera, while the Sources Chrétiennes volume of the *Defense of David* includes facing French translation.[92] These versions have helped me decipher many challenging passages.[93]

Ambrose's biblical text deserves special mention. Throughout my translation I render his Latin into English directly. Ambrose himself used different versions of the Bible, including forms of the Vetus Latina, that is, the Old Latin translation of the Bible common in northern Italy in the fourth century; but he also relies on the Greek text of the Septuagint, including, perhaps, any variants in his Greek sources, especially Philo, Origen, and Did-

90. *De Noe:* CSEL 32/1.413–97 (Vienna, 1897); *Apologia prophetae David ad Theodosium Augustum:* CSEL 32/2.299–355 (Vienna, 1897); *Apologia David altera:* CSEL 32/2.359–408 (Vienna, 1897).

91. Hadot, Introduction, *Apologie de David,* 44–45; I also take most of the notes on biblical and classical sources from these editors and translators.

92. SAEMO 5 (Milan: Biblioteca Ambrosiana, 1981), introduction, translation, and notes by Filippo Lucidi; *Opere esegetiche* II/I, SAEMO 2/1 (Milan: Biblioteca Ambrosiana, 1984), introduction, translation, and notes by Agostino Pastorino; there is a recent German translation of the *Apol. David:* Felix W. Heinrichs, *De Apologia Prophetae David ad Theodosium Augustum; Die Verteidigung des Propheten David, gewidmet Kaiser Theodosius* (Oberhausen: Karl Maria Laufen, 2013).

93. Other readers have noted the challenges of these texts; see Savon, *Saint Ambroise devant l'exégèse,* 1.7, who suggests that the many "obscurities" of *On Noah* may have limited its popularity.

ymus.[94] Furthermore, Ambrose often works from his memory of the scriptural text rather than from any particular edition. Thus the English version included here departs often and even radically from contemporary biblical translations. While I generally attempt to remain close to biblical versions that will be familiar to modern readers, at times Ambrose's wordplay depends on a literal rendering of his original (mis)translations of the Greek. Note also that Ambrose's numbering of the Psalms departs from modern versions. This difference matters most in his treatment of Psalm 50, which is typically numbered 51 in translations that depend on the Hebrew text. While I try to follow modern numbering, in the case of Psalm 50 I follow Ambrose in the body of the translation to make sense of his numerology, while including the modern numbering in my references.

The translation that follows stays close to the Latin original, which results in occasionally awkward phrasing and unfamiliar linguistic choices.[95] I have often decided to shorten Ambrose's long, meandering sentences to make them easier to follow. Another challenge has been the range of terms to signal an allegorical or spiritual reading. Often Ambrose speaks of a "certain" (*quidam* or, adverbially, *quoddammodo*) object or relationship to qualify or soften the identification; thus, for instance, Peter covers his triple denial with a "certain" triple veil of love.[96] I often substitute phrases such as "as it were" and "sort of" to capture the resonance of the term. Last, throughout all three treatises, Ambrose often identifies certain figures, including Noah and David, as *sanctus*. The term should not be taken to refer to a "saint" in a strict, canonical sense, but rather to one who is a model of the virtues of Christian life.

94. For an overview of issues relating to Ambrose's biblical citations, see Hermann Josef Frede, "Problem des ambrosianischen Bibeltextes," in *Ambrosius Episcopus,* ed. Giuseppe Lazzati (Milan: Vita e Pensiero, 1976), 365–92.

95. Savon, *Saint Ambroise devant l'exégèse,* 1.7, suggests that the many difficulties and obscurities linked to *On Noah* help account for the treatise's relatively limited manuscript tradition.

96. *Apol. Dauid* 6.25.

TREATISES ON NOAH AND DAVID

ON NOAH

WE PROCEED to explain the life, the manners, and the deeds of the saintly Noah, and also the depth of his heart, as much as we can.[1] For when even philosophy would say that there is nothing more difficult than grasping the inner depths of the human being, how much more difficult is it to know the heart of the just man?[2] Since this is the one whom the Lord God set apart as the fertile soil of justice for the renewal of the seed of humanity,[3] it is worthwhile that we describe him in order to provide a model for everyone, and that, free from every concern of this world, which we suffer daily in various disturbances, we may rest in him. It is shameful for parents to outlive their children; it is exhausting to continue to exist when we hear of so many hardships befalling those most dear to us.[4] Who is there so strong that he can suffer patiently as he either undergoes the various present storms and struggles of the churches themselves or even takes them into consideration?

1. Throughout compare Philo, *Questions and Answers on Genesis,* 1.87–2.7, trans. Ralph Marcus (Cambridge, MA: Harvard University Press, 1953), 54–81; for the text of the parallels consult the notes to the Italian translation, Agostino Pastorino, *Sant'Ambrogio: Opere esegetiche II/I: Noè* (Milan: Biblioteca Ambrosiana, 1984), 346–519.

2. The precise source of this "philosophical" maxim is unknown; see Goulven Madec, *Saint Ambroise et la philosophie* (Paris: Études Augustiniennes, 1974), 53–54; Christoph Schubert, "'. . . nihil difficilius quam hominis interiora comprehendere': Zu einem bisher nicht identifizierten Zitat bei Ambrosius, Noe 1,1," *Zeitschrift für antikes Christentum* 7 (2003), 338–42, suggests a reference to Seneca, *Epistulae morales,* 88.13.

3. Cf. Gn 6.9; throughout Ambrose identifies Noah as a *seminarium,* the place for seeds, which I translate "fertile soil."

4. Most likely a reference to the aftermath of the defeat at Hadrianople (378).

And therefore we also needed this time for rest, so that while we consider the saintly Noah with more attention, we too might be refreshed, just as in him every race rested from its works and its grief.

1.2. For this is what "Noah" means; in Latin it is rendered *iustus* ("just") or *requies* ("rest").[5] Therefore, even his parents said, "This man shall make us rest from our works and from our sadness and from the land that the Lord God has cursed."[6] If perhaps you think that this saying should be applied to those things that happened when the flood occurred in his lifetime, it would seem that there was no rest for humanity but rather there was the introduction of death, not a relaxation of evils but rather a host of miseries. But if you consider the heart of the just man, you will note that the only real justice is that which, born for others rather than for itself, seeks not what is useful to itself but rather what is useful for all.[7] This justice makes us rest from the works of iniquity; this justice summons us from sadness, for when we are doing what is just in the security of a clean conscience, we fear nothing, and we do not ache with any heavy pain; for there is nothing that causes greater pain than the burden of guilt. Let us also rest from every worry about the mundane matters that harass our body and soul with frequent pains and that wear down our lives.

2.3. So this man Noah had three sons: Shem, Ham, and Japheth.[8] These names mean "good" and "bad" and "indifferent," for it seems that by the gift of nature he possessed goodness and in no way did he lack the trials that come through evils and he abounded in "indifferents," that is, <in things neither good nor evil> as though they were the furnishings for his virtues.[9] And it is clear why the author places evil in the middle:

5. Cf. Gn 6.9. The Hebrew name *Noah* means "rest," although some scholars have identified the term with the verb "console," which may inspire the identification of "Noah" as a "just" man; see Agostino Pastorino, *Sant'Ambrogio: Opere esegetiche II/I*, 349 n.4.

6. Gn 5.29.

7. Cf. Cicero, *Republic* 3.8.12.

8. Cf. Gn 6.1.

9. The distinction among goods, evils, and indifferents (*adiaphora*), here drawn from Philo (*QG* 1.88), stems from Stoic ethical theory; cf. Cicero, *De fini-*

because the goodness of nature is present in all people and does not cast them into the world like those who are shipwrecked, but even supports them with strength. In this way they are neither pressed down by the trials of evils nor do they succumb like the helpless; goodness protects and outfits them, as it were, with certain indifferents to serve as their protective garb. These are health, a good constitution, beauty, industry, wealth, honor, and nobility of birth, so that, shielded by all this blessing, people might guard the goodness of nature and shut up that evil so that it cannot harm them, and so they enclose and, as it were, strangle it.

2.4. Do we not recognize in this a kind of ordered ranking of virtues directed to battle, so that the weaker ones are in the middle, and the stronger ones are on the left and the right as though flanking the middle, and through them the entire rank acquires its strength? Thus even a certain Greek poet says: κακοὺς δ' εἰς μέσσον ἔλασσεν, that is: "He drove the evil ones into the middle."[10] Hence nature too is like a good general, with God in command; and she knows that we have been born for the battles of this world, and she considers the "goods" whatever she has established in first rank, whatever harms in the second, and whatever helps in the third. In this way the enemy, as though shut up in the middle, is hemmed in by the twin forces wherever he goes; and thus he cannot wear down one of the two in an evenly matched battle, in which case he might manage to escape from the limits imposed by nature and creep out more broadly.

2.5. This is the order given when the text treats how they are begotten; but when they beget, Japheth is written in the first place, and Ham in the third;[11] thus, so that no one think that we have said something contrary to what we say later, the logic of this order should also be explained. At any rate, the good,

---

bus 3.53. "Indifferents," examples of which are identified later in the paragraph, are the "givens" that can serve for either good or evil moral ends. The text enclosed by angle brackets supplies a lacuna in the manuscripts.

10. Homer, *Iliad* 4.299, which reads κακοὺς δ' ἐς μέσσον ἔλασσεν, speaks of the Greeks preparing for battle against the Trojans; Nestor aligns the "good" Greeks against the hostile (κακοὺς) Trojans and drives them "into the middle."

11. Ambrose is comparing the sequence of sons at Gn 6.1 to the sequence at Gn 10.2.

as that which exists in a certain lofty nature, goes first, but evil follows. And these are the contrary thoughts of the heart, which surely arise later. As long as these are somehow closed up within and do not sprout as though in the grass, they are nourished, as it were, by the bosom of the good heart, so that they do not escape. For as long as evil remains in the will and not in *entelecheia*—that is, in actuality and effect—the goodness of the heart, like a steersman and charioteer, periodically reins in and restrains the evil that is trying to escape;[12] but when the evil does burst forth and erupt into a wound, in order that it should not creep about more broadly and infect the surrounding areas, righteous providence steps in, and the indifferent element, which is commonly called a "secondary good," yields its place, as it were, since, now that the evil is boiling over, the indifferent [element] cannot offer any resistance. And thus, in order that the evil not pour forth the noxious virus more broadly and infect by generating more contagions, that "first good," which is the good by nature, changes its place and ranking; it bears aid, as it were, to the wing that is struggling and takes up the part of the front that is laboring more; for the warrior's strength is needed in the more challenging places, just as the presence of a good watchman is more common just at the point where the walls are weaker. And lest any portion lack a defender, while that first good is propping up the tottering areas, that indifferent element takes up the higher place. It is as though the more perfect good handed over that portion from itself; for nothing is more perfect than virtue. While the indifferent elements do not have the strength of authentic virtue, they still increase and distribute virtue's grace. Hence he was called "Japheth," which means "breadth" in English.[13]

3.6. And not only did holy Noah abound in fathering children, but at that time even the entire generation reproduced to the greatest extent, a point that is not made in vain.[14] For al-

12. On "entelechy" as "activity" or "perfection," see Aristotle, *Metaphysics* 1050a.21–23. Ambrose inserts the Greek term, which he would have found in Cicero, elsewhere in his writings; see *De Isaac uel anima* 2.4.

13. Gn 9.27; see also below 33.124, p. 102.

14. Cf. Gn 6.1.

though the flood was about to follow, one should not think that the gift of fertility was lacking to the generation overwhelmed by the floods. For the abundance of human generation should be attributed to divine grace, while the flood that followed should be ascribed to our iniquities; it is by our sins that we drive away the mercy of the Lord. So you will also find in a later section of the Bible that the fertility of an equal number of years preceded the sterility of Egypt that would follow.[15] It is indeed a principle of virtue to begin from blessings and to sow grace first. And therefore David says: "I will sing of your mercy and justice, Lord."[16] The gift of the blessing precedes, while the condemnation of sober discipline follows. For thus it is God's work that the goods are sent beforehand, but it is our work that they are altered.

3.7. God himself declares this, saying: "My Spirit will not endure in human beings because they are flesh."[17] The Holy Spirit is the Spirit of wisdom, the Spirit of knowledge. Thus the one who has wisdom also has learning, just as Scripture says concerning Bezalel—commanded by a holy oracle to build the sacred tabernacle—that he was filled with a Spirit "of prudence and of learning."[18] And hence this Spirit is given to human beings, but it does not endure. And the reason why it does not endure is reported, namely because human beings are flesh: for the nature of flesh, because it is subservient to pleasure, is opposed to learning. Therefore, it is written about the Lord Jesus alone: "The one over whom you will see the Spirit descending from Heaven and remaining on him, this is the one who baptizes in the Holy Spirit."[19] For it "remained" on him who was restrained by no burdens of fleshly corruption; thus the one whose flesh did not see corruption maintained the rank of uncorrupted and uncompromised learning.[20]

15. Cf. Gn 41.29.
16. Ps 101.1.
17. Gn 6.3.
18. Ex 31.3.
19. Jn 1.33.
20. After 3.7 there is a missing page in the archetype; section 3.7b is a fragment cited by Augustine at *Contra Iulianum* 2.2.4 and *Contra duas epistulas Pelagianorum* 4.11.29, which editorial reconstructions place here.

—

3.7b. Therefore, the salvation that would come to the nations was declared through the one Lord Jesus, who, while a whole generation went astray, could only be just if, born from the Virgin, he was not at all held bound by the constraint of a sinful generation. "Behold, I was conceived in iniquity, and in sin my mother bore me,"[21] says the one who was considered just beyond all others. Thus shall I now call just only the one free of these chains, whom the chains of common [human] nature do not bind? All were under sin from Adam; death was reigning among them all.[22] Let only the man who is just in the sight of God come forward, the one about whom it is now said without any qualification, "He did not sin on his lips,"[23] but rather "he did not commit sin."[24]

—

4.8. "But there were giants on the earth in those days."[25] The author of divine Scripture does not intend that those giants be considered in the manner of poets, as sons of the earth, but he refers to those born from angels and women, whom the author names "giants" because he wants to express the greatness of their bodies. Let us also consider whether perhaps men who strive for the cultivation of their bodies are like giants, since they have no care for their soul; they would be just like those who were born from the earth according to the poetic tale and are said to have disdained the gods, relying instead on the size of their body.[26] Or should they not be judged like those who, although they are constituted from soul and body, reject the acuity of their mind, which is the most precious possession of the soul, and show themselves to be imitators of the flesh as though they had inherited their mother earth's stupidity? Thus they labor in vain when they assail heaven with their haughty oaths and yet dwell among earthly deeds; for in choosing what is lower and

21. Ps 51.5.

22. Cf. Rom 3.9; 5.14.

23. Jb 1.22.

24. 1 Pt 2.22; i.e., Christ's sinlessness outstrips that of any Old Testament exemplar.

25. Gn 6.4.

26. Cf. Ovid, *Metamorphoses* 1.151–62.

in rejecting fellowship with the loftier, they are condemned with greater severity because they are guilty of intentional sins.

4.9. Scripture often calls angels "sons of god" because souls are not begotten from any human being.[27] Thus, too, God does not refuse to say that the faithful are his sons.[28] Furthermore, men of upstanding life are called sons of God,[29] and so, relying on the authority of the Scripture, those whose works are fleshly we call sons of the flesh. For John the Evangelist says, "As often as they accepted Jesus as Lord, he gave those who believe in his name power to become sons of God, who are born not from blood nor from the will of the flesh and not from the will of man, but from God."[30] And after this you find that the Lord was angry;[31] for although he thought—indeed, he even knew—that human beings, who are placed in the region of the earth and bear flesh, could not be without sin—for the earth is like a setting for trials, and the flesh is a net of corruption—even still, despite having a mind capable of reason and the power of the soul poured into the body, without a second thought they fall into ruin, from which they refuse to draw themselves back.

For neither does God think as humans do, as though some new thought would occur to him, nor does he grow angry, as though he were changeable, but these statements are written to express the bitterness of our sins, which deserve the wrath of the divinity.[32] It is as though the guilt had grown to the point that even God, who is by nature unmoved by either anger or hate or any other passion, appears to be provoked to anger.

4.10. Next he threatened to destroy man. He says, "I will destroy everything from man to cattle and from reptiles up to birds."[33] What harm have irrational creatures done? It is rather

27. Cf. Gn 6.2; 6.4.

28. Cf. Ps 81.6.

29. Cf. Jb 1.12.

30. Jn 1.12–13.

31. Cf. Gn 6.6.

32. On divine impassibility and biblical expressions of God's anger in patristic and contemporary theology, see Michael C. McCarthy, "Divine Wrath and Human Anger: Embarrassment Ancient and New," *Theological Studies* 70 (2009): 845–74.

33. Gn 6.7.

the case, given that those irrational creatures were made on account of man, that once the one on account of whom they were made was destroyed, so too those [irrational creatures] were destroyed, because there was no one to make use of them. But that teaching is shown according to a higher meaning because man is the mind that is capable of reason: for man is defined as a living, mortal, rational animal. Thus, when the governing faculty is extinguished, so too every sense is likewise extinguished, since once the force that is the foundation of health has failed, nothing that maintains one's health endures.[34]

And for the sake of condemning the rest of humanity and for expressing divine piety, it is said that Noah "found grace with God."[35] Likewise it is shown that the guilt of other people does not cast a shadow on the just man, when he is preserved as the seedbed for every generation, the one who is praised not because of the nobility of his birth but on the merit of his justice and perfection. For the offspring of a proven man is the stock of the virtues, because just as the offspring of human beings are human, so the offspring of souls are virtues. And just as human families are ennobled by the beauty of their offspring, so the grace of souls is glorified by the beauty of their virtue.

5.11. "The earth was corrupt before God, and filled with injustice."[36] The cause of earthly corruption is clear, in that the injustice of men corrupted the land. Hence even the Lord God says, "The timespan of all people has come before me, since the land is filled with their iniquities."[37] Indeed, the timespan of all people remains in the sight of God and in his will. For it is not the case, as they say commonly, that there is a decree of fate implied by this verse; yet I think it is mentioned here for a

34. Throughout this section, Ambrose refers to the human *principale* or "governing faculty" as the highest "principle" in human action and thinking. The Latin term translates the Greek ἡγεμονικόν, which is central in Stoic ethics and psychology; on the term in Christian use of the language, see Heinrich Karpp, *Probleme altchristlicher Anthropologie: Biblische Anthropologie und philosophische Psychologie bei den Kirchenvätern des dritten Jahrhunderts* (Gütersloh: C. Bertelsmann, 1950), 135.

35. Gn 6.8.

36. Gn 6.11.

37. Gn 6.13.

particular reason, namely that the Lord, who in his Gospel will redeem the race of humanity by the suffering of his body and will cleanse them by his blood and by the sacrament of Baptism, says: "Father, the hour has come, glorify your Son, so that your Son may glorify you."[38] Thus, because in the flood the remnant of the human race was preserved through the Ark of Noah as the fertile soil of future repair and renewal, so here it establishes: "The time of all people has come, because the earth is filled with their iniquities."[39] This is figural; but in truth it says: "The remnant has been saved through the love of his grace." Thus the Apostle exclaims when he says, "Sin superabounded so that grace might superabound."[40]

5.12. "For," it says, "all flesh corrupted its path."[41] Here it employs "flesh" for the earthly person in whom the allure of flesh has corrupted his path. If someone should have understood what gift he would have received from God, he would never have allowed the flesh to obstruct the virtues of the soul. Thus the flesh was the reason for the corruption even of the soul, for the flesh is like a certain region and site of pleasure, from which rivers of desires and evil passions erupt and flow out far and wide as though from a fountain. It is as though the skiff of the soul is submerged in these rivers after the pilot has been thrown overboard, when even the heart, as though conquered by violent storms and crashing winds, abandons its place. But it is also fitting that the text says man corrupted the path of his own nature. For his path was in paradise, in that crossroads of blessings, in that bloom of virtues, in that incorruptible grace, which path he stained with earthly footsteps. Other texts have: "the path of himself," that is, "of God."[42] Scripture often uses this term to mean "of the Lord."

6.13. But now I think we should speak about the Ark of Noah itself, which, if one would like to consider it more carefully, he will discover described in its construction a figure of the hu-

38. Jn 17.1.
39. Cf. Rom 11.5; 9.27.
40. Rom 5.20.
41. Gn 6.12.
42. By "others," Ambrose refers to Philo; see Pastorino, *Noè,* 367 n.4.

man body.[43] For why is it that God says, "Make for yourself an ark from square planks of wood"?[44] Clearly we call this "square" because it is fashioned together well from all its parts and it is fitting to itself. So too the God who is the author of our body is presented as the maker of the nature of the body, and the fact that the work itself is perfect is indicated by these words. As for the reason why the parts of man are "squared," it is obvious if you consider a human chest or you consider the belly, which are equal in measure in their length and width, unless, when the belly is distended through delights and feasting, the natural measure is exceeded. Now, who would not notice that, even at first glance, the feet and hands, arms, thighs, and calves are squared off? True, many of them are not of the same length and breadth, yet they preserve a kind of proportion so that in them a congruous measure and ratio agree, the length being greater than the width, and the width greater than the breadth. And just as the distances of the planks of the Ark are threefold—if indeed he ordered that the length of three hundred cubits and the width of fifty cubits and the height of thirty cubits be observed[45]—so also in our body the distances run greatest and middle and least, the greatest according to the length, the middle according to width, and the least according to breadth, but the whole body, constituted from the individual members, seems squared off. For this is our normal way of speaking, when we call those men "squared off" whom we judge to be not irregular in height and strong in the quality of their hearty bodies.[46]

6.14 But what the text means when it says, "You will make nests in the Ark,"[47] seems something that we should not ignore. For I believe that this is said in a natural way, namely that our

43. The "rationality" of the human body is a common theme in Stoic anthropology as adopted by Philo; see R. J. Hankinson, "Stoicism and Medicine," in *The Cambridge Companion to the Stoics*, ed. Brad Inwood (New York: Cambridge University, 2003), 295–309. For Ambrose see Ernst Dassmann, *Frömmigkeit des Kirchenvaters Ambrosius von Mailand: Quellen und Entfaltung* (Münster: Aschendorffsche, 1965), 50.

44. Gn 6.14.

45. Cf. Gn 6.15.

46. Cf. *quadratus* as "hearty" or "robust"; see Celsus, *De medicina* 2.1.

47. Gn 6.14.

whole body is woven together just like a nest, so that the life-giving spirit entirely penetrates the tissue of every part and flows out from our governing faculty through the individual limbs.[48] For some of the nests are our eyes, where vision plants itself. The cavities of our ears are nests, through which hearing pours and casts itself in as though into a deep pit. There is a nest of noses, which draws aroma to itself. The fourth nest is the opening of the mouth, an opening bigger than the others, in which one is nourished when the sense of taste is aroused and from which the voice flies forth; here the tongue is hidden, which, like an organ, modulates the sounds of the voice by its artful sweetness, and, although it is itself irrational, it expresses a rational voice. The skull is a nest; a nest too is that membrane that houses the brain and holds it within. Nests are the tissues of the lung and the heart. Indeed, the lung is a nest of our breath, that is, of that which we inhale and by which we are nourished in this life. The heart is also a nest of the breath as well as of blood. For it has two chambers, one where it receives blood as in a sort of pool and transfuses it to the veins, the other where it draws the flow from that upper chamber into the arteries by a continuous motion. The stronger bones also have nests; for inside they are hollow, and there is marrow in those openings. Furthermore, in the softer tissues there are nests of desire and pain. And if one considers all the rest, he will find even more nests in the construction of the human body. Thus I think that the author in the Psalm spoke not only mystically, but also naturally: "Even the swallow finds her home, and the sparrow a nest for herself where she can place her young."[49] For there is now a nest of modesty in this body in which there had been a nest of irrational desire. But where once lust was nourishing misshapen births, there now the inheritance of comely chastity is maturing.

6.15. The text says, "You will seal it with pitch."[50] The human body is made from many bones and tendons and all the rest. And thus interwoven it clings together inside and outside by a fitting arrangement, and it is held fast with an appropri-

48. Perhaps allusions to Vergil, *Aeneid* 6.726–27, and Gn 2.7.
49. Ps 84.4.
50. Gn 6.15.

ate ordering, which the Greeks call ἕξιν;[51] by this ordering the breath shut up within that is infused or the spiritual substance that works interiorly does not escape, as though bound by two chains, and is held together for a proper unity and a secure and harmonious connection. Thus it is commanded that the Ark be bound by pitch; for the nature of pitch is effective for binding together. Hence ἄσφαλτος ("pitch") in Greek comes from ἀπὸ τῆς ἀσφαλείας, that is, from "security," because it binds disjointed things and connects them in an indissoluble bond, so that you would think they come together with a natural unity.[52] Thus the Ark is bound with pitch both inside and outside, to prevent the connection from breaking easily.

7.16. But elsewhere, that is in Exodus, another Ark is also gilded inside and outside; in the Holy of Holies this image is an imitation of the intelligible universe.[53] For just as gold is more precious than pitch, so the Ark that is in the Holy of Holies is more brilliant than this Ark. Thus the Ark of Noah is from wood alone, but the Ark of the Holy of Holies is from "incorruptible wood," by which it includes the merits of the saints. But it also is added in Exodus that the supports are immobile, since the position of the saints is stable and firm; for they followed the path of an upstanding life by the guidance of virtue and rejected participation in corruption. But the Ark of Noah, so long as it is in the flood, is cast about here and there by an uncertain motion, in that the situation of sinners is mobile: their life dangerously drifts within a certain flood of overflowing passions in a corruption that is made inconstant through error.

7.17. Nor should it be overlooked that when he said: "And you will make the Ark three hundred cubits long and fifty cubits wide and thirty cubits high," he adds: "gathering the parts together you will make the Ark, and you will complete it on top with one cubit."[54] For here he adds on to the rest of the body, as though a royal citadel, the human head, which squares everything off with the beauty of a balance well suited for its elegance; from the head all the senses are extended to the other parts of

51. Cf. *QG* 2.4.
52. For the link to *asphaleia* ("security"), see *QG* 2.4.
53. Cf. Ex 25.10.
54. Gn 6.15–16.

the body; the eyes in particular, positioned by the providence of nature, like sentinels and guardians overlook from above nearly the entire situation of our city.[55] Indeed, the mind itself is located there according to the opinion of many, and most of all of Solomon, who says: "The eyes of the wise man are in his head."[56] It is as though the mind calls together a council of the virtues in the imperial hall, where, protected by a company and itself quite well defended, it commands the ranks of the whole body as though gazing from a sort of sanctuary; [it knows] what responses to offer, through which we may not only reflect back on ourselves and not only see what is in front of our feet, but even gaze on the mysteries of heaven itself from the profound insight of wisdom. Thus, precisely where there is the height of our entire safety, there is also our grace. This is the source from which watchfulness and even beauty are acquired by the whole body, the beauty that blossoms first in our visage: indeed, it is fitting that the brilliance of the royal hall be more excellent, for just as the activity there is greater, so also is the beauty.

7.18. For if you look at the individual elements which seem designed in the human body for a specific activity, such as eyes for seeing, ears for hearing, noses for smelling, the mouth for speaking, as much as they offer services, so they exhibit beauty. How ugly are the faces of the blind! And why is it surprising that the face of a man without eyes is ugly when the sky itself does not have its beauty without the sun? We consider sunless days grim, and nights without the moon offer no pleasure; but these are like the eyes of the world. Take away the light of the stars, and there is in heaven itself something like the ugliness of blindness. Lashes as well, which cover the eyeball and extend over it in a kind of battle line, so that the pupil not be harmed by some filth or by a speck of dust, also prevent harm; if something should enter that could harm the eye, if the eyes are penetrated with inflammation—how ugly!—if the eyelids become squinty, if someone shaves off the eyebrows, which shine out with the beauty of very precious necklaces as though dressed with gems.

7.19. The same is true of the ears, which are lovely in ap-

55. Cf. Cicero, *De natura deorum* 2.140.

56. Eccl 2.14.

pearance just as much as their function is necessary; if someone mutilates them, he brings ugliness to the whole face. In them nature has so worked out her own project that those circuits of the canals, which are twisted with a marvelous providence, bring a great deal of utility, lest a sound strike the recesses of the head suddenly. Thus we often see many distressed by an unexpected ruckus and shock, going pale with the sound of some voice or tumult. That very filth, which the canals bring forth in themselves, binds the hearing by a certain glue.[57] At the moment that there is a very violent blast of some sound, it is subdued and slowed, so that it is preannounced and it is tempered rather than shaking the insides suddenly. Also if worms try to penetrate the ear, they are held by a sort of stickiness in the earwax.

7.20. Snub noses seem to be against nature. If they were cut off, how could life continue with the respiratory canal taken away? It would be judged more the face of a beast than the countenance of a person!

7.21. With such a graceful garment the hair of the scalp dresses the head, as though the hairs were guardians of the royal hall, so that the winds do not damage the brain, rain does not strike it, and the sun does not burn it. Yet nature has made it so that hair is more attractive when longer (depending on one's sex) or with it cut back (depending on one's age or often on the quality of the season and the year). In old men grey hair is pleasing, in boys abundant hair is; in summer it is pleasurable to cut it more closely, in winter to keep it more bountiful; the hair is the ornament of the woman, but indecorous for men. Thus the Apostle expresses this quite clearly saying: "And does not nature herself teach you that if a man indeed has long hair, it is shameful to him, but if a woman has long hair, it is her glory?"[58]

7.22. What shall I say about the royal palace itself, through which princely speeches come forth as indicators of our heart and messengers of the mind? What about the very design of the teeth, which both offer strength to the whole body through their activity and are modulators of the voice itself? If one of them falls out, the voice stumbles.

57. That is, earwax.
58. 1 Cor 11.14–15.

7.23. We have spoken at greater length about the head, because it was fitting that all the senses be located in the highest point; from there all other faculties are divided through the remaining parts. For in the back, the neck is closest to our head, and then there are the left and right arms, which are like faithful guardians over the imperial citadel, and thus those members that are closer to the head are stronger and healthier. In addition, the chest is like a sacred vessel of wisdom, and the stomach is a sort of witness, as the doctors say, and it is aware of the secrets of the head and is a companion of its sympathy; to the head the stomach pours out all that is its own, whether healthful or sickly. The flanking femurs of the buttocks and the thighs indicate by their appearance the width of one's stature, and the strides of the feet, which might even seem quite small, still extend out when we step forward.

8.24. It is interesting that it added: "You will make a doorway on the side,"[59] identifying that part of the body through which we are accustomed to discharge any excess of food, so as to surround with more abundant honor the parts of the body that we consider more shameful.[60] This fact Scripture expresses much more pleasingly than what we find Socrates said in the book of Plato.[61] For since either Socrates himself, or Plato, who was in Egypt, could have read this in the writings of Moses, or have heard about it from those who had read them, Socrates was moved by the lovely discovery to realize that a gate was opened to him to preach the wisdom of our Creator, praising the fact that it was entirely fitting to human beauty that God redirect the pathways and the exits of our inner canals to the back, so that our vision not be offended by the purging of the stomach.[62] And indeed the Apostle says, "the members of the body that seem weaker are those that are essential," surpassing the descriptions of philosophy in a single statement, "And what

59. Gn 6.16.

60. Cf. 1 Cor 12.23

61. The reference does not appear in Plato, but in Xenophon, *Memorabilia* 1.4.6.

62. On the early Christian hypothesis that Greek wisdom derives from the more ancient Hebrew wisdom, see Arthur J. Droge, *Homer or Moses? Early Christian Interpretations of the History of Culture* (Tübingen: Mohr Siebeck, 1989).

we consider to be the humbler members of the body, we clothe these with greater honor, and what are dishonorable for us have more abundant honor."[63] Hence the mark of our sobriety and temperance is known chiefly in this fact: gluttons in fact are either bloated from their indigestion to the point of danger, or very often they are weakened when their bowels are emptied.

8.25. This claim the Apostle also fittingly applies to the members of the Church. For what things are dishonorable and superfluous if not our indulgences, our entanglements? If someone in the period of his youth is caught up in these things, and then, when he reaches a more mature age, comes to baptism, renounces former things and casts off his old habits, puts sins aside, is buried with the Lord Jesus, and has the world crucified to him as he is to the world,[64] does he, blessed with the remission of sins, not have more abundant honor than the catechumen whose life was judged more blameless? And so that we might use the example of the Apostle himself, he was a Jew, he was a persecutor: called to the grace of Christ he began to be an apostle.[65] And because more was forgiven him,[66] he began to love more and to labor more abundantly than all the [other] apostles,[67] and became a vessel of divine election, and was sent as the teacher to the nations. Did he not attain richer and more honorable glory than many of the apostles themselves, he who was previously both dishonorable and inglorious when he was persecuting the Church of God? That is the poor man, who, though lowly in the Church, has redeemed you by his prayers.

8.26. And that we might uncover even greater mysteries, what is as dishonorable as the gentile people? They were poor like the one who had none of the fine words of God and was weak and crippled in both feet, who believed neither in the Law nor in the Gospel; yet when called by God, he believed, and when baptized, he received grace. Thus because more was forgiven him, he loves more.[68] The people of the Jews remained, albeit

63. 1 Cor 12.22–23.
64. Cf. Rom 6.4.
65. Cf. Phil 3.5–6.
66. Cf. Lk 7.47.
67. Cf. Acts 9.15.
68. Cf. Lk 7.47.

stumbling in one foot, although that people stumbled even in the Law itself. Thus the people who were considered most glorious lost everything: they lost a marvelous counselor, a prudent architect, and a wise listener; and the other people, who were dishonorable, received everything and could boast in the title of the faith, in the reward of martyrdom, and in the fellowship of angels. Thus Plato showed brilliance in speech because he had the ability, but the Apostle, who possessed the Spirit of God, revealed the mystery.[69] Enough has been said about the gate, since those who were behind have become the foremost.[70]

9.27. Now let us inquire about this point: why it is that the Lord said: "Make the lower parts of the Ark double and triple-roomed."[71] Indeed, in saying "lower parts" we note that he wanted us to imagine in a fitting way that the receptacles of food should be judged to be in the lower place, that is, the bowels themselves, which finish off the food that is received. For food is corruptible, and what is corruptible should not be compared to what is above, but to what is below. Likewise the food is led downwards, a small portion of which profits the strength of the body and of nourishment, while the rest is led down to be purged in the belly.

9.28. For our maker established it that there are intestines, through which the excess of food descends; these were stretched from the stomach to the bottom, but they were twisting and turning, by which the enjoyment of our life might be extended. For if a person's intestines, which take in and expel the food, were made straight, the food would pass through with no delay, and it would be necessary that we constantly go hungry, constantly feast, and collapse right when the substance of the food ceased. But now in that twisting and turning of the intestines in two and three parts the food sticks, and in descending little by little it administers strength, it infuses liquid to the body, it contains a sufficiency, it delays the appetite for eating, and there is no sudden outflow or rapid evacuation, and there is no insatiable appetite, and there is no ceaseless desire for binging. First,

69. Cf. 1 Cor 7.40.
70. Cf. Lk 13.30.
71. Gn 6.16.

therefore, there would be lack and hunger, then from them would follow a continual eating without any break. But next, what is uglier than to be always striving for the sake of the belly, which would need to be emptied once it is filled, and once emptied would need to be refilled? Third, what would remain but death, mixed in among the food itself and the feasting? For how could those who are eating yet hungry, drinking and yet thirsty, extend their life for very long? Before they can be replenished, they have emptied all that they consumed, and yet they are immediately hungry. But, as it is, the food makes its course little by little; natural providence tempers hunger and indigestion. For the process is that first in that stomach that many call the upper stomach, the food is finished off, then it cooks in the liver, and it is digested by the heat itself. For its liquid is divided up in certain sections of the bowels, from which the whole body gains health. This is shown well enough by the development of the young and by the endurance of the elderly. The rest of the food flows into the stomach, which we all call the "stomach" without modifier, but many call the "lower stomach"; from here it is necessary that the dung, which is now full of waste after flowing down, is evacuated, through "the gate in the side."

9.29. Although these bodily structures seem organized elegantly by a natural arrangement according to the plan of God, unless we observe a limit to our eating and behaving, a sort of flood and corruption of the whole body is born from the overflowing passions; for intemperance ignites the desire, breeds indigestion, and creates corruption. Thus for gluttons either the intestines are stretched out through an internal rigidity and convulsed with pains, or else a certain inner covering of the intestines is worn down by the uncooked dampness of the food and by the harshness of indigestion. For the covering of the intestines is said to be doubled like a sheet of paper: one on the outside, which those who are experts or who have examined more carefully say is continuous, directed from the top to the bottom; and another on the inside, as though it is attached to the sides, which, they say, is why the covering is not entirely destroyed when it is rubbed down; for if the inner layer were continuous, a cut in it would be incurable. The remains of the food cling there because of the delay caused by the seams; if these seams were broken, half-eaten food and spilled drink would pass through. This is the "flood of a man."

9.30. Thus it seems to me that through the image of the Ark, God wanted to show us how we are free from this particular flood. For corruption is the cause of the flood. Where it slips in, the waters are unleashed, all the fountains of desires boil over, and the entire body is submerged in a very great and deep overflow of vices. For there is nothing that subjects man to so wretched a slavery as lust and its desires, of the type that weighs down the miserable conscience with a sort of burdensome yoke, so that the conscience cannot lift itself up seeing that it has lost the freedom of innocence. Thus the greatest cure in this flood is that you prefer justice and you choose it as the fulfillment of heavenly commands. What is justice in us if not the acuity of soul, which encloses inside the Ark every kind of living being that is above the earth? Thus you too should restrain all your irrational passions and subject all your senses to the mind and accustom them to the ordinances of the soul. Do not allow your desires to fly outside, nor your lust to go out in public: thus, through your rational mind you will be able to free even your irrational parts and your unclean sins from every peril of the flood.

10.31. "All things on the earth will die."[72] But what did the wordless animals do wrong? Why should those who have no knowledge of sinning be subject to a penalty? But in the same way that it happens in battle, when the emperor is killed by the enemy, his army dies with him, and all his military strength is shattered, so it does not seem contrary to justice that when the man, to whom the Lord God gave a certain ruling power over every type of living creature, so that he might preside over all the flying things, the beasts, and the wild creatures by a certain imperial authority, should die, even cattle and whatever irrational animals there were should die with him. So too, when a plague occurs upon "the pestilence of some infected sky,"[73] first of all a vicious disease infects the irrational beings, especially

72. Gn 6.17.
73. Vergil, *Aeneid* 3.138.

dogs, horses, and cattle, and it poisons whatever seems to interact with human beings, and in this way the power of the sickness also infects even the human race.

10.32. In my opinion this is the first reason for the justice of the pronouncement, but the second is that no one blames nature for the fact that the rest of the members of our body die when the head alone is cut off, although we see many people survive with their hands and feet amputated. But the rest of the members do not have the same authority as the head, and thus when it is cut off, that is, the source from which our senses go forth into the rest of the body, all the other members die with it, and this does not imply either that the designer's foresight is lacking or that one should blame the weakness of human nature. Thus likewise no one now disputes that the human being is the head and a certain governing faculty of the other animals, and so it should not appear surprising that when he dies all the other animals die with him.

10.33. But the third reason is that, since animals have no part in reason, they are generated not for their own sake, but for the sake of human beings; and they have been ordered to exist for the sake of man so that by their subjection human status might be exalted. Thus the prophet ascribed them to be made for the sake of man when he said: "You have put all things under his feet, all oxen and cows, and the cattle of the field, the birds of the sky and the fish of the sea,"[74] since all things are made for his sake: some for his use, others for his pleasure, and others for his desire. Thus it follows that when man was wiped off the face of the earth, all things, which were made for his sake, were destroyed by an equal calamity. This is enough for a simple exposition of the reading.

10.34. But a deeper and more profound interpretation adds to this:[75] that when the soul is bowed down by the weight of passions, as though overwhelmed by the heat of various desires, all earthly thoughts and longings rush headlong, because in the case of each sinner the more grievous the sins he commits, the

74. Ps 8.7–9.

75. On the higher and lower senses of Scripture, see Introduction, pp. 12–13.

more insolent he grows. For wickedness increases by practice and use, and rashness is nourished by impunity. Thus the sinner withdraws from all regard for honor, and all earthly things die in him by the bitterness of mortal sin, which destroys a sinner with a true and lasting death. For no one dies more grievously than the one who lives in sin. In him the individual passions die, sight dies, sight that announces sin, that looks on the deceiving woman, that is seized by the beauty of another's face, the sight which the eyes of an adulteress bind, which the appearance of the harlot ensnares. Or does he not seem to die who impresses the dart of lust on himself, who voluntarily rushes into the pit of death? Hearing dies, too, when it reports the crimes, when it announces the message of an adulterous proposition, when it smuggles the words of the harlot into the soul, words that seduce the young man by a very flattering remark, so it ensnares him with the nets of her lips. The voice dies through silence, if it does not confess to God; it dies through much speaking, since it is written to you: "You will not flee sin with much speaking."[76] It dies through wrath, when it goes beyond the limit of revenge. Every sense dies eventually if it is a servant of iniquity.

10.35. And thus all earthly things die in the flood, but only the just one remains forever, since it is said to him: "I will establish my covenant with you."[77] For he is himself the heir of divine grace; he is himself the possessor of the heavenly inheritance and partaker of the most blessed goods. And indeed when men die, they are accustomed to transfer their patrimony by means of a will, and the inheritance is not ceded so long as the one who makes it is still alive. God, however, since he is everlasting, transfers the inheritance of his divine substance to the just, and he himself, while being in need of nothing, gives what is his without any cost [to himself] of giving. The partakers of his goods do not weigh him down, and he enjoys his goods more by as much as we use them. Accordingly, the Lord Jesus became poor, although he was rich, so that we might be enriched by the poverty of him who fulfilled each covenant with his own blood, so that he might make us co-heirs of his life and heirs of his

76. Prv 10.19.
77. Gn 6.18.

death, by whom we have both the fellowship of his life and the benefit of his death.[78] For he attributes much to the just man in saying: "I will establish my covenant with you," so as to say that the rational and faithful man himself is the covenant of God. For he is himself the inheritance of God, he is the possession, in whom there is the strength of the divine covenant, in whom there is the fruit of judgment, in whom there is the inheritance of the promise, about whom David said, "Behold, sons are the heritage from the Lord, the fruit of the womb is his reward."[79] But now, reserving an exposition of a more profound mystery, let us proceed to the rest of the account.

11.36. It says, "Let all your household enter into the Ark, since I have seen that you are just among this generation."[80] Clearly the faithfulness of the prophetic utterance is demonstrated here, too, because the foolish one is foolish to himself alone, but the wise man is wise for himself and for many. Thus, by the merit of Noah the just, his house is also preserved in the flood. Likewise, sailors on the sea and soldiers in a war, if the former do not lack the expertise of a captain and the latter do not lack the astuteness of a general, are preserved from danger by the work of another. But since a good army is a mark of a good general, so too we observe that the praise of the just man is hardly unnoted in the fact that the just man established his own household such that it would shine forth by sharing in his virtue, and in the fact that his kin rightly found safety.[81] And the fact that the son or the wife of a just man afterwards committed an offense does not compromise this truth. For the just man was sleeping while his son was sinning.[82] And the woman, belonging to the weaker sex and troubled by the mass of dangers, believed that the whole world would perish by a heavenly fire. Why are you surprised if she could not follow her husband, when even that just man, although he was warned by angels, scarcely escaped?[83] But why is it surprising if error sneaks up on man or if

78. Cf. Rom 8.17 and 2 Cor 8.9.
79. Ps 127.3.
80. Gn 7.1.
81. Cf. Prv 15.6.
82. Cf. Gn 9.22.
83. Cf. Gn 19.26.

his attention is distracted? You maintain, then, that the just man was also a drunk. But I believe that this behavior was reserved to that one instance alone.

11.37. But now let us consider what remains. For it says fittingly: "Because I have seen you as a just man in this generation."[84] Many people appear just to men, but few appear so to God. They seem one way to people and another way to God: to people according to the appearance of life, but to God according to the purity of soul, the genuineness of virtue; people esteem what is outside, God examines what is on the inside. The text also adds attentively: "In this generation," so that it does not condemn earlier ones or exclude future ones, and it indicates that it was appropriate for the flood to result in the death of Noah's generation, which had no share in justice.

11.38. This is what it says according to the letter. But the higher interpretation prompts us to consider this acuity of mind to be in the soul, and the soul to be in the body just as the paterfamilias is in his household. What the mind is in the soul, so the soul is in the body. If the mind is safe, the household is safe, the soul is safe: if the soul is ill, the flesh is ill. For the sober mind reins in all of the passions and controls the senses. It governs speech. Thus the Lord says rightly to the just one: "Enter within," that is, "Enter within yourself," into your mind, into the governing faculty of your soul. That is where salvation is, there is the rudder, while outside is the flood, outside is danger. But if you would have been within, you are also safe outdoors, since there the mind is in charge of itself, and your thoughts are good and your deeds are good. For if no vice overshadows the mind, thoughts are pure. If there is chastity with zeal, if there is temperance in the heart, no flame of lust will burn, no wounds of sickness will sneak in; for the sobriety of the mind is the medicine of the body.

12.39. Now let us consider why he commanded that there be led aboard seven and seven, the male and the female, from the clean animals, but two and two from the unclean, so that their seed would be sustained throughout the whole world.[85] And, as

84. Gn 7.1.

85. Cf. Gn 7.2. This section develops Ambrose's use of numerology in exegesis; see Pizzolato, *La dottrina esegetica,* 279–80, for some background.

I myself think, the text adds that seven clean ones enter because the number seven is clean and sacred; for it mixes with no other and it is generated from no other. Thus it is called a "virgin" number, because it generates nothing from itself and rightly it has the grace of manly sanctification, for it is as though it is free from and has no part in a maternal birth and womanly couplings, even if "seven" is named with a feminine word.[86] For "every male that opens the womb will be called holy to the Lord,"[87] that is, a "holy man." And in the prophet you have: "She escaped and bore a male,"[88] that is, "a holy male." But the number two is not full because it is divided. And what is not full is considered empty. But the number seven is full because seven is like ten, and it is similar to that first number, because the alpha is in the likeness of him who is always, from whom flow forth and move the virtues that are in every kind.[89] This is the natural meaning [of the verse].

40. But that we might speak about the moral meaning of the verse, there is no doubt that the irrational faculty of our soul is divided into the five senses, and into the voice and into the means of generation; these seem to be feminine by nature, because our senses creep quickly into material and worldly matters. Hence the verse makes clear that these have a substance of a more pliant nature. But all things are clean to the learned and hardworking man, because the wisdom and virtue of an experienced man pour into them a manly foundation. Therefore, by the judgment of the prudent man and the decision of one who is in control of himself, they are transformed from the condition of the weaker sex into stronger material. For the opinion of a wise man is sturdy and fixed, not changeable, as it is for the unwise and the foolish, who totter with an uncertain decision, and for the wicked, who does not choose what is true and just, but whatever is easy or useful for himself he cuts off from the true and separates from the just. For justice is uniquely good,

86. Ambrose seems to be referring to the Greek ἑβδομάς ("seven"/"week"), which is feminine.

87. Ex 13.12; Lk 2.23.

88. Is 66.7.

89. Cf. Rv 1.18 and Acts 17.28.

esteemed in itself for its own value. But wickedness brings forth, as it were, divided things, now twisted in hatred, now twisted in desire for profit, and it confuses the things that should be distinguished. For the fool changes like the moon, and, deformed by the multi-colored variety of his inner fluids, he stains his own soul into the appearance of a leprous body by a filthy contamination, often blending healthy thoughts with guilty ones.

12.41. But perhaps the fact that you notice that clean and unclean animals were commanded to be led into the Ark could rightly upset you, because I said that unseemly judgments should not be mixed with honorable ones. And in fact I do not deny that in our soul there are some seeds and principles, as it were, of our irrational yet clean movements, and of some movements that are not clean. For the nature of the human is capable of contraries, as there can be an entryway into it both for malice and for virtue; it is correct that in the beginning of this book, namely, Genesis, you read, under the appearance of the tree in the middle of paradise, that there is knowledge of good and evil.[90] As for that tree of knowledge of good and evil, it is commanded that it must not be tasted, because of the fact that our mind, in which there are knowledge and discipline, acquires the concept of good and evil. Thus the Creator of nature, just as he set aside living things for propagating or even restoring the race in order that all the lands might be refilled by the seed of living things, so also he did not think the earthly substance of our body should be left empty of these kinds of passions, which are like the unclean animals; this substance, when it is overwhelmed with indulgences and luxury as though with the event of the flood, is driven about by the passions that I mentioned. But when someone drains out the flood of inundating passions with sobriety and continence and reseals the "dryness" of the soul, he begins to vivify his body and the purity of his soul, whose rudder is wisdom.

13.42. The next task is to ask with intensity for what possible reason the flood happened seven days after Noah entered the Ark and led in the animals. For it does not seem pointless that no more or fewer days intervened than as many as there

90. Cf. Gn 2.9.

were in the creation of the world. For the world was made in six days, and "on the seventh day God rested from his work."[91] By this sign he declared himself to be the Creator of both the world and the flood. He created the world on account of his own goodness; he made the flood on account of our sins. Thus people are warned, even from the number of the days in which the world was created, that they should reconcile with their Creator not only by their tears and prayers alone, but by the correction of their morals. Thus the Lord gave space for repentance because he wanted more to forgive than to punish, such that he compelled men, anxious in their fear of the imminent flood, to beg for their forgiveness, so that they would renounce impiety and injustice, provided that they feared the danger of impending death. The second point is this—and from this point we may gather that the clemency of the Lord is above every limit of a merciful man—because he wished to pardon an offense that lasted as many years as there were from the creation of the world in a span reduced to a few days, if only they would repent. For God is forgetful of sin, a rewarder of virtue, just as he himself says in the prophet: "'I am, I am he who blots out sins, and I will not remember them. But remember them yourself and let us discuss: speak your iniquities that you might be justified."[92] For when he noticed that the true virtue of the soul had been restored, he bestowed on it such great honor that not only did he indulge it with the forgiveness of earlier sins but he even offered grace and justification. Thus he waited also on the seventh day, the very day when he rested from work, so that if forgiveness were sought and correction would follow, he would rest from his indignation.

13.43. But it was also a concern not to pass over the fact that the flood happened, as he said "for forty days" and he added "for forty nights."[93] For we know that what is called a "day" is that which the sun shining on the earth designates, while "night" is that which the encircling darkness marks off from the brilliance of the day; very often "day" is understood by us so that

91. Gn 2.2.
92. Is 43.25–26.
93. Gn 7.12.

we do not include night with it, and often so that we do include it. For when we indicate the month as "thirty days," we also indicate the nights. Since it would have been enough for Moses to have said that the flood lasted for "forty days," one asks why he would have added "forty nights." And some who were before us have so understood it, that the death of both men and women was shown to have occurred in the flood, and they refer "day" to man, who is purer and like the light, while they refer "night" to woman, who is described as being created while the man slept; at the same time the man is prior, as though the source, who provokes the woman's power and rouses her to give birth, and he is more evident in public deeds, while she is darker as though she is sequestered within the household and closer to the night, born in the second place and formed in her creation from the rib of the man; she is thus dependent on the gift given to the earlier one; she is also subjected to the prerogative of the superior rank and likened to what is material in her practice of giving birth.[94] But the number of the danger agrees in regard to both of them, because their sins likewise agree, and it is right that the amount of time is no different between them, because the gravity of their sins is no different between them.

13.44. Many have investigated in no superficial manner why the flood lasted for forty days. And we can say that this particular number is assigned to sadder events, that is, for the destruction of creation, but the number seven is for the arrangement of the whole world, that is, for the happier events. But perhaps it refers also to the fact that the Law was brought forth in forty days. For Moses observed this many days on Mount Sinai, where he dwelt when he received the commands of the Law.[95] Thus it is fitting that the precepts of the sins that must be rejected were allotted in the same number of days as that by which the penalty for the guilt was paid off; thus we may know that the praise that comes from correction should be given during the period in the time of life when the crime worthy of punishment can be committed.

94. That is, the feminine supplies the "material" for the offspring. On ancient theories of reproduction see Joseph Needham, *A History of Embryology* (New York: Abelard-Schuman, 1959), 75–77.

95. Cf. Ex 34.28.

Thus even now forty days [of Lent] are not prescribed for penalty, but rather for life, so that by this number we might lighten the punishment for our sins with heightened prayer and fasting, and, intent through our faith and devotion to the prescriptions of the law, we might correct our error. And thus, because of the resurrection of the Lord, the fortieth day is now not considered the last day, but rather the first; and life is numbered from that day, when previously one computed the number [of days] of death until the consummation of the world and the destruction of the human race.

13.45. And he says, "I will wipe away every resurrection of the flesh from the face of the earth."[96] O the beauty of the heavenly words, if one should consider them with the fitting understanding of the reverent heart! God is indignant at our sins, but he does not forget piety; he threatens punishment, but he did not permit destruction: he tempers revenge, he checks his severity. He says that he will wipe away flesh not from "the earth," but rather from "the face of the earth." He cuts off the flower, he preserves the root: he permits the power of the human essence to remain in the depth; while it toils on the surface, it perseveres without suffering underneath, and, immune to harm, it is preserved for the new establishment of those who are not guilty of crime. But fittingly the text has "I will wipe away," as though he is speaking of the tracings of the letters, which are wiped off with no damage to the books and without wearing away the tablets. The ink is wiped away, but the wood remains. The elements are wiped away, so that much better ones may be written; the ink is removed, but the material is not damaged.[97] "I will wipe away," he says, "the corruption of flesh so that I might write down incorruption. I will wipe away the resurrection of the flesh from the face of the earth that I might write down those rising into heaven. I will wipe them away from the book of the earth so that I might write them in the book of life."[98] They are wiped away, O Lord, my Lord; the characters from the iron implement are wiped away quickly so that the characters of Christ might be

96. Gn 7.4.
97. Cf. 1 Cor 15.42.
98. Cf. Ps 69.28.

written. Let the earthly resurrection be abolished so that heavenly grace may redound. Come, Moses, prepare your bosom, receive the Law, receive the inscriptions that now divine mercy will not wipe away.[99] Receive the tablets that the Lord establishes forever. Would that you would not break them yourself! And my sin would have snatched them from me if the Lord had not returned them. Indeed rightly, Moses, you were indignant that those who do not offer deference should not have divine privileges, but I think that you would break them not for me but for the Jews. You broke them for the Jews, you received them for me. The former ones were broken so that the latter ones would remain. You broke them in the hearts of the Jews; for what good would it do them to have tablets whose commandments they could not observe? See, they say that they have the second tablets, but they do not have them. For they say that they read the divine words, but they do not read them. Moses says that the tablets were written by the finger of God:[100] they do not read the finger of God, they read the writing of a stylus. They see ink, they do not see the Spirit of God. But the Church does not know ink, she knows the Spirit. Thus Paul learned to write not with ink but with the Spirit of the living God.[101] O foolish sacrilegious people of the Jews! A man, indeed a man raised under the Law, writes by the Spirit of God, and they maintain that God wrote with ink, not with the Spirit.[102]

13.46. Thus let us return to the previous remarks, that God wipes away the resurrection of the flesh as though the writing of the inscriptions. By this it is clear that, under the symbolism of letters, God wiped away the useless birth of men on account of its unholiness, but, under the symbolism of the preservation of the tablets, he kept the essence and the condition of the human race so that from it he might grow the remaining seed. That statement seems even to fit with this point because he says:

99. Cf. Ex 32.19.

100. Cf. Ex 31.18; Dt 9.10.

101. Cf. 2 Cor 3.3.

102. Cf. Gal 1.14; Phil 3.5–6. On Ambrose and "literalism" of the Jews, see Maria Doerfler, "Ambrose's Jews: The Creation of Judaism and Heterodox Christianity in Ambrose of Milan's 'Expositio Evangelii Secundum Lucam,'" *Church History* 80 (2011): 769.

"I will wipe away," he says, "all resurrection of the flesh." But purification seems to be contrary to the resurrection that is normal according to the practice of nature, because by purification the profusion of regrowth is cut back and restrained. But all that is purged, while it loses its outer appearance, nevertheless preserves its essence and even improves it. Thus at that time, through the purification brought by the flood, the Lord restrained the use of the body and the condition of the generation that had declined from the beauty of its nature and from the loveliness of the gift received. This is the literal meaning. But as to what pertains to the higher meaning: the appearance of the flood is the type of the purification of our soul. Thus, when our spirit washes itself from the bodily pleasures of this world, by which it previously was delighted, it wipes off the stain of previous desire by means of its good thoughts, as though absorbing by purer waters the bitterness of what flowed turbidly before.[103]

13.47. And the text says, "Noah did everything the Lord God commanded him."[104] The just man accepts the words as charges, the servant accepts them as orders. The former is considered in the position of a friend, for he has done whatever he has accepted as a project to complete, while the latter, who hesitates to do his duty, is destined to the burden of servitude. Thus even the Lord Jesus says in the Gospel: "You are my friends if you do what I command you. I will no longer call you servants."[105] Thus Noah is commanded as a friend, he is commanded as one who carries out with hearty charity and with sober counsel what has been commanded. And the Lord's own judgment did not fail him. The just man fulfilled all things, not just a part of them, but all things that had been commanded to him, and for this he received the affirmation of divine Scripture. And do not consider it superfluous that the text placed together "Lord" and "God"—for God is both in the Lord and the Lord is in God—but you should take this as a commandment from the Father and the Son together. But some before us interpreted it in this way, that in speaking in this passage of "Lord" and "God" the

103. Cf. Ex 15.23.
104. Gn 7.5.
105. Jn 15.14–15.

text expressed the twin power of punishing and of forgiving;[106] but here because he first punishes sinners so the text first said "Lord," but since afterwards he forgives, so that the fertile soil of the just man might be sown, he named him "God" afterwards. Thus he is called "God" when he is about to make the world: "In the beginning God made heaven and earth; and God said, 'Let there be light.'"[107]

14.48. There is also the issue, which is not minor, that the flood happened in the six hundredth year on the twenty-seventh day of the seventh month.[108] There is no doubt that the seventh is the month of the springtime, when newborns are growing, when the field gives birth, and when the things that are to be born, both from the earth and from other living things, pour themselves out. For God made the flood at the time when the pain of those who were punished in their excess would be greater, when the vengeance would be more terrible, as though God said: "Behold, nature in its wealth has produced all things according to the grace of the generosity of divine providence, the earth in greater fertility has sprouted all things that are for human benefit, the rows of wheat can be seen, the fields are filled with barley, the branches of the trees are dressed with the flowers for the fruit that is to come. The earth does not fail in its obedience, the beasts in their obligations, since they are bearing their customary offspring so that humanity might lack nothing. Man alone fails in his roles, for he does not know his author, from whom all things are provided for him; he neglects the Creator. Man disdains his rewarder, although God has not despised his work. Let all things perish with the man on account of whom all things were born. Let man be consumed in his riches, let him die with his reward." Before man, the earth had never failed; in none of its bounty had it erred; in man alone did it know itself to have declined, bearing thorns and thistles instead of fruit.[109] The single gift that is truly marvelous, namely the governing faculty of the mind, perished. Why, then, are all those natural

106. Cf. *QG* 2.16.
107. Gn 1.1, 3.
108. Cf. Gn 7.11.
109. Cf. Gn 3.18.

things preserved? It is so that the water is not poured in after the fruit has been gathered, lest the land consider it more a benefit than a flood. Thus among the Egyptians, in springtime, the Nile pours forth, but in a different month, so that the land might soften for the seeds that are to be tossed in and the land might receive the seeds that have been cast with a more welcoming bosom and a more generous breast. But the fact that the flood happened in Noah's six hundredth year seems to point to the fact that Adam was created on the sixth day.[110] The same number, that is, the one that is said to be the same in both cases,[111] is preserved in the maker and the restorer, because the number six is the source of sixty and of six hundred. But the same is also said of the first and the seventh month. But we should observe the first especially because after the flood in the springtime, concern for harvesting the fields is restored and the seedlings of the smooth and bountiful soil begin to come forth. By this explanation it becomes clear that God would never have had human beings die in a number or time when he made their birth, unless he had been offended by their tremendous sins. At the same time, the rationale of the season and the number promises pardon, because even though God is angry, he is reminded by so many reasons for his previous gifts that he does not entirely destroy the essence of those whom he wished to forgive.

14.49. "And all the wells below broke forth, and the cataracts of the sky were opened."[112] Scripture expresses fittingly the force of the flood by saying that the sky and the earth are shaken equally, for from these elements every principle of this world exists. Thus the race of men is hemmed in from all sides, shut up by the gushing torrents of the waters. This is the literal interpretation. But this also relates to a higher interpretation, for the human mind is indicated by the symbol of the sky, while the body and the senses are indicated by the name of the earth. Thus the great shipwreck occurs when an upheaval and outburst of the mind and of all the senses and of the body are mixed together at the same time. Let us consider carefully what has been

110. Cf. Gn 1.27.
111. I.e., "six."
112. Gn 7.11.

said. Very often the deceit and fraud of the soul practice their poison, but yet the sobriety and continence of the body overshadow the wickedness of the mind. Often the mind is precarious, in the uncertainty of its faith and its own belief, but yet the flesh remains free of delights and indulgence, so that frugality absolves the error of the soul; likewise, there are many heretics who pretend to effect a continence of the body so that, by the witness of disciplined flesh, they might acquire credibility for their own claims; although they are unreliable in their thinking, yet they are considered a bit more justified inasmuch as they are less polluted. But sometimes the poison of the mind and the infection of bodily wretchedness confuse every sense and vitality, and the soul is tottering by an uncertain movement, rotted by the stain of malice, inflamed by the wrath of cruelty, and even provoked by bodily attacks; then a greedy attitude, unable to bear the weakness of the faculties in its desire for indulgence and its longing to pour itself out, is driven headlong into the crime of threatening another's well-being; then the flood rages, with every passion flooding in at the same time; then foolishness, injustice, rashness, wickedness, deceit seem to pour forth from the superior part of the soul as if they were cascades of the mind. At that point, from the spring of the earthly body, lust, drunkenness, indulgence, and ultimately the incitements to different crimes erupt; these weaken entirely both the strength of the body and the power of the mind.

15.50. "And God closed the Ark from outside."[113] The narrative according to the letter is obvious. The Ark had to be closed up and encircled with a safe protection so that no passing flows of the flood would enter into it. There is also interpretation according to the higher sense, which is not unfitting, if we observe that the human body, for which the Ark that is described serves as a figure, is bound by skin for the sake of defending it from cold and heat; for God the artist dressed it with natural coverings for the protection of all the members and covered it with a kind of surrounding handiwork, so that it may neither freeze up with the cold nor melt with the summer heat.

113. Gn 7.16.

15.51. Thus the water overflowed and raised the Ark, and the Ark was carried over the height of the waters.[114] Not without reason did the water "overflow," since the cascades of heaven opened and the wells and the rivers of the waters burst up from the earth. This is said with great emphasis. For when there is an eruption, then it must be that the effusion is uncontainable, and the pouring forth of the immense floods is not easily held back. Thus it is clear what is written. But if you want to look to a higher interpretation, consider that our flesh is agitated by different forces, and, in the manner of the sea, it is tossed by its passions, by which it is pitched here and there as though upon the waves of its own troubles: now in hunger, now in thirst, now in desire, now in joy, now in pain.

15.52. I also think another point should not be overlooked, because Scripture does not overlook it: that is, by how many cubits the water was above the earth. For it says that the water was fifteen cubits over the highest mountains.[115] Thus the simple interpretation is quite clear, but an allegory of the five senses is also included here, for they are in our body like the highest mountains, which overshadow this flesh with its passions, and they are often overrun by beasts and disturbed by their dark and shady crowds. Hence even the Lord, when he came to his Church, through the faith of the nations that believed, came from Lebanon, just as Habakkuk the prophet said: "The Lord will come from Lebanon, from a shady and dark mountain."[116] The Church also comes from Lebanon, as the Song of Songs has it. For there we read: "Come from Lebanon, O my bride, come from Lebanon. You shall cross and traverse from the beginning of the faith, and from the dens of lions and the mountains of the panthers,"[117] which are the people of the gentiles. Those who endured heavy attacks, as though of the bestial passions, now shine out in the height of the faith and the excellence of devotion. Thus through these mountains Christ comes, suppressing the movements of the wild body with his evangelical

114. Cf. Gn 7.17.
115. Cf. Gn 7.20.
116. Hab 3.3.
117. Song 4.8; Ambrose's text here differs significantly from the Vulgate.

instructions and breaking down that loftiness of the heart and the pride that exalts itself by means of his own obedience and humility; and rightfully those whom previously the floods of the heavy passions were submerging begin to bear the fruits of meekness. But regarding the number of cubits mentioned, certain writers before us have judged that the five senses have a triple perspective, by which sight sees the visible and hearing hears the audible and smelling smells the smell-able and taste tastes the taste-able and touch touches what underlies the substance to be touched.[118] For this reason, then, the five senses have been judged in a threefold way, or else because of this: "Write to yourself in a threefold way."[119] But I think this the more fitting reading, namely to interpret them as the senses of the earthly and animal and spiritual man, which those influxes of the flood overwhelmed.

15.53. Rightly it adds: "All flesh that moved died," which is clear according to the literal sense, and by the image of a storm-tossed disturbance the verse rightly and naturally expresses the corruption of the flesh.[120] For a disturbance is not vicious unless through the corruption of the disposition; and the flesh agitates the desires and is itself agitated by the desires, and such a disturbance then creates corruption. Thus the disturbance of this world is the cause of the corruption through which the individual soul deteriorates. For when the vicious passions upset the mind, corruption is brought forth; but when desires for virtues are aroused, there is progress in discipline. Thus "everyone who was on the dry land died"; for the ones whom the waves of such a great flood had overwhelmed could not avoid death. This is so according to what is written and the sequence of words.[121] Otherwise, if you look for the allegory, there is no doubt that it appears in the example of very dry wood, which burns up the minute that flame begins to touch it; so too the soul, unless dampened by the dew of different virtues, watered by a sort of drop of wisdom and a well of justice and a drizzle of chastity,

118. *QG* 2.22.
119. Prv 22.20.
120. Gn 7.21.
121. That is, the literal sense.

flames out with a burning of desires as though its living root has dried out, or else when dashed by the flood of the flesh it topples over. Hence the soul should always dine on the thoughts of good works, so that the mind grows fat, drunken with the nectar of prudence, by which it does not easily yield to the violence of the bodily flood and it does not perish when weakened by the dry neglect of carelessness. Therefore, the Lord warns us not to depart from the well of wisdom, and to drink from the cups of virtue, so that no one dry up in the sun of iniquity and fail to endure the storm of persecution. For it is written: "But if this is how they act in the wet, what will happen in the dry?"[122]

15.54. It says: "God wiped away everything that was on the face of the earth."[123] The explanation of the writing is clear, but the allegory shows that pride has been present to us, a pride that extols itself in this earthly and fragile substance and, heedless of divine things while despising human things, distorts the manner and the gait of the arrogant man. These sorts of people Isaiah describes as the daughters of Judah, fluttering with their blinking eyes and casting themselves high with a lofty neck.[124] For there arc those who raise their eyebrows in this way, with an inflated heart, a puffed-up breast, a twisted neck, who graze the ground with the bottoms of their feet, but who balance themselves in their whole body and poise themselves as though hanging in the void by a needle, who make their way with their footsteps ahead of them while they lean their heads back behind them; they gaze upon heaven, yet they despise the earth, as though they are affected by a pain in their neck, so that they cannot bend it. Thus God wiped these people from the book of life, saying:[125] "Everyone who exalts himself will be humiliated,"[126] and when heavenly things have been arranged, God will not have these people stand among the merits of the saints.[127]

15.55. When all who were outside the Ark had been de-

122. Lk 23.31.
123. Gn 7.23.
124. Cf. Is 3.16.
125. Cf. Rv 3.5.
126. Lk 14.11.
127. Latin unclear.

stroyed, "only Noah was left with those who were with him in the Ark."[128] The very simple statement does not need interpretation—the interpretation concurs with the letter—but the higher and inner meaning shows that the just man, the lover of wisdom, is like the fruitful tree among the ones now dead who used to devour his bounty, to overshadow his foliage, and to bind up the extension of his branches; as though free from the irrational passions, he remains alone with those familiar to him. For the judgments of his heart, which cling to virtue, are pure. And rightly he adds that they remained in the Ark, as though it is scarcely believable that, once his bodily passions were removed, he would seem still to live in the body; here, although he now lacked earthly contact, he preserved the substance of the body, though unstained, and in the body he was borne above the flood as though he were bodiless; he was not engulfed and, indeed, he bore the body as though placed in the heart of the Ark; but he was himself unassailable by the passions as though he were bodiless, and he steered the body itself in the midst of very great disturbances.

16.56. "The Lord remembered Noah and the beasts and the cattle,"[129] as the divine Scripture says. Many are disturbed because the writer does not say that God remembered the wife and sons of Noah, even though he remembered the beasts and the cattle.[130] But when he said that he remembered Noah, he included the rest of his relatives in the author and the leader of the household. At the same time, there seems to be expressed a certain unanimity among the surviving relatives. For when all are dear to each other, the household is one; but when they disagree, they are separated and divided into many houses. Thus when there is charity, the entire house is indicated in the name of the eldest, on whom the rest depend; just as if someone says "tree," then he includes the branches, too, and if someone names the branch, the fruit that are on it are also included in one and the same utterance.

16.57. And it does not seem pointless that first it says, "God

128. Gn 7.23.
129. Gn 8.1.
130. Cf. *QG* 2.26.

remembered Noah, then the beasts, and then the cattle," that is, why those animals that are milder are not mentioned after man, but rather the more ferocious ones are. The reason for this seems to be that the ones that were more ferocious calmed down by proximity to the other group. That also seems to be declared in that verse of poetry: κακοὺς δ' εἰς μέσσον ἔλασσεν.[131] For from this the poet also understood that he [Nestor] organized the arrangement of an army that was about to fight so that he located the weaker in the middle, by which they might be helped more by the stronger sides, and so that they might take up the fight of one side or the other. In this sense the account of what is written is clear. But it is understood by the higher sense that the just man restricts to the middle, not to the sides, the thoughts of his heart, and, for as long as he lives his life, he necessarily has fierce beasts in his body as though in that Ark. For there is no mind, no soul, that does not also receive the wild movements of evil thoughts. Thus the soul of the fool sharpens the beastly disturbances and incites the poisons of the serpents, but the vigor of the wise softens and binds them.

16.58. "And the Lord led the Spirit over the land, and the water ceased."[132] I do not think this is said in this way so that by the word "spirit" we should understand "wind." For the wind could not dry out a flood; otherwise, the sea would be entirely empty because it is shaken by wind daily. For would not the entire sea be emptied out by the force of such winds, to which yielded a flood that was spread over the whole world all the way to the so-called pillars of Hercules and was a great sea foaming up over the steep cliffs of the highest mountains?[133] Thus there is no doubt that that flood was made to subside by the invisible power of the divine Spirit, by the heavenly operation, not by a blast of wind. Hence it is written: "All things await from you that you give them food in due season. When you open your hand, the universe is filled with goodness; when you turn away your face, they will be troubled. Carry off their spirit, and they

131. "He placed the evil into the middle" (Homer, *Iliad* 4.299); see above, 2.4, p. 31. The repetition of the verse is found in Philo, as well.

132. Gn 8.1.

133. Cf. Gn 7.19.

will fail and they will be turned into their dust. Send forth your Spirit, and they will be created, and you shall renew the face of the earth."[134] Thus there is a Spirit, to whose action the cosmos seems to yield, in whom is the power of heaven itself, just as it is written: "By the word of the Lord the heavens were created, and by the Spirit of his face all their strength."[135] This Spirit is the Creator of all things, just as Job also says: "The divine Spirit who made me."[136]

17.59. Now let us consider what it means when Scripture says: "The springs of the waters and the cascades of heaven were closed."[137] I do not think the meaning is unclear. For the flood diminished for the same reasons that it grew. The springs of water broke forth, the cascades of heaven were opened, and then the earth was flooded with the waters flowing in from all sides. The things from which the source of the flood flowed had to be closed so that its decrease would commence. So the letter indicates, but a subtler interpretation expresses how it is that the flood of the heart bursts in with the fault of the mind and of bodily indulgence, so that malice is mixed with passion, and passion with malice. When the Word of God entered as the physician in order to visit the soul, which was laboring long in sickness with the wickedness of disputes and bitterness of the passions, first the causes of the sickness had to be cut out. For the principle of medicine is to cut out the causes of the weakness, so that whatever is harmful does not serve to increase the sickness any longer. The Law teaches us this as well.[138] For when the leprosy had reached the point at which it would not spread further, then he said that the stopping point, as it were, and residence of the leprosy was clean; for whatever moves against nature is unclean. For this is the cleanliness of the soul, this is the health of the mind: that the influx of the error should cease, that sin stay still and not slip in. When the incentive for sin and crime ceases, health is assured, and an undamaged vigor restores itself to the soul.

134. Ps 104.27–30.
135. Ps 33.6.
136. Jb 33.4.
137. Gn 8.2.
138. Cf. Lv 13.4.

17.60. And it says: "The Ark came to rest on the twenty-seventh day of the seventh month."[139] Unless you pay close attention, understanding this passage is difficult even according to the letter. And first of all you must be careful lest the quick repetition of "the seventh month" upset you. For it had said this: that the flood began in the six hundredth year; in the seventh month on the twenty-seventh of the month the flood began; and the flood of the waters lasted for one hundred fifty days, and the Ark came to rest in the seventh month on the twenty-seventh day of the month: afterwards by the mercy of God the waters began to subside, and the subsiding of the waters occurred for one hundred fifty days, and afterwards the peaks of the mountains began to appear; then after forty days Noah opened the holy gate of the Ark, the raven that was sent forth did not return, the dove that was sent forth returned empty, and again after seven days, when it was sent out, it returned with an olive branch, and when sent a third time it did not return after seven days, then Noah understood that all the water had receded. And so it is shown that the year ended in the seventh month on the twenty-seventh day of the month [and so the year is shown to have concluded in the six-hundred-and-first year of Noah in the second month on the twenty-seventh of the month].[140] But what pertains to the clear explanation is that the stability of the earth is restored after the flood on the same day of the same month on which it was destroyed when the inflow of the flood began. For every field flourishes in springtime, and the earth bears fruit. Then the trees begin to bud, and the fruit to sprout. Hence, the Lord recreated its bounty and restored its quality. Thus in the second month, that is, April—for the first month is March, when the just man has his birthday,[141] when the equality of days and nights is determined, that is the eighth as the Romans reckon or the fifth of the kalends of April as others reckon—I say in

139. Gn 8.4.

140. Manuscripts are unclear here; see Schenkl, *De Noe*, lxi.

141. In Philo, the reference is to Noah; see *QG* 2.31. Ambrose may also be observing the tradition that identifies the *dies natalis* ("birthday," but also the day of birth to eternal life, i.e., death) of Christ (the just man) in March (the 25th); see Alden A. Mosshammer, *The Easter Computus and the Origins of the Christian Era* (Oxford: Oxford University Press, 2008), 48–49.

the second month, that is, April, on the twenty-seventh of the month, the flood began. Thus the spring is reckoned to be the start of the year, not according to the practice of the season, but according to the prerogative of nature, because at that time the hope of the year begins and the fruit begins to show itself, and so it seems to be the beginning and source of the year. But the seventh month calculated according to its number is the one called September, because the year also seems to begin from the month of September, just as the practice of the present declarations (*indictiones*) shows—for then the seed is strewn—but indeed, from that point grace begins to show itself more fully, from the point when the origin of the year is determined;[142] and therefore what is called first according to one way of thinking is held to be seventh by another reckoning.

So, therefore, the Ark rests, that is, in the seventh month on the twenty-seventh of the month above the mount of Ararat.[143] From that point the flood begins to subside. Likewise, consider that with the same number by which some things begin they are resolved, so that the flood begins in the second month of the year on the twenty-seventh day of the month; the flood flows for one hundred fifty days; the flood subsides for another one hundred fifty days; for forty days the excessive force from the heavenly rain and the outbreak of the floods rages; forty more days pass, after which the peaks of mountains appear; in the eleventh month on the first day of the month the saintly Noah sends out his raven. Thus it shows that the flood is diminished by the same number during which it gathered. Hence Scripture teaches us that the order should be preserved.

17.61. But according to a bodily interpretation, it was stated above what the gate of the Ark that the just man opens is.[144] According to a higher interpretation, however, the passage seems to say that the senses of the body are like gates. For through

142. On *indictiones*, periods of fifteen years each observed in the Roman Empire and the early papacy, see Lesley Adkins and Roy Adkins, *Handbook to Life in Ancient Rome* (New York: Facts on File, 1994), 374.

143. Manuscripts are unclear here, but on the basis of the Vulgate reading, Pastorino suggests *Ararati* (*Noè*, 441 n.8).

144. Cf. Gn 8.6.

them, as though through gates, the comprehension of sensible objects in a certain manner enters into our mind. Thus our mind seems to gaze out through these senses, and most of all through vision, which is judged the most outstanding of all the bodily senses, because it is familiar to light and, through it, when gazing at the sky, the land, the seas, and the sun, the moon and the stars by which the sky is decorated, we understand that God is the maker and conductor of the world, and we believe that such great works could not have come to be or exist without God as the Author and Creator.

17.62. Thus through this window the just man sent the first raven.[145] The reason for this should be considered; and since it is not obscure as far as the letter is concerned, many interpret the raven as an augury of future things, and they observe its calls and investigate its flight. But the higher sense signifies that the mind of the just man, when it begins to purify itself, casts from itself first whatever is cloudy and unclean and heedless; indeed all that is immodest and sinful is dark and feeds on what is dead, as does the raven, but virtue is close to the light, which shines out in purity and simplicity of heart. And thus it is as though sin itself is sent out and put to flight and is separated from innocence so that nothing cloudy remains in the mind of the just man. Thus the raven that has departed does not return to the just man because every sin shrinks away from equity and does not seem to fit with uprightness and justice.[146] Thus when the just man has separated himself from his fellowship, the unjust man thinks that he has escaped, as though from chains, although he is now part of a kind of flood and corruption, just like the raven, who, when he did not find dry land nearby, did not return but remained outside.

17.63. One should consider also why it says that the raven did not return, "until the water dried from the land," as though afterwards he did return.[147] But this way of speaking is common in divine Scripture, and indeed even in the Gospel you find it written about Saint Mary that Joseph did not know her until she

145. Cf. ibid.
146. Cf. Gn 8.7.
147. Ibid.

bore a son, when indeed he did not even know her afterwards.[148] Then why is it put this way, since it says, “until the water dried from the land,” and not, “the land from the water”? Again, the ordinary way of speaking generally puts it the latter way. Yet some before us judged in the fact that a certain immoderate force of the passions seems expressed by this manner of putting it, because the soul is consumed by stormy and fervent passions, but once they weaken and, as it were, dry up, the soul gains its strength again.[149] For thus the appearance of sin does not return into the soul of the just, as though it is leaving it dry and dead, and it can no longer do it any harm.

18.64. And it is not for nothing that afterwards a dove is sent out;[150] for indeed, simplicity also undoes malice, and virtue undoes guilt. Thus malice loves the flood; it flees fellowship with the righteous mind, and it remains as though abandoned and without any home, since it has no fellowship with virtue; but virtue comes home because it loves fellowship with the just and it is more comfortable in extending its usefulness to others; for it confers what is healing and warns that whatever will do harm should be avoided. Just so the dove that was sent forth, when it saw that the water had stopped, returned as though full of justice, so that it might announce to him from whom it had been sent what he should still avoid and how he might be able to acquire better fruit by waiting. But the fact that the dove returned to him when it did not find rest gave a clear indication through birds of this sort how great the difference is between malice and virtue;[151] indeed, the raven that was sent out before, although it seemed that the flood overflowed a bit more, apparently found a place to rest. And clearly the raven does not belong to the same kind as the other birds that are accustomed to spend their life on water. Thus when the raven seems to have found a place where it might rest, but the dove did not find anything, the clear

148. Cf. Mt 1.25; Ambrose makes a connection between *donec*/ἕως (“until”) in Gn 8.7 and Mt 1.25 present already in Origen, *Commentary on Matthew,* frag. 22.1–4.

149. Cf. *QG* 2.37.

150. Cf. Gn 8.8.

151. Cf. Gn 8.9.

explanation is revealed by the higher interpretation, namely that malice generally mixes itself with the disquieting passions and lusts, by which the soul is corrupted, and delights in them as though they are friends and family and there finds its habitat; but virtue, in the very instant it has been offended by the vision that appears to it, hastens to return to the heart and mind of the just man. For there is found the safest dwelling place, by the fact that just like the dove, so virtue of this sort could not find the safest dwelling place elsewhere. Indeed, only gradually does simplicity manage to find a haven among the deceptions of this world and the floods of worldly desires.

18.65. Thus just as virtue, having departed a little for the sake of getting a glimpse, hastens to return to the best mind and does not depart far from the just man, so also the just man, the one eager for virtue, when he knows that virtue approaches, extends the bosom of his mind. For what else does it mean that Noah, the man eager for virtue, extends his hand and takes in the dove and draws it to himself?[152] But even if it seems clear according to the letter, yet you do not easily get the point, unless it is known to you that this is a custom of a wise man, who uses virtue as a spy and seems to entrust it with a certain prerogative for exploring and managing his affairs. Thus this virtue evaluates different natures, so that if one of them seems fit for itself, he can increase the nature's yield. For the goodness of wisdom is shared, and it is ample and generous with its usefulness, so that it associates with itself whatever it sees as docile. But when it sees that the nature of some people hesitates before its proposal, it flies back and retreats as though to a guesthouse that is familiar to it; opening his whole heart, the wise and diligent man hastens to receive this wisdom, as though with a certain hand extended from his mind, by which he held it even while it was absent; for the wise man can never be separated from his own virtue.

18.66. But what else would it mean that he held the dove for seven more days and sent it off again,[153] unless that you understand that the goodness and highest intention of the wise man strives always to join others to itself, to correct the wandering, to

152. Cf. Gn 8.9.
153. Cf. Gn 8.10.

fix the lost? If he observes someone recoiling at first, nevertheless he does not despair of progress in changing and correcting him. For just as the good doctor, even if it be not the time for the medicine, still fixes beforehand a lookout for the visit, and thus does not neglect to keep watch for an appropriate period of waiting, yielding for a little while to the passions as he awaits the occasion for healing, and when the occasion has been given he does not neglect his duty; so in this way the wise man also desires to heal contrary passions with words and reasoning, just as the physician desires to do with medicines. And because in everything one should employ the healing of God's good favor, so Noah waited seven days, the period in which the whole world is described as being completed and in which rest is provided to the Creator, so that instruction for human activity would be drawn from the very Author of all things.[154]

19.67. Thus "the dove returned in the evening, having the leaf and branch of the olive in its mouth."[155] Not for nothing does the verse have "the evening" and "returned" and "having the leaf and branch of the olive in its mouth," so that you may not think virtue flutters away from future progress, if it can achieve any, and so that you know that virtue was not again without light and hidden in some shadows, but that it was gleaming in the daylight, waiting until day's end, and then returned to him in whose company there are not even shadows of evening. And the leaf that the dove bore with herself, even if it might seem that she brought back a little leaf, indicates the hope of those for whom there is repentance for any error—hope that might not be great but is still some hope; for there could be no leaf without a branch. The dove carried, therefore, some sign, albeit a small one, of the budding reform that was taking place, and it was the leaf of an olive tree, in which tree the olive sprouts, and from which the oil is made, by which this material light is nourished and the darkness of night is put to flight. For what is more proper to virtue than light? Thus the leaf with the branch is a mark of reform, and reform has repentance as though its very root, for this repentance cannot sprout in tu-

154. Cf. Gn 8.12 and 2.2.
155. Gn 8.11.

multuous [souls], but only in those who have already received the spiritual word. And the fact that the olive branch is carried in her mouth seems not to be superfluous, since virtue and wisdom have a brilliance in the very mention of them, and their light gleams immediately in their appearance, most of all when peaceful things are spoken, since those seeking peace are accustomed to offer this branch. The dove brought the branch, because simplicity by means of purity and sincerity pours in certain seeds that are useful to our ears; and the teaching of good virtue either provokes to readiness and invites to the prize the one who is aware of the discipline that is good for him, or else it casts into the sinner the desire for doing penance and for pursuing conversion.

19.68. In addition, it seems worth considering how the saintly Noah knew that the water had left the land, just as it is written.[156] First of all, according to the letter: the fact that he could tell whether it was dry or wet when the leaf was brought forth, since the dove was not the sort of bird that could draw forth fruit that was hidden under the water. But you should consider whether that leaf had sprouted before the flood or during the time of the flood. If it was before the flood, the just man rejoiced that some fruit from the old seed had been preserved, and, in that, he recognized a sign of divine mercy, because now that the flood had subsided, which the fruit had demonstrated, there was something that the floods had been unable to damage. If the leaf was born during the time of the flood, the just man notes that the new seeds of heavenly mercy had borne fruit, so that the roots of the trees would live and the souls, as though reawakened, would sprout old seedlings and return to their accustomed production—all facts that sprouting leaves would demonstrate.

19.69. But it follows by a higher interpretation that the Lord our God, although he might be offended by the bitter errors of our iniquity, nevertheless preserves some small remnant or seed of our ancient heritage and homeland, lest every mark of his work and creation concerning the human race be completely destroyed. Thus even Isaiah says: "If the Lord of Hosts had not left us a seed, we would become Sodom and would be like Go-

156. Cf. ibid.

morrah,"[157] expressing in the name of one city a mark of blindness, in the name of the other sterility. For thus, in their native tongue, the Chaldeans use the names Sodom and Gomorrah to refer to blindness and sterility. And rightly the Lord, in the case of cities of this sort, destroyed human vices rather than judge men worthy of punishment.

19.70. For the third time after seven days the dove was sent off, and that one did not return. Thus we consider whether this is contrary to what we said above. If indeed this word "dove" in the text, which in reality is virtue, does not return to the just man, then would the just man be bereft and stripped of his reward? Not at all. For the man of this sort is never cut off from his virtue, and, when he sends forth justice from his mouth and prompts discussion of some virtue, he does not strip himself of the virtue and despoil himself of the equitable fairness that others should imitate, but in the manner of the sun, when it sends forth the rays of its light, he shines on others.[158] For surely fire warms those who approach, just as much as it possesses the heat of its nature. Does the light of day weaken when it illuminates the whole world with its brilliance? It maintains its own path unobstructed and its own nature undiminished. So too that same virtue, under the appearance of the dove while the flood was still raging, returned to the just man: while on the earth, [it does so] in the form of a bird; but in the passions of men, in the form of virtue, for virtue could not find any place where it could rest in the hearts of the wicked. And so during that second return, when the dove comes back, it stops and rests. But also when the floods of passions seethe and many are eager to be companions of the word they have heard and the doctrine they have discovered, then the teaching of virtue begins to be not the patrimony of one man, but a common good. Like a cup of wisdom, it is drunk by many who refused to drink when they were thirsty before; just so now the floods seethe in the hearts of the Jews, and although the water of heavenly teaching pours out and the drink abounds, they think they should not drink. The Gospel is

157. Is 1.9.

158. That is, when the virtuous man speaks about ("sends forth") virtue, the virtue does not somehow leave him.

read, the virtue comes forth from heavenly speech, the priest explains the teaching in the Church; but sometimes he even leaves the Church, so that it does not happen that he should be alone within the Ark where he could not be heard. He goes where the Jew happens to be, he admonishes, and he offers the example of heavenly Scriptures; they close their ears so that the spring not flow on those who are unwilling, and the dew from the Lord's word not sprinkle them. But those who have believed, they run to the spring, they seek the teaching, they desire that the Gospel be imparted to them, and they are not satisfied even by ravenous drinking. So they want immediately to be filled by the font of wisdom, which they were formerly contriving to escape. Which spring? Listen to him saying: "If anyone thirst, let him come to me and drink. The one who believes in me, as Scripture says, rivers of living water flow from his heart."[159]

20.71. In the six-hundred-and-first year of the life of Noah, on the first day of the <first> month, it says that the water has vanished from the face of the earth, yet in the second month, the twenty-seventh day of the month, it recalls that the land is dry.[160] What does that addition about the diminishment of the water mean, when the accounting calculated previously seems to have concluded the year, the year that begins from the second month and proceeds as far as the second month of the next year? Should we not here perhaps take it that the form of the just man has been indicated? Thus the first year was the year in which the flood began, and the first year after the six hundredth, as it were, is again the first year and first month after the six hundredth year, when the water was diminished from the face of the earth. The fact is that the just man in the generation of sinners, which was wiped out on account of sin, was first in virtue; and in the second generation, which began after the flood, he was first in order, because he was the first of the second generation. And rightly he emerged first. For rightly honor is granted to the one who also was the first of the first generation and the source of the later one, who deserved also to depart from that previous generation and to be perpetuated as the fertile soil

159. Jn 7.37–38.
160. Cf. Gn 8.13–14; "first" (*primi*) added by Schenkl.

for the next generation. But when the others had perished, he alone, by virtue of his outstanding life and by the prerogative of his virtue, was rich before God and had no part in wicked corruption, and through him it happened that the whole body of the human race seemed not to be destroyed on earth nor to be abandoned, cut off from the grace of God.

20.72. "And Noah," it says, "stripped off the roof of the Ark."[161] When we take the Ark as a type of the body, just as we interpreted it above, let us understand what it means to strip the body, that is, according to the higher sense. On the other hand, the verse makes clear, according to the letter, how the Ark could be opened. What, then, is the roof of the human body, which was closed during the flood, unless perhaps we take it to mean the delight that was covering this body of ours and roofing it, as it were, through that sin of Adam? And it is especially considered to be like a roof, because all the senses are in the head, from which comes the delight that holds each body subject. But when the mind of the just man is sober and secure from the corruption of the flood, and, inflamed by the desire for divine knowledge, it wants to leap out and fly forth into higher things, then it removes all things that were an impediment, while it uncovers and removes the allure of desire, which was covering the other parts of the body by a sort of drapery; hence, not only does it free the body from slavery to an ignoble mistress, but it also grasps the things that were incorporeal. For the things that are not seen are eternal.[162] And thus the just man, free of corruption and eager for eternity, seeks the Lord whom he did not see.

20.73. But why it then speaks of the first or second month and says this was a day in springtime,[163] you find it said elsewhere: "This month will be for you the first in the days of the year."[164] For the one who is first in grace after danger rightly receives the prerogative of the first month.

20.74. And so that you not be upset by what we said above,

161. Gn 8.13.
162. 2 Cor 1.14.
163. Cf. Gn 8.13–14.
164. Ex 12.12.

about the leaf found on the branch possibly being generated after the flood—even if grasses are very often accustomed to sprout under water—still, so that all doubt may be removed:[165] Why is it so impressive that, by God's command, on the very day when the water subsided, the land also sprouted right away, since the Restorer of the fruit is the same as the Creator and he did not forget the practice of his handiwork? Thus you have the text, right in the beginning, that he commanded that the earth sprout the grass for food and the fruit-bearing tree with its fruit[166]—and immediately the earth brought forth the grass for food with its seed according to its kind and the fruit-bearing tree[167]—and that was the only day when God commanded this or made it. Thus God, who is not forgetful of his gifts, but forgetful of our iniquity, repairs his handiwork in the same amount of time during which he began it.

21.75. And the Lord God said to Noah: "Depart from the Ark, you and your wife and your sons."[168] Thus when the water receded and the land dried, Noah could leave the Ark. Yet the just man attributes nothing to himself, but he commits himself entirely to the divine command. And it is especially true that one who had entered by heavenly command should await a response from heaven that he exit; for justice is reverent, since iniquity is irreverent, for it seizes what does not belong to it and it does not reverence the maker.

21.76. Now let us seek the reason why, in the time when they were entering the Ark, the order of those entering was that Noah entered first with his sons, then his wife and the wives of his sons; but when they left the order changed. For it is written: "He himself left, and his wife and his sons and the wives of his sons."[169] And the literal interpretation indicates that upon their entrance they refrain from procreation, while upon exiting they practice procreation. For at the time when the father entered first with his sons and his sons with their parent, and

165. See above, 19.68, p. 74.
166. Gn 1.11.
167. Gn 1.11–12.
168. Gn 8.15–16.
169. Gn 8.18.

afterwards his wife and the wives of his sons, that is, the sexes are not commingled at their entrance, but they are mixed at their exit. For clearly, through the order of their entrance, the just man sends out a sort of message, that the time when destruction was threatening everything was not appropriate for intercourse and delights. Hence in the Gospel the Lord says in rebuke that in the times of Noah they were eating and drinking, taking wives and giving their daughters in marriage, and thus on account of their intemperance the flood overcame them.[170] Thus that was a time of mourning, not of joy, and hence the just man was not delighting in the fellowship of a wife, and the just sons were not seeking marital union—for how unseemly that in the time when the living were dying, some who would then be born would perish!—but afterwards, when the flood receded, it was proper that the practice of and concern for marriage followed, so as to plant the seeds of other people. Thus men did not leave with men, but women left with men, so that the masculine mixing would be shown to be forbidden in itself, but that the masculine and feminine union, made legal by the bond of marriage, would be shown to be permitted.

21.77. But the higher interpretation is this: that when there is danger, certain masculine and stronger thoughts cling to the mind, and it is as if the mind is guarded by them as by some generation of sons, by which a masculine battle line might oppose the storms and the harsher passions. But when the danger is past, there is no harm if milder thoughts are bound to stronger ones, so the stronger ones are not feminized by the softer ones, but rather the softer senses are strengthened as though by masculine ones, when all of our counsels are directed to virtue, justice, integrity, and courage, and when virtue can be created, as it were, through habit and training, and stronger counsels can mature. Thus it is not helpful, when there is some confusion of the vices that occupy the mind, for the mind to sow other thoughts and to procreate and give birth. When, however, desires will have been stilled and the mind will have been at rest, then through the reception of a certain fertile soil of judgment, virtues and good works can also sprout.

170. Cf. Lk 17.26.

22.78. The next verse says, "Noah built an altar for God."[171] One might ask why previously the Lord commands all the things that Noah would do and did, but here Noah did something that God did not command. But indeed the Lord should not, like some greedy man, demand a reward of thanks, and the just man understands that the true thanksgiving is not that which is bidden, but that which is offered freely. Thus he suffered no delay. For the soul's power for gratitude refuses to allow any hesitation; but the one who owes thanks, who waits for it to be demanded from him, is ungrateful. But it says, "He built it for God," and it does not say he built it for the Lord, but for God; according to the interpretation of the name this thanksgiving does not seem to be coerced as though to a master, but rather the obliging and grateful virtue of the just man sets aside for God what is characteristically given to a ruler, and he gives the offering the name of blessing.

22.79. "And he took from the clean birds and beasts and he offered a holocaust," it says.[172] The literal meaning is clear, that we ought to offer things that are unstained, in which the attitude of the one who makes the offering shines out; the higher interpretation takes it in this way, that the meaning of the clean beasts are the senses of the wise man, while the birds are his insights, which are by far subtler and lighter.

22.80. But now let us consider more carefully what it means when it says, "The Lord God reconsidered and said: 'I will not again curse the earth on account of the works of men, because the heart of man remains firmly fixed on evils from his youth.'"[173] It will not thus add that he would strike all flesh, as he had done, for all the days of the earth. Even if he punished the race of men again, still he knew that punishment leads more to fear of the law and the knowledge of discipline than to the transformation of nature, which can be corrected in some aspects but cannot be changed in all. Thus the Lord punished them so that we might fear, but he spared us that we might be preserved, and at one point he punished us as an example to inspire fear;

171. Gn 8.20.
172. Ibid.
173. Gn 8.21.

in the future he will spare us, so that bitter sin not be restrained only through subjugation; also because when someone desires to punish sins more frequently, he is considered cruel rather than stern. Thus God says: "I will not again curse the earth on account of the works of men,"[174] that is, he punishes a few, and he preserves many, because he wants to declare his own devotion for all of humanity, yet he also should not impart to human hearts any laxity and negligence. Hence when it says: "I will not again," it shows that he alleviates the troubles of people rather than weighing them down, knowing that the sins in people cannot be entirely removed; as it appears in the proverb, the one who tries to remove evil from the human heart is like someone who desires to drink water with a woven net.[175]

22.81. The verse says, "I will not again curse the earth on account of the sins of men, because the mind of man remains firmly fixed on evils from his youth."[176] See how carefully God shows that we fail by saying the mind of man remains ever on evils, by which statement he seems to indicate that the heart of man addictively hastens to sins and that the slipperiness of sinning is present in our governing faculty and that the desire for worse things is never lacking. For thus it says "firmly," as though we are harassed so that freedom from sin cannot find its way into us. And it does not say "on one evil," but on many evils, and it adds "from his youth"; for evil increases from that stage of life,[177] even if we read elsewhere that a one-day-old infant cannot be without sin, and also infancy cannot be without sin, on account of a weakness of the body;[178] but striving and zeal for sinning begins from youth, so that a boy sins somehow through weakness, while the young man sins through wickedness, for he desires assiduously to commit sins and he glories in his crimes;[179]

174. Ibid.

175. The proverb, of unknown origin, appears at *QG* 2.54.

176. Gn 8.21.

177. I.e., youth.

178. Cf. Jb 14.4–5; the text would become a frequent source in the development of teaching on original sin.

179. On the different stages of life, which distinguished *infantia*, "infancy," from *pueritia*, "childhood," and *iuuentus*, "young adulthood," see Beryl Rawson, *Children and Childhood in Roman Italy* (Oxford: Oxford University Press, 2003).

indeed, among many young men, innocence is held to be scurrilous, and blame is considered to be praise. Thus young men often vaunt their excesses and their delights and the pleasures of adulterous relations. Therefore, guilt increases with the stages of life. Thus God declares that the race of men should not now be consumed, when he says: "I will not again strike all flesh," but punishment is reserved for one part.[180]

23.82. But what does it mean when it says: "Seedtime and harvest, cold and heat, summer and spring, by day and night they will not rest"?[181] According to the letter it signifies that the animals and all the groves will remain unharmed while the seasons remain according to the Lord's design and their own state of being. For when the seasons are harmed, so too are all those things that are born in their own seasons. And if there is a confusion of seasons, how can those things that are born remain once the confusion has occurred? Indeed, there are seasons that either corrupt or preserve, insofar as they have that quality in themselves. For thus the year is drawn from contraries: spring, autumn, summer, and winter. Just as the harmony of a song seems to consist in the mixture of the flats and the sharps, so too this world is held together from contraries: from air and earth, from fire and water. Our bodies also preserve a certain order to their nature, from cold and hot, wet and dry. And if the natural order and measure are confused, death necessarily follows. Thus the Lord promises that once the confusion of the flood is removed, there will be a fixed order of seasons for the perseverance of the world.

23.83. But the higher meaning is this: that by "the seed" we might understand the beginning, and by "the harvest" we might understand the end. In both there is the motive for salvation. One without the other is imperfect, because one says: "Where the beginning is, the end is sought, and the beginning cannot be without the end, and the end returns to the beginning."[182] Therefore, he remembers that the human race, while it is in this world, will always return to the same things, so that when

180. Gn 8.21.

181. Gn 8.22.

182. The source for this saying is unclear.

the year begins, it ends, and when it ends, it begins, and the world is not divided during the time in the middle. In the same way the mind, when it seems to begin something, strives all the way to the end and seeks the completion of its act. When the mind completes some project, it does not celebrate as though the work is complete. Rather, it returns to other works and always achieves an increase in virtue when it sees that the earth is always restored to bear its fruits, which are born differently in different seasons, either in spring and summer as in the regions of the East, or in summer and autumn as in the regions of the West.

23.84. In one season the seeds of the lands bring forth their sprouts, and in another season we pluck the fruits of the trees. Thus the fruits are distinguished between the necessary and the desired: the necessary are from the seeds of the lands, but the desired are from the fruits of the trees. Thus our body is fed by natural food in spring, that is, ἔαρι. But ἔαρ is a Greek name, which is called *ver* in Latin.[183] Thus Scripture took this example from the regions of the east, especially Egypt, through which the Hebrew people passed, or else from the regions of Phoenicia. But the soul is nourished by its pleasures, that is, by the fruits of wisdom; to wisdom, fear and anger seem to be opposed, just as cold and heat are contrary to our body. But since the soul is in the body, it is necessary that it have both anger and fear. It cannot be without this necessity of a bodily nature. And thus the mind of the wise man distributes balanced instructions, lest it should mix together fear and anger, and a certain confusion and flood occur in that man's soul.

23.85. The verse also says "by day" and "by night" so that you understand by "day" the virtue that illuminates, and by "night" you recognize cloudy foolishness. Thus virtue can be illuminating in fear as though it is in the cold. Likewise temperance can repress anger, so that someone is not entirely undone by fear, but rather by fear he is directed to works of virtue, for instance, if a persecutor pressures him, so that you fear God more and you think eternal punishments should be avoided more than present punishments; when you fear eternal punishments, you

183. Or "springtime" in English.

are angered at treachery and transgression, and so you are ignited for glory; on the other hand, enflamed in your wrath, you may also temper your agitation by the fear of God.

24.86. And the Lord blessed Noah and his sons, saying: "Increase and multiply and fill the earth and subdue it. And fear and trembling toward you will remain in all the beasts of the earth and all the birds of the sky and in everything that moves above the earth and in all the fish of the sea."[184] This prerogative of power over other animals seems also attributed to man in earlier sections, but in that place where it said that God made man to the image of God, it stated: "He made them male and female, and he blessed them, saying, 'Increase and multiply and fill the earth and subdue it. And receive power over the fish of the sea and flying things and beasts of the earth and crawling creatures.'"[185] I have brought this up so that you may understand that the twin creation of human beings is expressed: one according to the image of God, the other according to the formation from the mud of the earth. Thus that creation of human beings from the mud of the earth seems to have occurred after [the creation of] the world, after God rested from his works. It is somehow late that the formation of the earthly statue is brought forth. "There were no rains over the earth, and man did not work the land,"[186] and then, "God created man from the mud of the earth and blew the spirit of life into his face, and man was made into a living soul."[187] But that was he who on the sixth day, as though on the perfect number when all the works of God were completed, was made man according to the image of God, as though designed by a perfect operation. Thus the one who was found to be just in the flood is compared to him. And thus God set him up over all the earthly regions, just like the one made to the image of God, because both Adam and Noah abstained from earthly vices, the former who was born thus, so that he owed nothing to earthly contamination, the latter one who had been approved in dangers and was tested in passions

184. Gn 9.1.
185. Gn 1.27–28.
186. Gn 2.5.
187. Gn 2.7.

and was found not subject to confusion even when he was surrounded by confusion.

24.87. But the higher meaning holds that the just man is increased by a magnitude and multitude of virtue and teaching, and fills the earth as though it were a heart, in which there is a receptacle of intelligible things. Thus he allows nothing that is bereft of wisdom, nothing that could assault him with foolishness. Thus he subdues all the earthly passions, and by means of terror and fear he also subjects to himself even the bodily senses, as though they are beasts, in which the appearance of malice and wildness seem to be present. For all malice is savage and wild: it is puffed up by a kind of inflated tumor. And it is also obvious that certain reptiles have a sort of look of lethal passions, from which a kind of poison seems to pour into the mind. Thus the just man rules all these; he is not mixed with them, but he dominates them if his mind is not led by delight or desire, not broken by sadness and fear; nor does he lead the course of this life as though on a slippery and tricky path in indulgence and enticements. Rather, by means of continence and temperance the wise man drives out from himself passions of this sort.

24.88. But then it added immediately, "All the creeping things that are living will be your food,"[188] and lest it upset you that we said previously that reptiles are poisonous, know that some reptiles are poisonous while others are harmless. Therefore, take this point [about food] to be about harmless reptiles, which, even if they do not all slither on their stomach and chest like cobras, yet have tiny feet, so that they seem rather to slither than to walk. Thus understand that the unclean bodily passions are like the poisonous reptiles, but the suitable passions are like the harmless reptiles. For every affection that is beyond the snare of any ugly pleasure is in fact a passion, but it is a good passion. Unmanly desire and anger and fear, these are the harmful passions of the soul, but the good passions are the harmless affections. And from them a certain usefulness and reason for living is offered to us: we use their food for the sake of life, we delight in their feasts.

25.89. Why is it that it says: "Just as I have given the green

188. Gn 9.3.

vegetables, I have given all things to you"?[189] In this passage even those who understand simply, since they do not devote study to the language, do not seem to be opposed to us. For there are those who think that vegetables seem to be offered to us for food by a command of God, so that we should eat them more than we eat meals from meat:[190] but I defer to them gladly, since the use of vegetables helps the human race to grow toward greater frugality and temperance. Still, I might find among those who do not agree with this point something that could be objected to me, namely that not all vegetables are found fitting for human consumption; and thus not all of the human race is led by love of wisdom and continence so that it can pursue continence. And hence what serves as the general precept we cannot limit to a narrow group of a few people; for this precept is given for all people.

25.90. Therefore, let us consider why the verse said, "Just as I have given the green vegetables, I have given all things to you"—not, "I gave you all vegetables as food." Thus let those who eat meat as though they are eating vegetables not use it for the expansion or fattening of the body, which is what meals from meat generally produce. But just as not all vegetables are suitable for use as food, so also not every living reptile is fit for eating; since indeed we should abstain from all poisonous beasts, there is also a certain indulgence that ensues in this way, that someone has more regard for delight than for danger; for in many reptiles, once the part that is said to be naturally poisonous is cut off, one claims the part that remains for food; but even if this part is not full of danger, still it is close to danger, and some infection necessarily seeped into the sap of all of the meat. For many shoot deer and swift animals of this sort with poisoned arrows, and afterwards, once they have removed a certain part of the limbs, they use the rest of the body for food.

25.91. But what pertains to the higher sense, that is, a deeper reason for what was said, is that the irrational passions should be subject to the mind of the wise man as vegetables are subject to the peasant. And thus he uses these thoughts as reptiles in the

189. Ibid.
190. *QG* 2.58.

same manner as the farmer uses vegetables, which cannot actually do any harm, yet they do not have the quality of stronger food. For a general and common precept does not prescribe for everyone the higher kinds of virtue, which indeed are only for the few, but even if someone cannot acquire for himself meals of the stronger virtues, he still has passions of the sort that do not harm but rather delight.[191]

25.92. Therefore, in the beginning the saintly Moses informed us and instructed us about the inbreathing of the soul, so that we not slip into the diverse opinions of the philosophers, which cannot stand on their own. For many have held varying positions, such as Critias and his disciples, who say that the soul is blood, referring to that soul by which we live, which is sensible, and not that soul of the inner man, which is rational and intelligent. Yet Hippocrates, even if he did not value the talent of Critias and did not refute his argument, still did not accept his opinion. Aristotle called the soul an "endelechy" (*endelechia*), while others want it to be fire.[192] Let us therefore maintain a division of this sort, that we might distinguish what is rational in the soul, the substance of which is the divine Spirit, just as Scripture says: "Because he breathed into his face a spirit of life,"[193] so that there is in it a certain vital nourishment by which this body is animated, and it is also cause for delight. Therefore, the vital and delightful substance of these parts of the soul is called blood by some, and indeed even Scripture said, "The soul of all the flesh is blood."[194] Thus properly he called the soul of flesh "blood"; for delight and passion are in the flesh, not mind and reasoning. But if you pay closer attention, this passage explains that point. For in this passage, when it said that the soul is blood, it certainly indicated that the soul is one thing, blood another, since the substance of the soul is the vital spirit, but the vital spirit itself does not confer the state of living only on its own and

191. Missing folium in the archetype; Philo (*QG* 2.58) here considers questions of farming. See Pastorino, *Noè,* 477 n.4.

192. On the Greek term, see Cicero, *Tusculan Disputations* 1.10.22, who renders it "a continual and ceaseless motion."

193. Gn 2.7.

194. Lv 17.11.

without blood. But spirit is mixed with blood, because the things called arteries are like receptacles of the spirit, and these contain not only the pure air, but also the blood, although a much smaller portion of blood. For since there is a pair of vessels, one that is the vein, which is called *phleps* in Greek, another that is the artery, the vein has more blood than spirit, that is *phleps*, and the artery less blood and much more spirit. Now the exact measure depends on the differing natures of individual people.

25.93. But the higher sense should delight you, which indicates that the blood is called the soul because the blood is hot and fiery, just as is virtue; for whoever has been ignited by the desire for virtue and has taken up the exhalation of praise excludes all delights from his stomach. Immersed, then, as you are in the fervor of virtue, it says, reject the thoughts that are fleshy and earthly as though unfit for spiritual food. For he was not eating meat, as though he was thinking of [meat as] something earthly, who said: "My food is that I accomplish the will of my Father, who is in heaven,"[195] inspiring in men the desire for virtue and pouring into them eagerness for divine knowledge. Thus earthly thoughts are considered like weakened and sick ones and without the flow of blood, just as the man is called weakened who has lost a lot of blood; for he also grows cold when his blood is spilled. Therefore, whoever is a lover of virtue removes and casts out bodily foods, except as much as he knows is sufficient for his natural needs; but whoever is more negligent has followed the slippery and watery course of this life, and, as though he stands on faulty feet, he falls into the stomach and the gut. Thus separated from heavenly food he desires what is earthly, and he cannot say: "Our dwelling is in heaven."[196] Thus that he might incite us to hidden foods, he himself says: "'Do not touch, do not handle, do not taste'; all these things lead to corruption by their very use, according to human precepts and teachings; these instructions have a rationale of wisdom in the observance of religious duty and in the humility of heart, and in not indulging the body; not in any honor for the fullness and the love of the flesh."[197]

195. Jn 4.34.
196. Phil 3.20.
197. Col 2.21–23.

26.94. Thus the later sections affirm that this is the meaning: for thus he says: "Indeed, I will demand your blood and that of your souls from all the beasts and from the hand of man."[198] He compares [mankind] to bestial evil; nay, he even piles on the wickedness of man beyond the ferocity of beasts by saying, "from the hand of the brother of a man." And indeed, beasts have nothing common in nature with us; they are bound to us by no sort of fraternal law. If they harm people, it is as though they are harming foreigners, and they are not violating the bonds of nature; they are not forgetting the sentiment of brotherhood. Thus a man sins more gravely when he assaults his brother, and thus the Lord promises that he will punish him more severely when he says: "I will demand the blood of man from the hand of his brother."[199] Is not a brother the one whom, as it were, the womb of rational nature has brought forth and the procreation from the same mother has bound to us? For the same nature is the mother of all people, and thus we are all brothers generated from one and the same mother and bound by the same law of parentage.

26.95. And thus the Lord called "brother" also the brother from whom the brother's blood was demanded; by this he indicates that we should fear danger more from those who are bound to us by a fraternal bond. For from this source betrayals, from this source more frequent dangers for people are contrived, and, so that we grasp a particular case, consider that for particular brothers resentments often increase in dividing up an inheritance. Thus if more has been conferred upon a brother by his parents, the other brothers are more indignant and through murder try to snatch the gift conferred by the parents. Those wars are more feared, not the wars between cities, but the wars within individual households. Thus the Lord includes in his determination for punishment those who he knows will more likely assault each other.

26.96. The third reason he said "brother" in that passage, not so that a murderer would be worthy of a name connoting devotion, but so that the crime might be emphasized more by identification with a name connoting devotion, and therefore

198. Gn 9.5.
199. Ibid.

there would be an increase of the crime so that the heavenly punishment might be more just. Thus the Lord our God promises revenge, so that the one who has forgotten devotion may be so shaken by fear and may know that even if the murderer might escape from men, still he cannot avoid the judgment of God, but rather he is preserved for greater and eternal punishment.

26.97. But we understand this in a higher sense: not only must one be wary of the attacks from external forces but also from our own, that is from our intimate thoughts, and thus we must preserve ourselves not only from the evil of the mind but also from our own conversations. Thus he says: "In much speaking, you will not escape from sin."[200] Thus the point seems to be that an account must be rendered to the Lord not only of our work, but also of our speech, which is more intimate to us. And therefore we should consider more intently that we not provoke an offense in word or in deed, because just as confession on the lips leads to salvation, so a slip of the lips leads to death.[201]

26.98. And it says, "Whoever will pour out the blood of man, he will be poured out for the man's blood."[202] The manner of speaking is not incorrect, but there is an image in the words, because the very one who "pours out" the blood of man will be "poured out" as though he were blood, since this tears out from him the hope of posterity, because just as blood poured into the earth is scattered here and there, so the soul of the impious is dissolved in the manner of the weakness of the body. For it is said about the soul that corruption is its death,[203] so that it is stripped of the gift of heavenly grace and it hinders the body from its salvation as though [the soul] were dashed against the cliffs of wickedness.

26.99. Indeed it disturbs many that the verse said: "I made man to the image of God,"[204] and it did not say, "to my image," although he is himself God. But understand that he is both the Father and the Son. And indeed all things were made through

200. Prv 10.19.
201. Cf. Rom 10.10 and Prv 18.6.
202. Gn 9.6.
203. Cf. Jb 33.28.
204. Gn 9.6.

the Son, yet we read that the Father made all things and he made them through the Son, just as it is written: "You have made all things in wisdom."[205] Thus, either the Father is speaking, so that he created all things to the image of the Word, or the Son is speaking, and he created all things to the image of God the Father. And thus he shows that human nature, that is, the nature of the rational man, has something familiar and intimate with God according to which we are created in the image of God; and for this reason what God sees cruelly and recklessly committed against the living creature that is intimate with him does not go unpunished in his sight.

26.100. Thus this added reason for punishment implies that we first of all exclude the opinions of certain philosophers who deny that God has any concern for humanity; and hence, knowing that the prerogative of our punishment remains with God, let us not commit against others the punishment reserved to God's judgment, and let us ourselves not fear death too desperately, since we know that the death of an innocent man is not spurned by God.

27.101. The verse says, "There will not be a flood that destroys all of the earth."[206] There seems to be a doubt whether "there will not be a flood" should be understood as "a flood that destroys the earth"—for this is what floods generally do—or whether "there will not be such a flood, by which all the earth would be destroyed." What follows clarifies this point, when it says that not all the earth would be destroyed; for it shows that there will indeed be floods, but not such that all the earth will be destroyed by them.

27.102. But the higher meaning is that now the providence of the Lord will not allow there to be a flood of bodily passions so great that the whole soul will perish. Of course, I do not dare say that the Lord seems to determine that no one's soul can entirely perish. For what shall we say about a parricide? What about a murderer, an adulterer, a prevaricator? Which parts of their soul do we preserve for forgiveness? Hence I think rather that the Lord our God encourages us so that even if someone suffers

205. Ps 104.24.
206. Gn 9.11.

some other, moderate passions, he should not despair entirely of divine grace and be despondent that he will be overcome entirely; and even if someone is indulgent and cannot avoid the desire for excess, yet he can strive to refrain from adultery; let him take pleasure in feasting, but not in committing rape. But even if there is someone or other who is greedy, who snatches others' goods, who casts out orphans and evicts widows, at least afterwards, after he has returned in repentance, let him return what he took. Therefore, Zacchaeus deserved pardon, because not only did he promise that he would make restitution, but he promised fourfold to those from whom he had taken anything, and he promised that he would give half of his patrimony to the poor.[207]

27.103. Then let us consider more carefully what it means when it says: "I will set my bow in the cloud, and it will be a sign of the everlasting covenant between me and the earth; and it will happen that when I send clouds over the earth, my arc will appear in a cloud, and I will remember my covenant."[208] For it is not as most people think, that he calls a "bow" that which people speak of; it is not the phenomenon when some signs of rains appear, in which different colors sometimes glisten as though of the rays of the sun, and other times are shaped by the more brilliant light of what shines, and by which even future rain is indicated, in the apparent inconstancy of the tranquility shown through the bow's many-colored appearance. Some call this arc a "rainbow," but it is not at all as we say the arc of God to be: for this arc, which is called a rainbow, usually appears in the day but does not appear at night. And even during the day itself, if the air should be covered by black clouds, the arc does not in fact appear, unless perhaps the heavier clouds begin to dissipate.

27.104. Therefore, let us consider whether it is because of the "bow" by which arrows are shot, which is at one moment taut and at another released, that Scripture should seem to indicate a certain tension and release, and thus the universe is not entirely broken through too much tension, but there is a certain measure and a certain balance of divine power. There

207. Cf. Lk 19.8.
208. Gn 9.13–16.

is therefore the power of the invisible God, which even in the appearance of that bow, taut and released, is tempered by the divine will, mercy, and strength; this power does not allow all things to be confused by too much dissolution or to be broken up by some great burst. Thus the verse says that this arc is placed in the clouds, because in the clouds there is special need for the help of divine providence, since the battle lines of clouds are driven during gusts and storms. Therefore, it says, "I will place my bow in the cloud"—not, "I will place my arrow." For the bow is the tool for shooting an arrow; thus the bow itself does not wound, but rather the arrow does. And thus the Lord places the bow in the clouds rather than the arrow, that is, it is not something that wounds, but something that gives a hint of intimidation, while it does not generally have the effect of wounding.

28.105. Why then, when in the first place Noah numbers three sons—Shem, Ham, and Japheth—does this passage include the offspring of only the middle son, that is, when it says: "But Ham was the father of Canaan; these three were the sons of Noah"?[209] This is especially noteworthy because the other two sons were just, while the middle one was unjust. Thus the offspring of the unjust is observed before the offspring of the just ones. In fact, we cannot deny what has been written, but Canaan's birth is added so as to pile on Ham's crime, because, since Ham had a son and he was a father, the one who most of all should have recognized his father Noah was the only one who did not recognize him. Therefore, because he was wicked to his father, he deserved to have a wicked son. Likewise, the verse indicates that from that same Canaan were the Canaanites, who, after being oppressed by the righteous people for many generations, submitted to their control. Thus it is clear that Canaan, who was the son of this Ham who arose impudently against his father, was the source of the Canaanites.

28.106. But the higher meaning is indicated by an interpretation of the names. For Ham is "heat," and Canaan "their disturbance." For one who gets hot is immediately upset and disturbed, and thus it is shown most clearly that the father of men was not a man like this, but that evil passion is the mother

209. Gn 9.18–19.

of wicked passion, which comes from the morality of the father; that is, it is a stranger to the practice of virtue.

29.107. "And the man Noah began to be a farmer of the earth."[210] It seems indeed that the just man Noah is compared in that first appearance to that Adam who was made from the earth, because just as it is written about Adam, that once he was cast out from paradise, he began to work the earth, so too it says about the latter that he also became a farmer, when he departed from the Ark.[211] And in like manner, in both cases a certain kind of flood preceded, that is, for both Noah after the flood and Adam in the fashioning of the body after the creation of the world (for as the world came to be, the water was gathered into one pool, that the earth might appear; earth could not have appeared previously on account of the confusion of the waters).[212] Thus, just as that firstborn seems to have worked the land as its master, so also, after departing from the Ark, Noah became the master of sowing and cultivating. These things are considered to be similar. But if you consider the words, which now express the force of the higher meaning, one is the "worker of the earth," and the other is a "farmer"; for one acts like a mercenary while the other acts like the head of a household. Thus Cain, who killed his brother, was a worker of the earth.[213] And so that you might know that to work the earth is more servile than free, the work of the murderous one is characterized with a curse: "Since you will work the earth, and it will not increase its power to bear fruit for you. In sighs and shudders you will be on the earth."[214]

29.108. But the earth is our flesh, which the wicked man "works," but which the good man "cultivates"; the former seeks from the earth something like payment, the latter reaps the fruits and grace of good discipline, so that he makes his farm abundant, and it can respond to the cultivation of the Lord and show the generosity of the cultivator. But what can serve as nourishment for the worker, who seeks nothing other than food for

210. Gn 9.20.
211. Cf. Gn 3.23.
212. Cf. Gn 1.9.
213. Cf. Gn 4.2.
214. Gn 4.12.

his body alone, who strives more for the benefit of the stomach and is happy to satisfy it alone? But the cultivator feeds on the quality of the fruits. You know which fruits the just man has. The fruits of the Spirit are charity, joy, peace, patience, goodness.[215] Thus the good farmer has continence and chastity, so that if there are trees that bend over quickly to the earth and spread seed widely, he cuts these off as though with his temperance as a sort of knife. And so the trees discard what is ailing, and they sprout what is fitting.

29.109. Why is it that the just man plants a vine first and not either wheat or barley? And why vines after a flood and the destruction of the earth? But we have already spoken about this above, that in the springtime the roots of corrupt things can also sprout vice. Thus I think the fact that the just man first seeks for what is desired rather than what is necessary should be considered with greater care. For the necessary fruits are wheat and barley, without which we cannot live, but wine is desired, given for the sake of delight. But precisely because he is just, he claims this for himself, that is, what is secondary rather than what is primary. For he offered to God the foods that are necessary for living [because he had no part in producing them];[216] wine is superfluous, however, and not necessary for people.

29.110. But perhaps you say that people cannot live without drink just as much as without food. Thus is not drink just as necessary as food? I do not deny it. Indeed, is drink not constituted by the Lord as necessary for quenching thirst? I do not reject this. And therefore it is fitting to draw the necessary drink from springs and rivers, things that are not made by human hands, but flow by the bidding and working of the Lord our God. And lest to the fact that we speak of the Lord's "working," you retort that Cain's "working" seems to have brought curses, consider that the working itself did not receive the term for curse, but rather because it is written that he "worked the earth." For the one who "works the earth" is a mercenary. But the Lord is not a mercenary, but the Lord who says: "My Father has worked until

215. Cf. Gal 5.22–23.

216. Based on Schenkl's conjecture. See his note on p. 487 of the Latin text.

now. And I work."[217] Hear what a worker of this sort accomplishes: "My bread is that I do the will of my Father who is in heaven."[218]

29.111. The text says, "He drank from the wine and got drunk."[219] It did not say that he "drank the wine," nor that the just man "drank up" the wine, but that he drank "from the wine," that is, he poured it from his own portion. For it is characteristic of the drunk man to imbibe all the wine, and of the intemperate man to empty out all that he took, but the continent uses the legitimate measure. Thus there are two forms of drunkenness: one is that which brings staggering to the body and upsets its footsteps and disturbs the senses; the other is that which lightens the mind by the gift of its power and seems to carry off all infirmity. Thus the Apostle says: "Use a bit of wine for the sake of your frequent infirmities."[220] For just as in such a moderation in drinking, wine does not bring infirmity but rather health, and removes all infirmity from the body, so too that noble drunkenness drives out every weakness from the flesh, about which it is written: "How excellent is the cup that inebriates."[221] What is that inebriation? "Do not grow drunk with wine," he says, "in which there is indulgence, but be filled with the Spirit,"[222] just as the Apostle says. Thus according to the literal meaning there is a caution while according to the higher meaning there is praise for the wise man. Cautious is the man who, if he should be naked, yet is naked in his own home, where there is no lack of hangings and coverings, as it were, for his drunkenness, so that he can hide his own vices.

29.112. Thus bodily things cover the naked body like walls and a roof, but let us see what the hangings of the soul are. We will, however, understand these hangings only if we have first discussed his disrobing. And the disrobing of the wise man is twofold. Thus our mind is dressed with a twin covering, either

217. Jn 5.17.
218. Jn 4.34.
219. Gn 9.21.
220. 1 Tm 5.23.
221. Ps 23.5.
222. Eph 5.18.

when it had committed sin thoughtlessly—for that is a nakedness as though of the drunken mind, because it does not know that it failed, and it is as though it falls, led from ignorance into vice by a kind of tipsiness—or, on the other hand, it does not know its own error, buried in the sleep of negligence and ignorance. When we fell into these sins, or, rather, when we fell into many sins even when we were perfectly aware of them—for there is a certain natural drunkenness also from our innate infirmity, such that we are led into vice by the impetus of delight, just like many who are ignited by youthful heat or inflamed by indulgence and thrills or seized by avaricious desire—then clearly a medicine for all these sins was sought, so that someone might cover this sort of weakness first by a certain modesty and shame. Thus, even if he is still placed at the risk of failing again, he might give some sign of improvement. And so it is very different if he desires to boast of his sins: for in this case there is filthy shamelessness, while in the prior case a tolerable modesty gives hope of future reform.

29.113. But another kind of disrobing is the disrobing of the soul, by which one casts off the burden, as it were, of the body and leaves it behind, as though fleeing the tomb of the flesh. "For their throat is an open grave,"[223] Scripture says, in which grave the soul is buried, weighed down by different delights and passions of the desires. Thus the soul extracts itself from earthly pressures; it rises up from and pushes off what surrounds it like nets; it strips off from itself every snare of the passions and drives off all of that ugly appearance of earthly disgrace, so that it might see the light of eternal beauty.

30.114. I ask now why it does not say simply: "Ham saw his father's nakedness," but rather: "Ham the father of Canaan saw."[224] Indeed, Canaan was not yet born. Why then did he add the name of the son if not so that the descendant would be deformed by the vice of the progenitor and the progenitor would be weighed down by the wickedness of the son? Thus both the father in the son and the son in the father are rebuked, since they both have common participation in foolishness, wicked-

223. Ps 6.10.
224. Gn 9.22.

ness, and impiety. And it could not happen that one who himself stood out as a wicked son to a noble father and a degenerate in nature and learning would father a noble son.

30.115. This is according to the letter. But what pertains to the higher sense, all wicked practices delight in others' errors, not only in their errors, but also in the things that appear to be evils in themselves, even if they are not. For Noah did not realize that he was nude, because he had been clothed in the covering of wisdom. Thus not even Adam placed in paradise thought himself nude except after he committed the sin of lying.[225] And stripped of the covering of wisdom and denuded of justice and the heavenly commandments by his lie, he saw that he was nude, and he thought he should be covered by leaves. In this way, Ham laughs when he sees his father stripped naked. For every wicked man, since he himself has abandoned self-control, not only perceives the sins of others as a consolation for his own error, because he has found companions for his guilt, but he also rejoices in his wicked attitude, as though he himself had corrected his own sins. Thus the evil mind rejoices because something unforeseen happened to the wise man; yet in fact the fall of the body should not count as a vice, even if it is considered a lapse, unless the soul also consents to the sin. Finally, the errors of this sort are considered forgivable; they should not be hunted in hatred, nor held in mockery. Yet the wicked-minded, as I have said, when he thinks that the wise man has erred, thinks that he must insult the one whose morals he considers contrary to his own; for his sin is rebuked by a certain quiet witness of the wise man. And he thinks he should rejoice because the just man's learning brought him no benefit, nor did his justice support him, nor did his material possessions provide him with a prosperous outcome. For such things, identified with wealth or honor, are considered by the wicked to be the highest goods, which nevertheless confer no fruit as the praiseworthy basis for virtue. Thus those who think that the lover of virtue has been defrauded of his right to prosperity appear as defenders of foolishness, because they believe that every good thing must be judged according to temporal rather than eternal criteria.

225. Cf. Gn 3.7.

31.116. But why is it that "Shem and Japheth placed a garment on his shoulders and looked behind themselves and covered their naked father, and they did not see his nakedness"?[226] The letter expresses the manifest attitude of devotion, because the good sons avoided looking at their father stripped of his clothing, lest their reverence for their father be diminished even by a single glance; for indeed respect is often offended even by a silent glance. Hence it is said even at Rome that the ancient custom was that children, and most of all adolescents, do not enter the bath with their parents.[227]

31.117. But the higher meaning takes it in this way: that the foolish sees only the present things that are in his eyes; he does not consider the future and does not think about the past. But the wise man both remembers the past and considers the future. Thus every wise mind walks backward, that is, it considers past things and is not impeded by a certain practice of nature; it allows none of its deeds to be empty, none to be naked. It covers the things that have been accomplished in another way with a kind of garment and with the grace either of a present or future deed, so that nothing passes by undressed; it leaves behind nothing unadorned. Hence even the Apostle would forget what was past, and would strive for what was higher, but he would forget them so that he might cover over the sins of his acts of persecution, so that he might cover his previous faults and overshadow them with good works.[228] For it says, "Blessed are they whose sins are covered,"[229] that is, covered by good deeds and works, and veiled by the resulting practices of the virtues.

31.118. "And Noah became sober from the wine,"[230] Scripture says. It is clear that men sober up from drunkenness after sleep intervenes, but the mind is also sober when it knows both past and present things. Thus the mind of the just man was sober even when it was considered drunk; for it is the famous

226. Gn 9.23.

227. Cf. *Off.* 1.18.79, where Ambrose treats the covering of Noah and identifies a similar custom of modesty in Rome, but also in other cities.

228. Cf. Phil 3.14.

229. Ps 32.1.

230. Gn 9.24.

"cup" that inebriates the just.[231] But that man who laughed at his father was really the drunk one. For he did not consider the past gift of his birth nor the present reverence for his father nor the future penalty for injustice to his father. He was truly drunk and thought that he saw what he did not see. The blindness was profound in the one who could not see his father. For if he had seen his father, he would not have laughed; for the father should not be mocked but revered. But even more than this, the fool could not see the mind of the just man. For how can one who thought that there was in Noah the sin of drunkenness see, when Noah possessed the complete aura of wisdom and of all other virtues? For so it is written: "She is the breath of the virtue of God."[232] For when is the mind soberer than at the moment when it contemplates the nature of all things and the matters of present and future times, so that no momentary tipsiness of drunkenness appears in it?

31.119. But I ask for the reason why, although it said previously that Ham was the middle of the sons, it now defines him as the younger. For so it is written: "Noah knew all the things that his younger son did to him."[233] Surely the earlier Scripture erred in the order of the birth? Not at all. Why then? Are contradictions written here? I do not think so. How is this then resolved, unless you take "younger" not in age, not in chronology, but defined as immature in his thinking and in a sort of infancy of his intellect? He is one who has not imbibed the teaching of a more advanced age and has not perceived the counsel of the elderly. For indeed a certain human sensibility belongs to the white-haired. And thus it says: "When you come to the council of the elders, shut your mouth,"[234] as the opinion holds elsewhere, "You must learn before you speak."[235] Thus have your ear ready, that you might obtain something from the counsels of the wise. The tongue should be restrained, while the hearing should be readied.

231. Cf. Ps 23.5.
232. Wis 7.25.
233. Gn 9.24.
234. Sir 32.13.
235. Sir 18.19.

32.120. Blessing his son Shem, Noah said: "Blessed be the Lord God of Shem. And Canaan will be his servant."[236] And Noah said both "Lord" and "God" and, in particular, the God of his son whose name is Shem, that is, the God of the just, that is, the God of the mountains, which have the grace of lofty virtue, not of the valleys. Next, why is it that Noah did not condemn his son Ham, but rather Ham's son, to servitude, when it was Ham who had sinned? Perhaps it is because the father[237] is more affected by wrongs done by his son, and especially those of which he is himself guilty and the culprit, and he is more deeply saddened at the punishment paid by his son for his own sin, who is punished not so much for his own responsibility but for that of his father: in addition it may be that, since he had been a student of his father's teaching and an imitator of his terrible thoughts, both used a single body and mind and the same wickedness. Thus it makes no difference whether the son pays the price for his own or for his father's malice, since there is common fellowship in the wickedness. But there is no doubt that he paid for his father's wickedness, and he paid for his own, as guilty for his crime, or at least the penalty would be drawn out longer, since it extends as far as the son, and the affliction of his successor is carried forward for a long time. This is according to the letter.

32.121. Otherwise, here the verse indicates not so much individuals as characteristics, of whom one nature is in each. For Ham is "heat," Canaan "commotion" and "disquiet." But indeed, whoever is hot is also disquieted and upset. Thus there was one passion and one disposition in the two men. Thus when the one is named, both are condemned.

32.122. Why, when blessing his son Japheth, did the saintly Noah say: "The Lord will enlarge Japheth, and he will dwell in the houses of Shem, and Canaan will become his servant"?[238] We said above that Japheth signified in a certain way the "good indifferent." But indifference contains an extension, which is present in health and vigor and beauty and courage and riches

236. Gn 9.26.
237. In this case, Ham.
238. Gn 9.27.

and grace and nobility, friends, powers, and other things. But although these indifferents are goods, yet they have harmed many who possess them without wisdom and justice.[239] For riches have made many drunk; nobility and power have made many proud; and beauty has made many indulgent, since by beauty's help many have corrupted the chastity of another's heart. Therefore, in regard to the one using the disposition toward these things characterized by what we called "indifference," their use is either governed by the virtues or then indeed, if they lack governance by the virtues, what could be beneficial becomes wicked.

33.123. Now we do not think it is a point to be passed over in vain, that after the flood Noah is said to have lived three hundred fifty years.[240] For in the number three hundred it is clear that the Cross of Christ is signified; by the type of the Cross the just man was freed from the flood. In fifty there is the jubilee, the number of forgiveness, when the Holy Spirit was sent from heaven pouring grace into human hearts. Thus the just man fulfills the course of this life by the perfect number of forgiveness and grace.

33.124. About the generation of Japheth it says: "Rhodes and other islands are of the nations."[241] The term "extension" is not included pointlessly, since Japheth's offspring also proceeded into another part of nature, that is, into the sea. For indeed, as though they were "extension," they were not content with what nature had prescribed for human use, that is, the possession of the earth, but they also entered the sea and proceeded all the way to the islands. This is according to the letter.

33.125. But according to the higher sense, it means that the things that are beyond, which are called goods, riches, powers, honors, are diffused more broadly, and that rich men are content not only with the things that are in their hands and before their eyes, but they spread their desires far and wide, when they seek payment of money from more remote peoples, or honor from many, or power that extends more widely, or pleasure.

239. See Introduction, pp. 8–10, on the influence of Stoic thought.
240. Cf. Gn 9.28.
241. Cf. Gn 10.4–5.

34.126. Now I ask why Scripture recalled that Cush was the older son of that wicked Ham.[242] There are two types of earth, one that is the sandy and dusty, that indeed I will even call dust, and another kind of earth that is fruit-bearing and fecund, land that is more solid and deep. But what then does the wicked man beget unless dust, from which there can be no offspring? Thus the prophet compares dust to the wicked in saying: "Not so the wicked, not so, but they are like dust, which the wind casts from the face of the earth,"[243] so that even according to the higher sense the soul of the wicked is infertile, since it cannot generate useful fruit.

34.127. Why then did Cush beget Nimrod the giant, who was a hunter in the sight of God? For the verse said: "So Nimrod the giant was a hunter in the sight of God."[244] What else, then, do the dust and sand beget unless the earthly man, insofar as the unholy man places earthly things before heavenly ones? For giants in the tale are introduced as having desired to fight against the heavenly beings, and they contrived to ascend to heavenly things by ascending from the earth.[245]

34.128. But according to the higher interpretation it means that anyone who loves earthly desires and pursues them and thinks that he can come to the grace of God by means of them and that the heavenly reign is to be handed over by sins of this sort battles against heavenly things with a rebellious disposition. In this sense, then, there is in the proverb a statement about the one who sinned: "So Nimrod the giant was a hunter before God." But the name "Nimrod," when interpreted, means "Ethiopian." The color of the Ethiopian indicates the shadows and messiness of the soul; he is against the light, lacking in brilliance, encircled in shadows, more like night than day. The practice of the hunter is in the forest; therefore, his interaction is among beasts and wild things. Thus the irrational [man] is min-

242. Gn 10.6–7.

243. Ps 1.4.

244. Gn 10.8.

245. A reference to the mythological *gigantomachia,* or battle between the giants and the gods; see Apollodorus, *Biblioteca* 1.6.1–2.

gled with irrational passions, and the hunter of this sort is accustomed to seek those things that are of wild and hardened malice and to drink from them and to delight in them. Thus Nimrod is the beginning of this reign of Babylon, that is, "confusion," in that malice and power exist not in simplicity and purity, not in the discrimination of virtue, but in the confusion of vices.[246]

246. Cf. Gn 10.10.

A DEFENSE OF THE PROPHET DAVID

TO THEODOSIUS AUGUSTUS

In the present composition we have undertaken to write a defense of the prophet David—not because he needs our support, for he shone forth with plentiful merits and he abounded in virtues—but because, after the reading of the narration of his deeds, many who do not carefully consider the meaning of the Scriptures or the hidden aspects of the mysteries wonder how so great a prophet did not reject the stain first of adultery and then of homicide.[1]

1.2. Thus it has been our task to review the scriptural account, which appears to have attributed sin to him. For we read in the second book of Kingdoms[2] that, while he was strolling in his royal home, David gazed upon a woman bathing—her name was Bathsheba—who was lovely to behold, pleasing both in her charms and in her countenance, and very striking in appearance.[3] And by these enticements David's affections were captivated so that he conceived a desire to make her his own. The woman, however, was married to a man; her husband's name was Uriah and by royal decree the stage was set for his murder. For even if his life was judged to be no obstacle to the king's lust, surely it would stand in the way of the utmost disgrace of adultery.

1.3. But then, in order that we proceed from more obvious

1. Most likely a reference to the liturgical setting of the oration, during which portions of 2 Samuel 11 would have been read.

2. 1–4 Kingdoms (LXX and Vulg.) are divided as 1–2 Samuel and 1–2 Kings in modern Bibles.

3. Cf. 2 Sm 11.2.

facts, the one whom God has justified may you not judge.[4] "I count it nothing," says Paul, "that I be judged by you or by a human court, but I do not even judge myself."[5] Paul was still then in the body, still liable to temptation, and yet he did not judge himself for the very reason that the spiritual man is judged by no one but by God alone.[6] Thus he adds: "The one who judges me is the Lord. Thus do not judge anything before its time."[7] But David's time was already completed, and he merited grace and was justified by Christ, from the moment that the Lord himself rejoiced that he was called son of David and those who confessed him to be so were given sight.[8] Why would you call a man of God out of his reward and into condemnation? The Lord had already passed judgment about him, when he spoke about him to Solomon: "If you walk in my sight, just as David your father walked in holiness and justice of heart, so that he acted according to all things that I commanded him."[9] Is this one who acted according to all the heavenly commandments, walking in holiness and justice of heart, worthy of condemnation or of reward? At the moment when the sins and vices of others lie hidden, then David receives the divine affirmation of his virtue and glory.

And we quibble idly about the sin of the one by whose merit and grace the sins of others have been pardoned! For when Solomon committed offense, because he did not observe the commandments of the Lord, and God had determined that his kingdom should be split into many parts, God said to him: "Yet indeed I will not do these things in your days on account of David your father. I will take the kingdom from the hand of your son. Nevertheless I will not take the entire kingdom; I will allot

4. As discussed in the introduction, Ambrose draws heavily on Didymus the Blind (c.313–398 AD) as well as Origen of Alexandria (c.185–254 AD); for the text of the parallels see Pierre Hadot, *Ambroise de Milan: Apologie de David,* SC 239 (Paris: Cerf, 1977), 49–58, who includes French renderings of the parallels in the course of the translation.

5. 1 Cor 4.3.

6. Cf. 1 Cor 2.15.

7. 1 Cor 4.4–5.

8. Cf. Mt 9.27–29; 15.22; 20.30–34.

9. 1 Kgs 9.4.

one tribe on account of David my servant."[10] And so, who is there who judges so great a man when the Lord justifies him? "What God has made clean," Scripture says, "you shall not call impure."[11]

1.4. Yet setting aside heaven's judgment, by which even you would honor so great a prophet, investigate more closely David's actions and way of life. Are you not amazed that such a man, most of whose life, you judge, must be likened to that of the angels, succumbed only once to sin, even though from his childhood he was surrounded by power, riches, and honors and beset by many temptations? And he succumbed to the very sin for which even the angels of heaven, as Scripture recalls, had once been cast out from their grace and power?[12] To be sure, we read that he was also guilty of another sin, namely that he ordered the people to be numbered in a census.[13]

2.5. How many times has each of us sinned hour by hour, and yet no one of us thinks his sin should be confessed in public: but that king, so great and so powerful, did not allow the awareness of his crime to stay hidden with him even for a moment, and instead, by means of a hasty confession and through immense distress, he offered up his sin to the Lord. Can you easily find me someone now who is honored and wealthy, who, when he is shown to be guilty of some crime, does not bear it as a nuisance? Yet David—who was outstanding in his royal rule and approved by so many divine oracles—when he was accosted by a private individual because he had sinned gravely, did not rage with indignation, but confessed and groaned from the pain of his guilt. And the ache of his inmost feeling so moved the Lord that Nathan said: Since you have repented, "the Lord has also taken away your sin."[14] Thus the alacrity of the pardon, which removed the offense of so great an error, demonstrated that the king's repentance had been profound.

10. 1 Kgs 11.12–13; following the Greek text, Ambrose has *sceptrum* (literally, "scepter") for the "tribe" that the Lord will preserve.

11. Acts 10.15.

12. Cf. Gn 6.2.

13. Cf. 2 Sm 24.10.

14. 2 Sm 12.13.

2.6. Other men, when they are corrected by priests, make their sin worse as long as they desire to deny it or justify it, and then their fall is greater precisely when one hopes for their correction. But the saints of the Lord, who long to complete a holy battle and to run the race of salvation, if at any point they have fallen in their humanity—more by the weakness of their nature than by the desire to sin—they rise up again more swiftly for the race.[15] Prompted by their shame, they take up even greater challenges, and one would judge that not only did their fall bring with it no obstacle [to progress], but also that it seems to have added to the incentives for hastening [in their race]. In the same way, if the runners' race and the wrestlers' struggle are not brought to an end when by chance some of them should fall, but rather the contests continue unhindered—and, in fact, many, after one fall or another, have gained a victory with an even greater prize—how much more should we not condemn those who, once they have undertaken the struggle for holiness, suffer the offense of a single lapse? For then [we recall that] the one who can repair himself after a fall is blessed because the reward of the blessed is that they rise even after death.

2.7. In other cases we can also recognize that a sin is actually beneficial and that through the Lord's providence sins have sneaked up on saints. Saints are proposed to us for imitation, and there is a concern that even they should fall on occasion. For if they would manage the course of this life among so many enticements without committing any offense, they would give to us weaker people the excuse to conclude that the saints had been of a higher and divine nature, so that they could not have any fault or complicity in any crime. This belief, of course, is one that would prevent us from undertaking an imitation that is impossible, because we would have no share in their nature. Thus the grace of God passes them by just a bit, so that their life might become a model for our imitation and we might draw from their actions a lesson as much in repentance as we have in innocence. Thus when I read of their failures, I recognize them as companions in weakness: when I believe that they are companions, I presume that they should be imitated.

15. Cf. 2 Tm 4.7.

2.8. The Apostle Paul likewise advises us to look upon the Lord our God, lest the merely human sensibility in the saints be elevated because they received lofty revelations or they advanced ceaselessly in their accomplishments, and lest they assign to themselves and attribute to their own virtue what would have been conferred on them by divine operation.[16] And to prevent them from falling into great condemnation and stumbling into the pit of deceit, the Lord permitted fault to steal into them so that they too might recognize that they need divine help and might know that the captain of their salvation must be sought out. Thus Paul gives witness that his weakness served for his own gain when the Lord replied to his request that the thorn of his flesh might leave him: "My grace is sufficient for you; for power is perfected in weakness."[17] And he was right to boast in his weaknesses; for he knew that many, even saints as they abounded in strength, had fallen without any hope of a cure. Therefore, how much more appropriate it is to yield to one or two faults than to carry around a single offense against divinity forever!

3.9. Shall I then add to my defense those conclusions that we can draw from reflection on daily practice, namely that most times when we esteem people in a particular capacity, we want to test them to see if they are diligent and persevering in a different challenge? How many athletes, once they have prevailed in one sort of struggle, are then called to another type of test! Why is it any different if the Lord your God wishes to prove you in the other virtues once you have given some evidence of one type of virtue?[18] He allowed holy Job, who was going through his life without hindrance, to be tested nevertheless by the slaughter of his children and by the sores on his entire body, so that he might prove his mettle in this situation as well;[19] he wanted to see if the dedication of Job's commitment would not fail when he was oppressed by injuries and afflictions. Is it not obvious that he also wished to test holy David, who was noble in his fidel-

16. Cf. 2 Cor 12.7.
17. 2 Cor 12.9.
18. Cf. Sir 2.5.
19. Cf. Jb 1.9; 2.7.

ity, outstanding in gentleness, and strong in arm, to see how he would cover over his guilt and correct his fall, so that he might teach us in what way we can cover a sin we have committed?

3.10. But lest perhaps this explanation seem flimsy to anyone—that a great prophet sinned simply for the sake of our correction: when Christ took up our infirmities for the redemption of all, he who knew not sin was made sin for us.[20] And should one judge it unfitting and believe it to be unlike what is appropriate, namely, that David, for the sake of the progress of his posterity, fell into the reproach of a single lapse, although the Lord himself was made a "reproach" for us, just as he himself says: "But I am a worm and no man, the reproach of men and the outcast of the people," and elsewhere: "the reproaches of those who reproach you have fallen upon me"?[21] Thus in his own lowly servants the Lord prefigured the mystery of the future dispensation, while they in fact bore the sins of their own condition, since even they could not be free from sin; but the Lord took up another's burden, since he alone was free from fellowship in sin.

3.11. In short, by the teaching of the Apostle we know that many deeds that were performed in earlier times are figurative.[22] For when he said that the fathers in the desert who were wounded by serpents could not be healed unless Moses hung the bronze serpent by which, when looked upon, their lethal bites and infusions of poisonous venom were cured, he adds: "But these things happened to them as figurative for our instruction."[23] The bronze serpent is figurative, depicted as though it were fixed on the Cross; and thus was made known to the human race the true one to be crucified, he who countered the poisons of the serpent the devil; he was cursed in a figurative way, while in truth he was the one who wiped out the curses of the whole world.

Also elsewhere, namely, in the letter to the Galatians, it says, "Abraham had two sons, one from the slave woman and one from the freewoman," and it adds: "But indeed his son from

20. Cf. 2 Cor 5.21; Is 53.4.
21. Ps 22.6; 69.9.
22. Cf. 1 Cor 10.11.
23. Ibid. Cf. Nm 21.6–9.

the slave woman was born according to the flesh, but the one from the freewoman according to the promise. These things are said by way of allegory."[24] What he means by "allegory" he clearly explains in what follows, when he says that those two offspring generations, one from the slave woman, the other from the freewoman, are the two covenants, one from Mount Sinai giving birth to slavery, the mountain on which Moses received the Law from the Lord, but the other from Jerusalem, which is free; and through Isaac this covenant gave birth to sons, that is, in the freedom of grace, not in the slavery of the letter.[25] For a penalty is decreed for slaves, but grace is conferred on free children. Did not Jacob receive the two wives from whom he produced divergent offspring typologically, to stand for the twin people?[26] Why is it written that the patriarch Judah, after the death of his own son, sought relations with his own daughter-in-law, who gave birth to twins?[27] Is it not so that the figure would precede both covenants of the Lord Jesus: one child is established as the type of his future death, another for the truth of the Gospel, either because two people had to be born, of which the later, born in the sign of the Cross—that is, the people prior by the reach of the hand, but later by birth—would cut through every hedge and barrier of the earlier people, or because the Lord Jesus himself, born from the tribe of Judah, pre-established his works before he was born for us from the Virgin?[28]

3.12. What shall I say about Joseph, who was assaulted by his brothers, stripped of the garment given by his father, cast into a pit, sold into slavery, and in this way gave clear indication of the Lord's Incarnation:[29] for the one beloved by the Father, since

24. Gal 4.22–24.

25. Cf. Gal 4.24.

26. Cf. Gn 29.25.

27. Hadot, *Apologie de David,* 59–61, provides an appendix explaining this "nearly incomprehensible" section of the text, which treats the birth of the twins Zerah and Perez from Tamar. Ambrose treats the episode in a similar fashion in *Eu. sec. Lucam* 3.17–29, which follows Eusebius of Caesarea, *Quaestiones euangelicae ad Stephanum* 7.5–6. In brief, Zerah, who was to be second of the two but stretched out his hand first, prefigures the anticipation of the Christian Church through his hand, while his birth signifies the definitive revelation in Christ.

28. See the genealogy at Mt 1.3.

29. Cf. Gn 37.23–28.

he was in the form of God, did not judge that equality with God was robbery, but emptied himself, so that, receiving the form of the slave, he came down and he lowered himself all the way to death on the Cross; and, having been both bought and sold by his brothers for the price of the Cross, he has redeemed the human race?[30]

In the type of Christ, David, although the youngest, was chosen from among his brothers, and he alone was anointed for the kingship;[31] he freed all the people by his singular struggle in a gravely dangerous war, and triumphed against tens of thousands, so that the girls sang with their tambourines: "Saul triumphed against thousands, David against tens of thousands."[32] What do those young girls mean figuratively but that they are the souls that sing a psalm of triumph to Christ? David then begot sons, one who was incestuous and the other who was a parricide, to signify that the incestuous and parricidal people would violate the flesh of its own Author by nailing it to the yoke that is the Cross.[33] Thus the third Psalm is prefaced with the title "Absalom," and the Passion of the Lord is prophesied.[34]

3.13. What shall I say about the saintly Solomon, whose later years were not without serious sins, and yet someone whom the Jewish people believed had come as the anointed, the Christ? And how many others did the offense of a serious sin convert? Thus his greater fault resulted in a greater profit, since one who did not lack human vice is not considered superhuman. And so in him we find an enviable wisdom but also a compelling fault, which showed that he was also a human being.

3.14. What, then, prevents us from also believing that Bathsheba was linked to the holy David in a figurative manner?[35] Their union would signify that the assembly of the nations,

30. Phil 2.6–8.

31. Cf. 1 Sm 16.11–13 and 17.32–54.

32. 1 Sm 18.7.

33. Ambrose refers first to Amnon, who raped his sister Tamar (cf. 2 Sm 13.1–14); second to Absalom (cf. 2 Sm 17.1–18.15), who attempted to kill David his father.

34. Ambrose refers occasionally to the inscriptions to the Psalms; for Psalm 3 the LXX has "The Psalm when David fled from before his son Absalom."

35. Cf. 2 Sm 11.27.

which was not joined to Christ as though his legitimate spouse through the faith, because she would have entered into his grace by means of hidden back entrances, outside of the prescriptions of the Law; in her, the naked sincerity and exposed simplicity of heart, accomplished through the justifying sacrament of baptism, would attract the attention and arouse the love of the true David and the eternal king.[36] Rightly, then, Christ came hidden, since he would deceive the prince of the world, identified as the man Uriah, whose name means "my light" because he transfigures himself into an angel of light.[37] I am saying Christ came into this world and he came hidden, as an adulterer would sneak in, so that he might claim his legitimate rule.

4.15. We have analyzed some effective interpretations, and we have demonstrated, we think, that the text of this history was figurative; now let us return to the foregoing matter, and let us examine the sin itself now that it is stripped, as it were, of its spiritual decoration. David sinned, something kings often do, but he did penance, he wept, he sighed, which is something kings rarely do; he confessed his guilt, he sought indulgence, he prostrated himself on the ground, he mourned his trial, he fasted, he prayed, and by making his pain public he handed on to all future ages the example of his confession.[38] The king was not ashamed to make a confession, something that even private citizens are ashamed to do. Those who are bound by the laws dare to deny their sin, they refuse to ask for the mercy that the one who was bound by no human laws sought out. The fact that he sinned belongs to his human condition, that he made supplication belongs to his repentance. His fall is ordinary, but his confession is exceptional. Thus to fall into guilt belongs to nature, but to wash it clean belongs to virtue. "Who boasts," it says, "that he has a pure heart?" For it is demonstrated by the witness of Scripture that not even the one-day-old infant is pure.[39]

4.16. Show me someone who does not fall into sin. It is written that Samson is the sturdiest of them all, he who even stran-

36. Cf. 2 Sm 11.2–5.

37. Cf. 2 Cor 11.14. For Uriah as "Uri," n.130 on p. 181 applies here.

38. Cf. 2 Kgs 12–16.

39. Prv 20.9 quoted here. For infant impurity, see Jb 14.4–5.

gled a lion with his own hands; but would that he could have smothered his own impassioned love! For he burned the crops of foreign tribes, but he himself burned with the flame of just one woman.[40]

Jephthah returned from the enemy as a conqueror, but as he was returning with the triumphal standards he was himself conquered by his own oath, since he decided that the devotion of his daughter who was running toward him should be repaid with murder.[41] What need was there to swear so recklessly in the first place, and to vow an uncertain offering, whose outcome he did not know, as though it were certain? Is there anyone who would render such grim offerings to the Lord God, so that he would fulfill his vows with bloody murder?

4.17. Yet I do not think we should be silent about priests lest I appear to try to hide our own sins. Aaron himself was a high priest; he was equal in standing to Moses as a leader to the Hebrew nation when they crossed over the Red Sea by foot. When the people asked him to make gods for them to worship, he demanded their gold and cast it into the fire, and the head of a calf was created, to which sacrifices were then offered. By this sign Aaron showed that greed for gold is the source of infidelity and that sacrilege is often born from the lust of avarice.[42]

So great a priest fell into sin yet again together with his sister Miriam. For at the very moment when the two of them were berating their brother because he had taken a foreign wife, Miriam erupted with the infection of blemished flesh.[43]

4.18. The account here demonstrates the prefiguring of a mystery: the priestly people of the ancestors would in later times disparage a fraternal people because they did not understand the sacramental role of that Ethiopian woman.[44] For if they had known, they would not have disparaged what was in accord with the ancient mystery. And thus when the Jew identifies as impure the one from among the gentiles who came to believe, and

40. Cf. the episodes at Jgs 14.4–16.4.

41. Cf. Jgs 11.30–40.

42. Cf. Ex 32.

43. Cf. Nm 12.

44. I.e., Moses's wife; Nm 12.1.

when he seeks to separate that one from the Law, he gets leprosy; he cannot avoid this unless he acquires a spiritual knowledge of the Law, which would have brought him to repentance.

4.19. And so too David, who knew that he was a man born to fall, sought forgiveness, and he did not despair of the Lord's mercy.

5.20. And the parable [from the Gospels] seems to show no discrepancy with this mystery.[45] For who is the rich man unless Jesus our Lord, who speaks about himself, as was read [in the liturgy] today: "There was a certain rich man who went into a faraway region to receive his kingdom and to return"?[46] And the Son was truly rich, enjoying the wealth of his majesty and the fullness of his own divinity; angels and archangels, virtues and powers and principalities, thrones and dominions, Cherubim and Seraphim served him with tireless submission.[47]

But although he was rich, he left ninety-nine sheep on the mountains, and he sought out the one sheep, which had remained behind from exhaustion.[48] The prince of this world, who was himself needy and poor in regard to that rich man, was nourishing this sheep with his own rations as though she were his daughter.[49] So then the sheep collapsed because its existence was sustained by the food of this world. This sheep was lost, harassed in Adam by the plots of the serpent.

5.21. Yet she was not a wicked sheep, for she was "filled" with the Word, since she was a daughter of the spiritual "seven" and a gift of her sacred Creator;[50] yet she was not being fed by what is valuable, but for a long time by the wretched rations of a poor man. Thus Nathan says, "She ate from his bread and drank from his cup and rested in his lap."[51] For the food of

45. The reference may be to the Gospel reading of the Parable of the Ten Talents (Lk 19.11–27) in the liturgy.

46. Lk 19.12

47. Cf. Col 2.9; 1.16; Eph 1.21.

48. Cf. 2 Cor 8.9 and Mt 18.12–14.

49. Cf. Jn 12.31 and 2 Sm 12.3.

50. According to Hadot, *Apologie,* 98–99 n.34, a reference to the etymology of "Bathsheba," with the number seven signifying the perfection of the Old Testament.

51. 2 Sm 12.3.

the Ethiopians is not good; poisonous is the golden chalice of Babylon, which intoxicates the nations;[52] slumber is not helpful for sleepers; I prefer to stay awake. And "all the foolish of heart have been disturbed; they have slept their sleep, and they have found nothing."[53] Thus for the sake of hospitality—the fact that he received a guest—in order to offer him a feast, he stole that sheep from the poor man;[54] for if he had offered a beast from his own flocks or herds, it could not have profited us; if he had not offered a sacrifice for us, he would not have redeemed us.

5.22. Thus he took up the weaknesses of our limited condition in his flesh by a kind of affectionate hospitality, and for the sake of relieving or rather refashioning our fragility he offered his flesh to that saving Passion, so that he might provide for us the food of eternal life. And rightly Scripture calls him "ewe lamb," because he was born of a virgin. Rightly does the prophetic judgment proclaim that rich man was "worthy of death,"[55] because even Caiaphas prophesied saying: "It is better for one man to die in place of the people."[56] For the Lord Jesus alone was chosen to be worthy of such a death, by which he would take away the sin of the world. It fittingly adds: "He will restore the lamb."[57] Because he raised his own flesh, he returned that flesh born from virginal integrity. And it is not for nothing that it says: "He will restore it fourfold,"[58] for the resurrection of the dead is quadrupled, just as the Apostle says when he teaches: "[The body] is sown in corruption, it rises in incorruption; it is sown in ignobility, it rises in glory; it is sown in weakness, it rises in power; the natural body is sown, the spiritual body rises."[59] And it is clear that he will restore the lamb fourfold also in the way by which a man can now say: "If I have stolen anything from anyone, I return it to him fourfold."[60] And he

52. Cf. Ps 74.14 and Jer 51.7.
53. Ps 76.5.
54. Cf. 2 Sm 12.4.
55. 2 Sm 12.5.
56. Jn 11.50.
57. 2 Sm 12.6.
58. Cf. Lk 19.8.
59. 1 Cor 15.42–44.
60. Lk 19.8.

fittingly adds this point: "Because he did not have mercy."[61] For Christ did not have mercy on himself, so that he might bring help to all.[62]

5.23. Thus it was spoken by the Lord Jesus Christ to his servant David, that he might make known the mystery: "Since you have done this in secret, I will make this claim before all of Israel in broad daylight."[63] And at first, when David did not grasp the sacramental meaning, he was upset with indignation, but he did not err in his attitude. In fact, afterwards, when he knew the great mystery (*mysterium*)—for it was the great mystery (*sacramentum*) of Christ and the Church[64]—seeing the future remission of all sins, and foreseeing the brilliance of grace through the washing of regeneration and the infusion of the Holy Spirit, he trusted in his pardon and said: "I have sinned before the Lord";[65] so that he would also enter into fellowship with those who would profit from the remission of sins. Do you notice how he deplored his own sin? Who would be surprised that his sin was forgiven him?

6.24. Now let us consider the good works by which he could cover over his sin. For even if it is not possible for human fragility to be without sin, one must take care that there not be more sins than works of virtues. Holy Paul expresses this with the great force of his wisdom when he says, "The sins of some are obvious, reaching the place of judgment ahead of them; the sins of others trail behind them";[66] that is: there is no one found unharmed by sin; each person has good merits, just as he also has vices and sins. Thus all our deeds are weighed as though in a balance. And so if our sins weigh more than our good deeds, they press on to judgment; for sins sink, as it were, all the way to the bottom; when manifest, they sink by their weight and their gravity, or their number. "But the sins of others trail behind," Paul says; that is, there are those who manage themselves with

61. 2 Sm 12.6.
62. Cf. Rom 8.32.
63. 2 Sm 12.12.
64. Cf. Eph 5.32.
65. 2 Sm 12.13.
66. 1 Tm 5.24.

moderation, but by the fragility of their condition they have succumbed to error at some point, so that their good deeds go ahead and the evil ones trail behind. These people are more honorable, yet they have fallen by milder vices and mistakes. Thus the sins "trail behind" the just—they do not precede them: they precede the unjust. The sins that weigh one down are heavier, while if there are deeds that were done rightly, they trail behind, as though they have been burdened by the precedent of the sins that came first. Likewise, "good deeds are also evident."[67] For the works of virtues shine out, and the splendor of their merits, "and those things cannot be hidden which are otherwise distinctive."[68] Thus such deeds are not obscured, and the "charity" which "covers a multitude of sins" does not overshadow them; the grace of good works does not conceal them, the multitude of virtues does not hide them;[69] but they are revealed, as though naked and uncovered. For there is no one among them who says: "Protect me under the shadow of your wings";[70] for the Cross of the Lord abolishes and hides all errors.

6.25. Thus who has covered and hidden more than the saintly David, who also elsewhere says: "Even in the shadow of your wings I have hoped, until the wickedness passes by"?[71] Thus he has so loved the Lord that by an abundance of charity he might cover over every sin and hide it. For even if the holy apostle Peter had already overcome his fall by the confession of his love, he too was tested by the Lord when he said to him the third time, "Simon son of John, do you love me?"[72] Hence, the one who had denied him three times might confess him three times, and thus with a triple veil of love he might cover over the fall of a triple denial. If it is true that when Peter wept just once he received pardon, how much more is it true of David, who washed his bed and flooded his mattress with his tears for nights on end, whose tears were as his bread day and night, who ate

67. 1 Tm 5.25.
68. Ibid.
69. Cf. 1 Pt 4.8.
70. Ps 16.8.
71. Ps 57.1.
72. Jn 21.16.

ashes as though they were bread and mixed his sobs into his drink![73] And if Jesus has mercy on the one who cries out once he has repented, if he looked on Peter and Peter wept, how much more would the one who wept for so long not disappear from the sight of the Lord? For Peter denied Jesus once and did not weep, because Jesus had not looked upon him; he denied a second time and did not weep, because the Lord had not looked upon him; when he denied a third time, Jesus looked at him, and immediately he wept and wept bitterly. Thus David, who was always weeping, said: "My eyes are always on the Lord";[74] he who was always seen by Christ said: "My eyes have flowed down through floods of waters."[75]

6.26. But now let us also consider his deeds. Who would not cover over the hostility born from a single crime with the acclaim of so many virtues? Chosen through divine testing, David proved straightaway that he was not unworthy of such an election.[76] He went forth into battle, and, standing alone while all the others were trembling in fear, he drew on both his faith and his strength to cast down the foreigner Goliath, who was terrifying in the display of his words and in the bulk of his enormous body.[77] The courage of one became the victory of all. Let one juxtapose, if you please, the sin of a private individual and the triumph achieved for all, the death of a single man and the life of many peoples whom he freed from death.

6.27. Let us proceed to other matters. He endured ambushes from King Saul; the king sought to end [David's] life, but when the king was handed over by divine providence into his power and Saul was entirely vulnerable to a blow, the saintly David opposed his companions as they were about to strike him, and he turned back the lethal wound from the body that was to die, saying: "Do not touch the anointed of the Lord."[78] In fact, he

73. Cf. Ps 6.7; 42.4; 102.10.

74. Ps 16.8.

75. Ps. 119.136; the verse, which has textual problems, suggests to Ambrose that the eyes themselves are flowing; see Filippo Lucidi, *Opere esegetiche V: Le due apologie di David* (Milan: Biblioteca Ambrosiana, 1981), 83 n.3.

76. 1 Sm 16.11–13.

77. 1 Sm 17.1–38.

78. 1 Sm 24.7.

even avenged the death of his great enemy; he wept copiously as he lamented [Saul's] death, and for a long time he refused the power that was owed to him;[79] for he knew that it was owed only with God's approval. By this fact alone he made it known that all people should not preemptively snatch the kingdom, even if it is owed to them, but they should wait until it is handed over in its proper time. Would that later rulers had imitated this man! We would not have undergone so many bitter experiences of wars. You argue that he killed a man, but you do not consider that he taught us how perpetual peace might be preserved in the Roman world. How severe a devastation do we even now endure, how much public bloodshed, even of the entire world, have we paid for the murder of a slaughtered king![80] Alas, what harsh punishments! From that point until now the barbarian enemy assails us, while the arms prepared against them are turned against ourselves. Thus the communal power has collapsed; thus Roman virtue, broken down by its own uprisings, has grown old; for [the state] is seized by public murder, while it should be supported by the observance of paternal concern. And David was so concerned to avoid this that when he discovered that his son Adonijah had planned to take the reign for himself and was organizing an alliance, he would not choose the one who was snatching authority away in haste but rather the one who would wait for it to come to him.[81]

6.28. The most powerful of kings was leaping before the Ark of the Lord, and, when he was criticized by his own wife because he stripped himself within the sight of young girls, he responded: "I will continue to be stripped down before the Lord, and I will be a trifle before your eyes, so that the Lord might be glorified," he said, "who recognized me for the kingship instead of your father";[82] he thus teaches that one should not be concerned with the trappings of royal authority when obedience is

79. Cf. 2 Sm 1.14–27.

80. Probably a reference to the emperor Gratian (367–383), who generally favored Ambrose and who was assassinated by the forces of the usurper Maximus; see Hadot, *Apologie,* 36–37.

81. Cf. 1 Kgs 1.5–39. The "one who would wait for it to come to him" is Solomon.

82. 2 Sm 6.21–22.

being shown to piety. For it is honorable to do something for the sake of piety even if it is unbecoming to one's authority.

6.29. Consider another fascinating point. His son, the parricide, had violently invaded the kingdom of his fathers.[83] At first his father yielded to his [son's] rage and avoided the fighting, so that in this manner the reckless one might recover from his rage. David also refused to engage in war, and he requested that those who were going forth to battle should spare his son. The one who asked them to spare his enemy was certain of victory, and the one who believed that even an impious son should not die was no stranger to piety. He even wept with loud mourning and deplored the death of that murderer, saying: "My son Absalom, who will grant death to me instead of you, my son Absalom?"[84] He thought that the one who killed Absalom to satisfy paternal obligation should himself be punished.[85]

6.30. How much indeed did David himself suffer through injustice and pain! As I said, even when he was fortified on the left and the right by hearty warriors, he yielded to the fury of his son Absalom; the man whose name was Shimei cursed him, calling him violent and a man of blood who was cast off from the kingship by a just judgment of the Lord.[86] But David was not at all upset by these insults, even when his companions were upset. Thus one of his companions—Abishai was his name—threatened that he would take off Shimei's head as the price of his insult. But the king turned to Abishai and said, "What does it matter to me and to you, son of Zeruiah? Thus he curses me since the Lord told him to curse me."[87] See how he taught us the moral that the periods of our injuries and our perils are tests through temptations and the trials of tribulations, and therefore they are not usually imposed apart from God's edict. The good athlete is trained through insults, he is trained through struggles and dangers, that he might be worthy to have the crown

83. Cf. 2 Sm 15.1–14.
84. 2 Sm 18.33.
85. Cf. 2 Sm 18.14; 1 Kgs 2.5.
86. Cf. 2 Sm 16.7–8.
87. 2 Sm 16.10.

of justice bestowed on him.[88] Therefore, whatever is considered hostile must be borne patiently. Thus even elsewhere Holy Scripture teaches you the same thing, when the just man says: "If we accept good things from the hand of the Lord, why should we not accept what is evil?"[89]

6.31. And the saintly prophet says in addition: "Behold my son who went forth from my loins, he seeks my life. But then if this Benjaminite curses me, let him curse; the Lord told him to do this that he might look upon my humility, and the Lord might requite me for this curse."[90] O height of prudence, O mark of patience, O marvelous recognition that an injury should be accepted eagerly! He says: "Are you upset, Abishai, that an outsider curses me, someone whose own son seeks to kill him? The Lord told him to curse me." But the Lord is not a slanderer and does not take pleasure in insults.

6.32. See how David observes each detail carefully. He does not blame the Lord as though he were the author of the injustice, but rather he praises him because the Lord allows us to endure lesser things so that we might acquire forgiveness for greater sins. See how the insult of the words lightened the bitterness of the [attempted] murder, and David absolved the insolent one, whose curses yielded more profit because they were forgiven according to divine recompense. Who would not consider such injustice recompensed, since God comforts by means of a much greater repayment the one whom a human being has wounded?

7.33. Let us also consider his other deeds. He battled against the progeny of giants, when one of them nearly struck the king as he was turned around in the fighting, a brazen act that the enemy paid for by means of his own death.[91]

7.34. Once he had accomplished the triumph of conquest over the brutal nation, he again undertook a massive war in the valley of the titans, no less against the enemy than against nature itself.[92] For when he was thirsty while he was waging battle, he

88. Cf. 2 Tm 4.7–8.
89. Jb 2.10.
90. 2 Sm 16.11–12.
91. Cf. 2 Sm 21.15–21.
92. Cf. 2 Sm 23.13.

did not have anything to drink. He said, "Who will give me drink from the well that is at the gates in Bethlehem?"[93] For the enemy was poured in between the well and holy David, and the middle was fenced around by enemy camps. Three men cut through a multitude of the enemies and filled up [their vessels] with water from the well that was in Bethlehem, and they brought it to the king to drink. But the king refused to drink and poured it out for the Lord—for it was worthy of so great a gift, that the water that was a sign of lively power should become a sacrifice of devotion—and he spoke this laudable opinion in a prophetic spirit: "Far be it from me to do this, lest I should drink the blood from the lives of the men who departed."[94] Thus he conquered nature, since he did not drink when he was thirsty, and he gave himself as an example by which the entire army might learn to endure thirst. He also instructed those who were his subjects in the demands of virtue, so that the soldiers might willingly submit to the royal command even in the midst of dangers. Indeed, by the fact that he refused to drink he declared that he had given the command in order to test the soldiers, and not because he was overcome by the demands of thirst; and he also was concerned that no future king look to their own need for drink by putting others in danger. And, finally, the pain of a devout conscience was avoided, in that the water procured with the loss of so many men's lives could not be sweet to drink because it depended on the horror of the death that was demanded.

7.35. But if you wish to look for a higher meaning and to investigate the mystery, David was not thirsting for water from the well that is in Bethlehem, but he foresaw the Christ who was to emerge from the Virgin in the Spirit. Thus he did not wish to drink the water of the river, but rather the draught of spiritual grace; that is, he was not thirsting for the element of water but the blood of Christ. Therefore, he did not drink the water that was offered, but he poured it out to the Lord indicating that he thirsted for the sacrifice of Christ, not the flow that comes from nature; he longed for that sacrifice in which there is the remission of sins, and he thirsted for the everlasting fountain, which

93. 2 Sm 23.15.
94. 2 Sm 23.17.

is not sought in what is perilous to others, but one that drives out what is perilous to others.

7.36. Do we not then conclude that the blood of one man was covered over with so many wondrous deeds? Rightly the voice of the blood of Abel the just cried out to the Lord, because the wicked Cain was protected by no good works of his own, because he was murderous, because he did not confess his crime, but rather denied it.[95] Although David killed a man who was not at all guilty, he did not kill him because he was driven by a lust for cruelty. Rather he hoped to hide his shame and cover over the humiliation of his lust. I do not dare say that he was constrained by the force of the crime—for a person who knew how he could possibly lift himself from the ruin of that sin is hardly constrained—but I still maintain that he was bowed down by the force of temptation: for he had said above: "Test me, Lord, and try me, burn my insides and my heart,"[96] and elsewhere, "But I said in my abundance: I will be forever unmoved,"[97] and also, "You have tested me by fire, and iniquity has not been found in me."[98] The Lord wished to subject David to temptation so that he would not claim for himself something that is beyond man: for "power is perfected in weakness."[99] Thus David did not act with bloody intent: nothing could be less properly attributed to the holy prophet. For when he was departing from this life, with his final words he summoned his son Solomon, telling Solomon to remove innocent blood from himself;[100] this was the blood that Joab, the leader of his army, had poured out when Abner, who was attempting to draw up a truce although he was the leader of the other army,[101] was killed by treacherous acts.[102] David wept over him, and after his burial he went forth after removing his insignia of power, observing the obligations of Abner's funer-

95. Cf. Gn 4.9–10.
96. Ps 26.2.
97. Ps 30.6.
98. Ps 17.3.
99. 2 Cor 12.9.
100. Hadot, *Apologie,* 119 n.46, suggests an allusion to Theodosius's crimes.
101. That is, Saul's army.
102. Cf. 1 Kgs 2.5.

al rites.[103] By this action David made it clear that vowed commitments must be observed even for enemies, and that virtue, even in one's foe, must be honored. Did David not remove the wart of even this error by handing on his devotion that was so gentle?

7.37. And how brilliant he was when the three options were offered to him to choose from (since he had committed the offense of numbering the people): that there be a famine over the earth for three years, or that they flee for three months before the face of their enemies in persecution, or for there to be a pestilence on the earth for three days. David chose the third option, because he preferred to commend himself to the power of the Lord rather than to the power of men. For the Lord in his mercy would immediately forgive him.[104] Thus he said: "My anguish is great in these three choices, but better for me to fall into the hands of the Lord, since great is his mercy, than for me to fall into the hands of men."[105] By this humility, prudence, and meekness he made clear, if I may use the words of Scripture, that the Lord has repentance for his own wrath. Thus so it is written that "the Lord had repentance for his malice."[106]

7.38. But even more marvelous than that is the fact that David offered himself to the angel who was smiting the people, and he said: "What did that flock do? Let your hand come upon me and upon the house of my father!"[107] By this deed the one who was judged unworthy of absolution was immediately judged worthy for sacrifice. It is no wonder that he received pardon for his sin by such an offering of himself for the people, when we consider that Moses also wiped away the sins of the people by offering himself to the Lord in the name of the people's folly.[108]

7.39. Did he then cover over his own sins or not? But who would deny that he did, when the prophet himself has indicated that his iniquities are forgiven, his sins are covered over, and they are not imputed by the Lord?[109] He himself taught that the

103. Cf. 2 Sm 3.31.
104. Cf. 2 Sm 24.12–14.
105. 2 Sm 24.14; 1 Chr 21.13.
106. 2 Sm 24.17; 1 Chr 21.15.
107. 2 Sm 24.17; 1 Chr 21.17.
108. Cf. Ex 32.11–14; Dt 9.18–19.
109. Cf. Ps 32.1–2.

sin was forgiven him, just as it is written: "I acknowledge my sin, and I have not covered over my injustice. I have said: Against myself I will profess my injustice to the Lord, and you have forgiven the impiety of my heart."[110] If he said, "I will profess," and he earned pardon even before he had professed, how much more is it true that when he professed about himself the words "I acknowledge my iniquity," every sin was forgiven him?[111] Indeed, the prophet Nathan addressed this specifically when he responded to David: "And the Lord has taken away your sin."[112]

7.40. Thus he also earned the remission of his iniquity, and he covered it over with charity, and he concealed his sins and covered them over with good works. And his sin was not reckoned to him, because there was no deceitful malice in him, but only a fall due to error. Hence it was not the fire of wickedness that was in him but only the shadow of a mystery. And he confessed his sin, he acknowledged his iniquity, he saw the washing; he both saw and believed it.[113] He loved much, so that he could cover over any error with abundant charity.[114]

8.41. But at this point let him defend himself; for he wrote the fiftieth Psalm to record this account.[115] And when he laid down the history of the events of his life, such as his betrayal by Doeg the Syrian, who is inscribed at the head of Psalm 51 [52], and the betrayal by the Ziphites, which seems to be implied by the inscription to Psalm 53 [54], he placed the history that is earlier first, since both Doeg and the Ziphites betrayed him before the prophet David took up the reign.[116] Indeed, he was still fleeing King Saul throughout various hiding places as he wandered about in exile, but he took up Bathsheba when he was already reigning.

8.42. Then why does the order of the Psalms not square with the order of his deeds? Because he seeks not so much to make

110. Ps 32.5.

111. Ps 51.3.

112. 2 Sm 12.13.

113. Cf. Jn 20.8.

114. Cf. Lk 7.47.

115. Ps 50 in the LXX is numbered Ps 51 in the Hebrew text. Borrowing from Didymus, Ambrose here treats the inscriptions of other Psalms.

116. Cf. 1 Sm 21.8; 22.9–10.

the order fit the historical sequence as for the mystery to correspond with his deeds; therefore he wished to fix to this historical account the number that is symbolic of remission. For the fiftieth number is a number of forgiveness, just as the Lord himself teaches us in the Gospel when he says: "Two people owed money to a certain moneylender. One owed him five hundred denarii, and the other fifty. Neither of them had the money to pay him back, so he forgave the debts of both. Now which of them will love him more?"[117] And in the Law you find that the Jubilee is said to be the recurrence of years fifty in number, which is celebrated in extraordinary fashion;[118] then debts are forgiven, and the liberties of the Hebrews and the restitution of properties are established. Joyfully we celebrate this same number after the Passion of the Lord, when the debt of all sin is forgiven and we are freed from every bond when the debt-collection is made null; we receive the grace of the Holy Spirit that comes upon us on the day of Pentecost, the fast is relaxed, praise is sung to God, and the alleluia is chanted.

Thus [according to the Law] even the father of the girl who was violated by force while she was espoused to no one receives fifty silver drachmas, and she herself will remain married [to the man who raped her].[119] And so by this number even vices are turned into grace. Truly great is that Psalm by which we learn how penance should be done.

8.43. David says, "Have mercy on me, Lord, according to your great mercy. And according to the multitude of your mercies wipe out my offense. Wash me thoroughly from my injustice, and from my sin cleanse me. For I know my iniquity, and my sin is against me always. Against you alone I have sinned, and I have done evil before you, that you may be justified in your pronouncements and prevail when you are judged. For behold, I was conceived in iniquity and my mother bore me in sins."[120] Who of us, even if he confesses his sin, does not consider the confession something to be minimized rather than repeated?

117. Lk 7.41–42.
118. Cf. Lv 25.10–11.
119. Dt 22.28–29.
120. Ps 51.1–5.

Who repeats it a second or third time? See in how many verses the great prophet re-proclaims his own sin, how there is no verse that does not contain a confession of his sin. He heaped it all up, compiling together his iniquities, and by proclaiming his injustice he adds his faults to his sins, and by rightly repeating these things again and again he seeks abundant mercy, and not only abundant mercy but also a multitude of mercies. What sin, then, does such a pleading not wash clean, what guilt does a prayer of this sort not purify? David beseeches a multitude of mercies for one sin, while we believe that for our many sins God's mercy should be requested scarcely once.

Thus we read that in his "great" power and with his lofty arm he freed his people from the land of Egypt when he led them through the Red Sea, in which baptism is prefigured.[121] Thus if his "great" power was revealed in the prefigurement of the sacraments, how much more is his "great mercy" revealed in their reality? It is also fitting that a multitude of mercies is requested precisely where there is a multitude of sinners.

8.44. "Wash me thoroughly from my injustice, and from my sin cleanse me."[122] For David seeks not so much to be washed more often as to be washed more completely, so that he can slough off the hardened filth. He knew that according to the Law there were indeed many aids for cleansing one, but none was complete and perfect.[123] He thus hastens to that perfect cleansing with utmost intent, to reach the time when all justice is fulfilled; that moment comes in the sacrament of baptism, just as the Lord Jesus himself teaches. For when he had come to John, the Baptist said: "I should be baptized by you, and you come to me?" The Lord responded: "Allow it now; for so it is fitting that we fulfill all justice."[124] But after this exchange, Christ was baptized, and the Holy Spirit descended upon him like a dove, and the Father from heaven identified his Son, then all justice was fulfilled.[125] Thus the prophet says: "Wash me thor-

121. Cf. 2 Sm 17.36, Ex 14.15–31, and 1 Cor 10.1–2.
122. Ps 51.2.
123. Cf. Heb 9.1–10, 18.
124. Mt 3.14–16.
125. Cf. Mt 3.16–17.

oughly from my injustice," for the filth is great and the pollution is removed not by a small but by a great washing.[126]

8.45. But if anyone wishes to interpret the phrase otherwise, he can form his own understanding in the following way. The divine speech cleanses, and our confession cleanses: the former when it is heard, and the latter when it is uttered; good thinking cleanses, honorable work cleanses, as does the practice of a good way of life. Each one cleansed by these means imbibes the glory of spiritual grace more easily, and it is as though he seizes it for his own benefit. Thus precious dye does not immediately color fleece by means of a single infusion, but first the fleece is infused by a second-rate substance and then by other sorts of substance; after frequent washings the natural color is changed quite often to a different color. Thus the dyeing is afterwards applied as a more thorough washing, so that a truer and more perfect brilliance of the purple shines forth. Therefore, just as a multitude of murexes[127] is used to infuse the purple, so in the washing of regeneration a multitude of heavenly mercies is needed so that iniquity might be washed away. So too the one who is washed "thoroughly" from injustice is cleansed from sin, and he casts aside the practice and he forgets the manner of sinning that has, as it were, permeated his desires and his practices. And rightly is he "washed clean" from the vices of injustice and iniquity, which are the greater evil; so also he is "cleansed" from any particular sin (*delicto*), which is less important.

9.46. He then adds: "Since I know my iniquity, and my sin is always against me."[128] It is no small matter that each one recognizes his own sin. Thus also he states above: "Who discerns his own falls?"[129] He means, Who is so great that he understands them? Consider this: "Who will dwell in your tent?" and, "Who will ascend to the mountain of the Lord?"[130] He does not mean that no one will, but that only the rare one will; for he who can acknowledge his fall can avoid it, and he can choose what he will pursue.

126. Ps 51.2.
127. A mollusk used for dyeing.
128. Ps 51.3.
129. Ps 19.13.
130. Ps 15.1; 14.1.

And many boast in their falls, and they think actions that are blameworthy deserve praise; for instance, if they defile another's bed and conquer the affections of a chaste lady, if they undermine the commitment of a widow by some trickery; someone thinks it is a point of power to live by the slaughter of men, by the deceits of robbery, and by theft; some reckon it is a mark of wisdom to trick and swindle. No one of these can say, "Since I know my iniquity," but only the one who can mourn what he did and condemn what he failed to do, the one whose vices elicit regret. Hence the prophet also says: "Regret what you speak in your hearts and in your private rooms."[131]

Most horses, when they have fallen, are accustomed to toss themselves around, and the ones that the fall did not wound grow lame and are crippled on account of the tossing. Others (and this is said to be characteristic of Greek horses), when they are cast from the chariot in battle or they fall by chance, are in no way accustomed to move themselves, and they maintain a certain practice of quiet and patient waiting. If the fall has not harmed these, the rest helps them heal; and at least the offense is not made worse. When the fall is a matter of a sin, shouldn't those who toss about in their sins and consider it a mark of their power be considered worse off than speechless animals? Thus it is said, as though to a speechless steer: "You have sinned, be still."[132]

9.47. Hence David fittingly adds: "And my sin is always against me."[133] For the foolish one delights in his errors, and by covering over the old sins with new ones he thinks that he is helped; he even exults in his crime. Yet truly the wise man judges his sin to be against himself and thus reckons the sins into which he has fallen to be standing against him now as though they were an enemy line. Whatever he hums, whatever he squeaks, his own sin always rushes against him; whatever was said or read he thinks was said against him; whatever he looks upon, he believes that he is betrayed by gestures or looks. If he feasts, if he thinks, if he prays or beseeches, his own error is always before his eyes,

131. Ps 4.4.
132. Gn 4.7.
133. Ps 51.3.

and the guilt strikes his conscience at every moment and does not allow him to rest or to forget. As though a harsh judge, he upsets himself with perpetual fear. Thus the one who is displeased with himself considers all things to be against him;[134] he is his own accuser, he is a witness against himself, and he who drives himself and goads himself on finds nowhere to flee. But it is the characteristic of the good heart to sense the wound of sin. For those who do not experience pain do not sense the bitterness of a wound, and that is part of an untreatable sickness. But those who are pricked by some pain, inasmuch as they do not lack sensitivity to pain, so too they do not lack the prospect of health. For where there is a feeling of pain, there is also a feeling of life; for feeling is a mark of vigor and vital functioning. Hence even the one who does not know his errors rages, goes mad, and is delirious, but he who recognizes them indeed comes to his senses; he does not spit out the remedies that bring health; rather, he reins himself in, he repents of his sin, he thinks about it always and by thinking about it he condemns himself: "for the just man, once he begins to speak, is his own accuser."[135] The one who accuses himself is just; whoever is just is sober, he is healthy. The just man does not know how to prefer himself to others; he does not even know to bend the rigidity of judgment in his own favor; he shudders at the memory of his own fall; and he blushes at his own error; he fears, he dreads, and he shrinks before every memory of it; he believes that it weighs heavy on himself; he flees from serving as his own judge; and he does not dare commit himself to himself, because he thinks no one more severe to him than the one from whom he cannot hide, whom he cannot deceive, whom he finds no way to flee and avoid, unless he should "deny his very self and take up the Cross" of the Lord.[136]

9.48. There is great power in a guilty conscience, and a great punishment. Eve and Adam were afraid, and, when they heard the voice of the Lord walking in the garden, those whom no one

134. Cf. Prv 18.17.
135. Ibid.
136. Mt 16.24.

was seeking desired to hide themselves.[137] Cain also was fearful that anyone who would find him would kill him. In this way he was carrying his own verdict against himself because he was not worthy that anyone would forgive him.[138] David therefore expresses it well: "And my sin is always against me,"[139] that is: without any break, the memory and very appearance of that error of mine assail me. Consider how it confounds us when we fail somehow, how it invades our eyes, how it always returns to our memory. The one who is ashamed about something that he has committed knows to avoid committing afterwards something similar, which would shame him in a similar way.

9.49. But iniquity precedes, sin follows. Iniquity is the root, but a fault is the fruit coming from the root. Hence iniquity seems to refer to the wickedness of the heart, sin to the error of the body. Thus iniquity is heavier, as though the material for sins, while sin is lighter. Thus iniquity is remitted through washing, while sin is covered over by good deeds and overshadowed by good works as though by wings. Hence he says this well above: "Blessed are those whose iniquities are forgiven and whose sins are covered over."[140] For charity covers error and "hides a multitude of sins."[141] Indeed, great charity even remits sins themselves, just as it is written about the woman who poured oil over the Lord: "Her many sins are forgiven since she loved much."[142]

9.50. Indeed, there are those who take the first part of the verse[143] to be about the washing, and the second part to be about repentance. For the same reason, Peter, who had already been baptized, was asked, after he had been known to have denied the Lord: "Simon son of John, do you love me?" He says to him: "Indeed, you know, Lord, that I love you." And again he is asked: "Simon son of John, do you love me?" And again he responds: "You know that I love you." And the third time he is asked: "Simon son of John, do you love me?" "And he was sad

137. Cf. Gn 3.8.
138. Cf. Gn 4.9.
139. Ps 51.3.
140. Ps 32.1.
141. 1 Pt 4.8.
142. Lk 7.47.
143. That is, from Psalm 51 (50).

because he said to him a third time, 'Do you love me?' and he said to him: 'Lord, you know all things: you know that I love you.'" And it is said to him a third time in turn: "Feed my lambs; follow me,"[144] as though he were addressing one who had covered over his sin with a very great love.[145] And one should note that it is after his confession of very great charity that Peter, who, even when he was upset, had not lost the means of governing himself, is commanded to govern the people. We have said this on account of the grace of charity, the grace by which he covered over his sin. Thus there are some who have therefore said that the triple question of love took place because the denial had been threefold, so that the profession of charity was repeated as many times as would wipe out the fall of the triple denial.

10.51. Then the Psalm continues: "Against you alone I have sinned."[146] In fact, David was a king, himself bound by no laws, because kings are free from the bonds connected to crimes; and indeed those who rely on the power of their authority are not called to charges by any laws. Thus he did not sin against an individual, to whom he would not be held accountable. But although he was safe through his authority, he was yet subject to God through his devotion and fidelity, and, knowing that he was subject to God's law, he could not deny his sin. And so, as though he were guilty, he confessed with bitterness; for he knew that he was held by even greater bonds because he owed more, since more is demanded of him to whom more is entrusted.[147]

We can also interpret the passage in this way: Who condemns me when all are under sin?[148] Thus the Lord stated about that adulterous woman, "Whoever is without sin, let him cast the first stone."[149] And no one stoned her. Thus the prophet says: "Against you I have sinned," you who alone are without sin.[150] But the one who is guilty in sin cannot condemn someone else as a sinner. For every man who condemns in another what he

144. Jn 21.15–21.
145. Cf. Ps 32.1; 1 Pt 4.8.
146. Ps 51.4.
147. Cf. Lk 12.48.
148. Cf. Rom 3.9.
149. Jn 8.7.
150. Ps 51.4.

himself does has no excuse; in judging the other he condemns himself. He says, "Against you I have sinned, and I have done evil before you, that you may be justified in your pronouncements and prevail when you are judged."[151] I have sinned against you who called me to the pursuit of virtue, you who taught me in your law. "Against you alone I have sinned," whom alone the hidden things of our thoughts and the concealed matters of the heart do not escape.

10.52. And "I have done evil before you," to whom only holiness is appropriate.[152] We avoid the witness of man, but in your sight we commit those things that are unworthy of you. It is an affront to someone to look on their crimes; we know that God is the judge of all and that we sin while he himself is the witness. And yet in these actions the Lord our God is justified because our injustice commends the justice of God and our deception celebrates the truth of God;[153] for "God is true, but every man is a liar."[154]

10.53. "That you may be justified in your pronouncements."[155] The pronouncements of God are full of truth and justice, and therefore whatever the Lord has spoken about human weakness is true, that human hearts are inclined to wickedness, that they hasten to deceive. And because by that fact he has defined that there is no man who does not sin—for "all have gone astray and become unprofitable"[156]—therefore he prevails when he is judged, since by the fall of all he has demonstrated whatever he has judged about our mistakes. Thus if we said that we have committed iniquity, we justify God in his pronouncements; but if we say that we have not sinned, we make God a liar, and yet it is impossible for him to lie.[157] Thus it is clear that all are under sin.[158]

10.54. Thus how great is the crime when a man denies that

151. Ibid.
152. Ibid.
153. Cf. Rom 3.5.
154. Rom. 3.4.
155. Ps 51.4.
156. Ps 14.3.
157. Cf. 1 Jn 1.10 and Heb 6.18.
158. Cf. Rom 3.9.

he is a sinner, since insofar as he can, he seems both to oppose and refute as a lie the words of the Most High God, who is so moderate and patient that he prevails even as he is judged.[159] For when judgment is reached, God says: "My people, what have I done to you or how have I saddened you or how have I troubled you? Because I led you out of the land of Egypt and I have freed you from the house of slavery and I sent before you Moses and Aaron and Miriam. My people, have in mind what Balak thought about you."[160] He places for your viewing his benefits one by one, so that you might judge in these matters what you should have preserved; thus you are made even guiltier because you could not remain in divine benefits. He says, "What have I done to you?" and sets you up as the judge and himself as the guilty one. "Or how have I saddened you?" He does not deny the charge that comes from your offended visage, if you have been saddened by God your Creator. "Or how have I troubled you?" He admits the injustice of the objection, if it is judged too troublesome. He lists his benefits, on account of which the one who appears ungrateful hardly blushed.

For this reason consider also how the Lord shows himself to be judged by David himself, that he might prevail: for Nathan says: "Thus says the Lord God of Israel: 'I have anointed you as king over Israel, and I have freed you from the hand of Saul, and I have given to you all things that belonged to your lord,[161] and I have handed his wives into your embrace, and I have given to you the house of Israel itself, and, if these are small things, I will add to them for you. And why do you consider the Lord as nothing, that you practice iniquity in his sight?'"[162] Confronted by the record of these events, when David saw that he was very much in the wrong when God judges, David says: "I have sinned against the Lord."[163] Thus he justified the Lord because he did not dare deny his own sin.

10.55. So we can also understand the text in this way: The

159. Cf. Ps 51.4.
160. Mi 6.3–5.
161. That is, King Saul.
162. 2 Sm 12.7–9.
163. 2 Sm 12.13.

one who confesses his sin justifies the Lord. Hence, in the Gospel you find that "the tax-collectors justified God when they were baptized by the baptism of John."[164] For John the Baptist performed a baptism of penance. But the one who does penance does not deny his sins. Thus the fact that David always had his sin against him means that he did not deny what also put him to shame, he did not deny what he also acknowledged. But, in fact, by not denying his sin he did penance for the error he committed, and by thus confessing his sin he justified the Lord and was himself justified by the Lord. For the Lord is justified when his justice is proclaimed and pardon is requested from him. At the same time the Lord himself justifies the one confessing and is justified in his pronouncements, just as it is written: "Speak your iniquities that you might be justified."[165]

11.56. The text continues: "For behold, I was conceived in iniquities, and my mother bore me in sins."[166] Who does his penance with such great passion? He casts himself down prostrate on the floor streaming with tears; he tastes no food at all; he refuses to bathe.[167] What now shall I say about the rest of the account—that he abstained from the splendor and the trappings of royalty? He added to that the confession of his own iniquity and he handed on for all ages a confession to be sung throughout the whole world. He says, "Behold, I was conceived in iniquities, and my mother bore me in sins. Turn your face from my sins, and blot out all my offenses. Do not cast me from your face, and do not take your Holy Spirit away from me. Free me from bloodguilt, O God, God of my salvation."[168] Before we are born, we are marked by a stain, and before we enter into the light, we receive the injustice of our very origin. We are conceived in iniquity—he does not express whether the iniquity belongs to our parents or to ourselves—and each one's mother bears him in sins.[169] And he does not clarify whether the mother bears the child in her own

164. Lk 7.29.

165. Is 43.26.

166. Ps 51.5.

167. Cf. 2 Sm 12.16–22.

168. Ps 51.5, 9–14.

169. This text, from "Before we are born" through "single stain only," is quoted by Augustine in *Contra Julianum* 1.3.10.

sins or whether there are already sins in the one who is born. But consider that both could be understood here. Thus the conception itself is not without iniquity, since even the parents are not without fault. If the one-day-old infant is not without sin, how much more are those days of the mother's pregnancy not sinless at all.[170] Thus we are conceived in the sin of the parents, and we are born in their sins. But even that birth has its own pollution, and nature itself does not have a single stain only. Of course marriage is a good thing, and intercourse is holy; but yet those who have wives should live as though they have none.[171] The marriage bed itself is unstained, and neither spouse should deny it to the other, unless perhaps for a limited period when they make time for prayer; yet according to the Apostle no one is free for prayer in the periods set aside for that convention of the flesh; the garment of the menstruating woman is polluted, and she cannot offer sacrifice in the days of her purification, and on the day of giving birth and for more days the woman who has given birth is forbidden to make sacrifice, until the birth-giver is cleansed by the lawful rite.[172]

11.57. Thus to the one in whom the Lord wished there be no original stain, the Lord says: "Before I formed you within your mother's womb, I knew you, and before you came forth from her belly, I sanctified you, and I established you as a prophet to the nations."[173] Who is so great, to whom have such great things been granted? Is this not Jeremiah? But Jeremiah was never established as a "prophet to the nations," but at that time he was in Judea, while even now he is in the nations that have believed in the Lord Jesus. Yet consider whether this statement was made to the one who, before he was born from the Virgin, existed already and existed always and was working even in the womb of Mary; so he was also established as sanctified so that he might sanctify his prophets. In him alone the virginal conception and birth occurred without the stain of any mortal origin. For it was fitting that he who would not have the sin that comes from the

170. Cf. Jb 14.4–5.
171. Cf. 1 Cor 7.29.
172. A reference to purity laws (cf. Lv 12.2–7 and 15.19–28).
173. Jer 1.5.

body's fall would experience no natural stain through being born. Thus rightly David, in complaint against himself, mourned the very pollution of his nature, namely that stain should first appear in the individual before life does.

12.58. While David says these things and confesses the filth of both particular and general sins, suddenly the splendor of the truth and the brilliance of spiritual grace shine out for him. Having surpassed the shadow, he sees by the prophetic spirit the sacraments of the heavenly mysteries, whose type Moses prefigured in the Law.[174] Thus, wounded by the wound of charity and seized by the desire for investigating the truth in the heights of his mind, he extends his gaze and, looking into the future, he sees the treasuries of wisdom and knowledge in Christ;[175] as he foresees the sacrament of baptism and marvels at its grace, he calls out at once, saying: "For behold, you have loved the truth; you have shown me the secrets and uncertain things of your wisdom."[176] The mysteries are not uncertain, since they are certain, nor are the secret and hidden depths of wisdom uncertain, but rather they are not shown forth. For David means rather that the secrets had not been revealed to any one; for "what eye has not seen and ear has not heard and has not entered into the heart of man, God has prepared for those who love him."[177] Seeing this is the case, David says: Behold, now the light shines out in manifest truthfulness, no longer in shadow, nor in figure, nor in type: behold, now I gaze on the truth; I recognize the splendor of the truth; now I adore you with greater devotion, Lord our God. [For he said,] "Behold, you have loved the truth":[178] not through a mirror, not in an enigma, but face-to-face you have shown yourself to me, Christ; I have discovered you in your sacraments.[179] These are the true sacraments of your wisdom, by which the hidden things of the mind are cleansed.[180]

174. Cf. Ex 24.8.

175. Cf. Song 2.5; Phil 3.13; Col 2.3.

176. Ps 51.6. Ambrose seems to have translated the Greek term ἄδηλα ("unclear") as *incerta* or "uncertain." See Lucidi, *Due apologie,* 117 n.2.

177. 1 Cor 2.9.

178. Ps 51.6.

179. Cf. Song 3.4.

180. Ps 19.13.

12.59. Therefore, he is joyful and secure because the fullness of wisdom has shone forth for him, and he says to the Lord: "Sprinkle me with hyssop, and I will be cleaned; wash me, and I will be whiter than snow."[181] It is appropriate both that he does not nullify the sacraments of the Old Covenant and that he asserts that the Gospel mysteries should be preferred. He begs to be cleansed with hyssop according to the Law, while he desires to be washed [in baptism] according to the Gospel and he judges that he will be whitened brighter than snow, if he will be washed. The one who wanted to be cleansed by the prefigurement of baptism was sprinkled with the blood of the lamb by means of a bundle of hyssop.[182] But whoever is washed is cleansed by the infusion from the eternal font, and the one to whom sin is forgiven is whitened above snow. And therefore Scripture says about his very soul: "Who is this, who ascends whitened?"[183] Before the soul was baptized, she was herself the one who said: "I am black and beautiful, daughter of Jerusalem."[184] For she was black, ugly by the shadowy horror of sins, but after she was made clean through baptism she earned the remission of her sins, and, after she was whitened, she ascended to Christ. Hence the Lord spoke also through Isaiah, when he said: "If your sins were as scarlet, I will make them white as snow";[185] that is: If they are bloody, if they are offensive, I will cleanse them. The "snow" refers to the snow of understanding; speaking in this way, the Gospel says that the garments of the Lord Jesus shone like the snow, that is, because he did not know sin, and the flesh that he wore when he came into this world was free from every sin.[186] Why are you surprised that David saw the sacraments of baptism when he described the Passion of the Lord in what he said in an earlier Psalm: "The Lord is my shepherd, and nothing will be lacking to me; he has placed me in the verdant pasture, he has led me above the water of refresh-

181. Ps 51.7.
182. Cf. Ex 24.6–8; Heb 9.13–14 and 19–20.
183. Song 8.5.
184. Song 1.5.
185. Is 1.18.
186. Cf. Mt 17.2.

ment,"[187] and at another place where he said, "The voice of the Lord has resounded above the water, the God of majesty"?[188] And he spoke even more clearly about the sacrament itself: "You have prepared a table in my sight; you have anointed my head with oil," and, "your intoxicating cup, how splendid it is."[189]

13.60. It is right, then, that David rejoices in these things when he says: "You will give joy and gladness in my hearing; my bones, once cast down, will rejoice."[190] Lord Jesus, you have proven that your words never pass away; you have proven the Gospel passage where you said:[191] "Many prophets and just men have wanted to see what you see and to hear what you hear."[192] Note that David rejoices only in the hearing, because the remission of sins was yet to come, and he prophesies that his bones, cast down, will rejoice. Just as the bones of the just man will say, "Lord, who is like you?"[193] likewise, "the bones, once cast down, will rejoice," that is to say, the bones of the just man who humbles his soul. Thus virtues are called "the bones"; they are called "the bones" because they are certain movements of the soul or the spirit; these movements are brought low through sins, but rejoice with the bestowal of heavenly grace. The bones are also said to be the people of the churches, as you have it spoken in the Psalm: "My bone is not hidden, which you made in the hidden places."[194] He calls his own "bone" the Church and the holy gatherings of the devout people, since we are members of the body of Christ, coming from his very flesh and from his bones.[195] Thus he says this so that the Church of the Lord might know all God's works and accept faith in the resurrection.

13.61. The text continues: "Turn your face from my sins, and blot out all my iniquities."[196] It is a customary request to

187. Ps 23.1.
188. Ps 29.3.
189. Ps 23.5.
190. Ps 51.8.
191. Mt 24.35.
192. Mt 13.17.
193. Ps 89.8.
194. A literal translation of the Greek of Ps 139.15; see Hadot, *Apologie*, 162–63 n.108.
195. Eph 5.30.
196. Ps 51.9.

ask those whom we have wounded to forget the offense done to them. Thus, speaking in a moral way, the prophet asks God that he turn his face from his sins and that he adopt, as it were, a stance of forgetfulness toward them. But because God gazes upon all things and overlooks not a single one of them, he cannot forget as we do; for the memory of the things we have learned slips away from us in a brief span of time. Thus David speaks well when he says that God should turn away his face not from David himself, lest he be abandoned and fail, but from his sins, so that his sins could not have any strength.[197] For those whom the Lord looks upon he illumines; and piety and gentleness are in the countenance of the Lord. Thus David says this as well: "May my judgment proceed from your face";[198] for pardon, not penalty, comes from the face of the Lord. Thus he should be beseeched that he look on us, but [at the same time,] that he turn away his face from our sins, so that he might wipe them out. For what he does not look upon he wipes out, and what he has wiped out is buried in his memory, just as the Lord himself says: "I, even I, am he who blots out your transgressions, and I will not remember them; but may you be mindful, and let us decide the matter."[199]

13.62. For a sin is either forgiven or wiped out or covered over. It is forgiven through grace, wiped out through the blood of the Cross, and covered through charity. This is true of iniquity as well, which is taken to be the condition of a wicked mind, as John in his letter said that he who had committed sin also committed iniquity, just as we find it written: "Everyone who commits sin also commits an iniquity."[200] A sin is an iniquity, because iniquity is present in sin itself; yet, as it seems to us, a sin is a work of iniquity, but iniquity is the worker of guilt and crime. Thus it is more important that iniquity itself be wiped out, that the root and the seedbed of sins be cut off. Let the wicked root be ripped out, lest it produce evil fruits. Let every sinful attitude be abolished; let every sort of iniquity be destroyed.

197. Cf. Ps 104.29.
198. Ps 17.2.
199. Is 43.25–26.
200. 1 Jn 3.4.

13.63. Thus in the same way that the instruction of wisdom, upon entrance into the soul, destroys imprudence, and the knowledge of wisdom destroys ignorance, so does perfect virtue destroy iniquity, and the remission of sins abolish every sin. Hence the Apostle says brilliantly that the Lord Jesus "forgave our sins," "wiping away the record of the decree that was against us," and he says, "fixing it to the Cross, he bore it from your midst."[201] By his blood he wiped away the blackness of Eve, he wiped away the debt of the inheritance of guilt. Thus faith diminished sin. And thus the Lord, when he cast sins aside, said: "Let it be done to you according to your faith."[202]

14.64. The text continues: "Create a pure heart in me, God, and renew within my bowels a steadfast spirit."[203] Above he seeks to be cleansed from the hidden faults; here he asks that a pure heart be made for him, one that comes to him who is renewed in spirit;[204] for the heart is clean in the new man, in whom the filth of old sins was wiped out and no sort of image of iniquity remained engraved.[205] For purity of heart is a great gift. Hence it is fitting that Solomon says: "Who will boast that he has a chaste heart?"[206] And the Lord says in the Gospel: "Blessed are the pure in heart; for they will see God."[207] Furthermore, David also desired to have a pure heart lest he be cast from the face of the Lord.

14.65. But in the one whose heart is pure, the spirit is renewed in what is within. The bowels are, as it were, the inward parts of the body; so too the bowels of the soul are the interior intelligible realities, as are the "bowels" of mercy,[208] and what is within blesses the Lord, about which it says: "Bless the Lord, my soul; and all that is within me, bless his holy name."[209] For

201. Col 2.13–14.

202. Mt 8.13.

203. Ps 51.10.

204. Cf. Ps 19.13.

205. Cf. Eph 4.22–24.

206. Prv 20.19. Tradition identifies Solomon as the author of the biblical book of Proverbs, along with Ecclesiastes and the Song of Songs.

207. Mt 5.18.

208. Cf. Col 3.12; Lk 1.78.

209. Ps 103.1.

the "bowels" of the soul are the discoveries of the meanings, they are healthy thinking, they are the pursuit of the virtues, perseverance, and, finally, they are what are called ἔννοιαι in Greek.[210]

14.66. But the spirit is "steadfast" that guides well, that guides one in the right path;[211] this is the Spirit of truth or even the just conscience of man that is twisted by no sins, or the spirit that is in man.[212] We have not passed over what others think; yet it seems to us that, since the reading speaks about mysteries and since the grace of future rebirth is expressed, the infusion of the Holy Spirit is intended here.

14.67. Thus the text continues: "Do not cast me from your face, and do not take your Holy Spirit away from me."[213] If one of our slaves offends us, we are accustomed to turn our face from him. But many of the rich are accustomed to banish their slaves and to relegate them to very small estates, and this penalty is considered quite harsh. Therefore, the slaves are accustomed to give themselves over to lashing instead. If among men this punishment [of exile] is considered so harsh, how much more so would it be before the Lord our God? Is it not from this source that Cain's murderous resentment (which, of course, should have been repressed, if any filial respect could have tempered it) erupted, because God turned his face from the gifts of Cain, while he looked upon the gifts of Abel?[214] Thus, although his lips were silent, God pronounced one of them innocent, the other a sinner. Therefore, as though he were the lowest of servants, David humbles himself, and, as though he has been caught in the act of sinning and is guilty of an offense, he begs God that he be lashed rather than cast from the face of the Lord.

14.68. To learn how it is that God casts someone from his face, you must hear the one who says: "Take him into the outer darkness, where there will be weeping and gnashing of teeth."[215]

210. On "conceptions," see, e.g., Plato, *Timaeus* 47a.
211. Cf. Ps 51.10; 143.10.
212. Cf. 1 Cor 2.11.
213. Ps 51.11.
214. Cf. Gn 4.3–5.
215. Mt 22.13.

He who is not corrected is cast away from his face into the darkness. Thus the just man, lest he suffer in darkness, says: "I will seek your face, Lord."[216] For where there is the face of the Lord there is light, just as it is written: "Send your face as light on your servant."[217] So when Christ first gazed on Peter, looking at him, he shed light on him.[218]

14.69. Thus it is a great punishment to be cast from the face of God. Adam was cast from paradise, and not without deserving it; for he had previously hidden himself from the face of God.[219] And Cain departed from the face of God not only after the murder was committed, but even after he thought he could trick God, to the point that he denied the crime.[220] Thus the sinner is shut off from the face of God, but the just man says: "Here I am."[221] Thus David himself, when he saw the people dying, offered himself, saying: "Here I am, I have sinned and I have done evil as a shepherd";[222] and thus the anger of the Lord was tempered and pardon was granted.[223]

14.70. At the same time David shows that the saints remain while the criminals are cast out. And in this way we should preserve spiritual grace in us, lest it be taken away from us on account of our sins. For the one in whom the Holy Spirit dwells is not cast out, but by the sinless fruit of the gift he has received, he desires to offer himself always to the Lord; he is just like the one who responds to the Lord who said to him: "Surely you too wish to depart?" He responds: "To whom shall we go? You have the words of eternal life, and we believe."[224]

14.71. At the same time one should consider that the Spirit is not removed unless by the will of the Lord, just as it is not granted unless by the will of the Lord. But when indeed the Spirit is granted, he works not as though being coerced, but he is por-

216. Ps 27.8.
217. Ps 119.135.
218. Cf. Lk 22.61.
219. Cf. Gn 3.8 and 3.24.
220. Cf. Gn 4.16.
221. 1 Sm 3.4.
222. 2 Sm 24.17.
223. Cf. 2 Sm 24.25.
224. Jn 6.67–69.

tioned out according to his own will, just as it is written when the Apostle says: "But the one and same Spirit works all these things, apportioning them as he wills."[225] Thus since the Spirit is not withdrawn unless by the will of the Lord, it appears that the will of the Trinity is one.

15.72. "Grant me the joy of your salvation, and with your guiding Spirit confirm me."[226] To the one to whom it is due, it is also granted: the joy of salvation is granted to a rational nature. But joy and gladness are fruits of the Spirit;[227] in addition, the guiding Spirit is our foundation. Therefore, the one who is confirmed by the guidance of the Spirit is not condemned to servitude, does not know the service of sin, does not know instability, does not know errancy, and does not waver as though unsteady in his zeal, but he is confirmed and stable on the rock, with his solid stance.[228]

15.73. Who do we think is the one called the "guiding Spirit"? Many refer the "steadfast Spirit" to the Lord Jesus, who took away the sin of the world and renewed the entire human race by the outpouring of his blood.[229] And thus it is said: "And renew within my bowels a steadfast spirit."[230] But the "Holy Spirit," about whom David says: "And do not take your Holy Spirit away from me,"[231] they interpret as the "Spirit of truth," while they judge the "guiding Spirit" to be God the Father.[232] But in a moral way he says: "Do not cast me from your face!"[233] Faithfully he fears that the grace that he has received might be taken away from him. And thus elsewhere he says: "My eyes are always on the Lord,"[234] and in later sections: "Behold, as the eyes of servants are on the hands of their lords, and the eyes of the handmaid are on the hands of her mistress, so are our eyes on the

225. 1 Cor 12.11.
226. Ps 51.12.
227. Cf. Gal 5.22.
228. Cf. Rom 6.6, 17, 20; Eph 4.14; Jas 1.6; Mt 7.25.
229. Cf. Jn 1.29.
230. Ps 51.10.
231. Ps 51.11.
232. Cf. Jn 15.26.
233. Ps 51.11.
234. Ps 25.15.

Lord our God, until he has mercy on us."[235] Clearly this Spirit is the leader and guide, who governs the mind, confirms the intention, carries it where it wills, and leads it to higher life.[236]

16.74. There are those who have understood this to be the spirit of man that is in him. About this spirit the Apostle says: "For who knows the things of men which are of man, except for the spirit that is in him?"[237] The one who can know all things, the one whose notice the hidden things of man do not escape, he can have the governance in man.

16.75. The text continues: "I will teach the wicked your ways, and the impious will be converted back to you."[238] The one who steers the ship by the craggy shore is the chief pilot; the one who sharpens duller intellects to advance in learning is the good teacher; the one who incites the very fearful for battle and who supports them by investigating the features of the terrain, so that he may compensate for the weakness of his forces by the advantages of a favorable post, he is the outstanding warrior, the marvelous leader. Similarly great, too, is the preacher of the faith who teaches the wicked. Hence he says fittingly: "I will teach the wicked." He does not say: "I will teach the just," for the just know the ways of the Lord; but he says, "I will teach the wicked," and so the author of prudence and the teacher of all says: "I have not come to call the just but sinners."[239] And the heavenly physician, "The healthy have no need for the doctor, but the sick do."[240]

16.76. Thus, whether it is spoken in the person of the one who called the nations or whether it is spoken in David's own person, he asserted well, "I will teach the wicked," because the heavenly teaching can transform the innermost emotions and convert their intention, and the divine activity can pour the desire for piety into wicked hearts. In this way those who were living apart from the Law are converted to the true Lord, the

235. Ps 123.2.
236. Cf. Ps 139.24.
237. 1 Cor 2.11.
238. Ps 51.13.
239. Mt 9.13.
240. Mt 9.12.

ones who were previously turned away and were committing injustices and wicked crimes are corrected by the example of a king's penance, and once they are converted in faith and in good works they receive the cure of salvific instruction; so they enter the ways of the Lord, along which they stumble upon no tortuous pathways of error, no alleyways that threaten them with headlong collapse. For just as we find a model of a good life and an example of virtue in these men who navigate the course of their lives without causing offense, so those who have renounced the crimes that they committed previously or their errors of unbelief and have amended the course of their later years are proposed for imitation to those who are slipping in their actions or thoughts.

16.77. The text continues: "Free me from bloodguilt, O God, God of my salvation."[241] And this could refer to the death of Uriah, because, acknowledging the death that he ordered, David sought forgiveness for so great a crime, and although as king he was free from the laws, still he was guilty in his conscience. Eager to loosen himself from these chains, he requested divine help for himself, so that he might be cleansed from every stain of the sin he committed. And, indeed, because, being mild and humble in heart, the holy prophet gave outstanding signs of his humility and piety,[242] to the extent that he frequently forgave his adversaries and thought that he should abstain from killing them, it is no marvel that he mourned so heartily the fact that the sin of pouring out innocent blood had sneaked up on him.[243] Thus he prayed that he should be free from bloodguilt, that is, from mortal sins. He praised the Lord his God, he preached the justice of the Lord, and thus he added: "My tongue will rejoice in your justice."[244]

17.78. "Lord, you will open my lips, and my mouth will proclaim your praise." For whoever praises the Lord will be safe from his enemies, as it is written. And above he said clearly in Psalm 49: "But God said to the sinner: 'Why do you speak of my

241. Ps 51.14.
242. Cf. 1 Sm 30.21–25.
243. Cf. 2 Sm 19.16–24.
244. Ps 51.14.

justice?'"[245] Since it is the case that through his own lips David said that God had prevented the sinner from recounting God's acts of justice, indeed by the very fact of narrating the justice of God he made clear that what he had done was not at all imputed to him as sin.

17.79. And he adds: "You will open my lips, and my mouth will proclaim your praise."[246] God shuts the mouth of the sinner so that he does not speak of the just deeds of God; he opens the mouth of the just man so that he speaks of them. Therefore, the one whose lips God opens, he absolves from the guilt of sin. But the Lord opens the lips of him who receives the word in opening his own mouth.[247] Hence even the Apostle asks that he be aided by the prayers of the people, that the entry of the word might be opened for him in order to speak of the mystery of Christ.[248] But we interpret "tongue" as the speech of the one who exults in the praise of God. And thus we can interpret the following as the speech infused into the prophet: "My tongue is the pen of a scribe who writes quickly."[249]

17.80. But if we take this as spoken by the person of Christ, note that the tongue is not the scribe who quickly writes the word of God that runs through the bowels of the spirit and penetrates and inscribes in them the gifts either of nature or of grace, but the tongue is that holy body born from the Virgin, by which the poison of the serpent has been emptied out and the works of the Gospel have passed throughout the whole world, to be celebrated. He adds that for the sake of nullifying sin, because he took up humility, he cast down his heart because God prefers a sacrifice rather than the holocaust for sins that was typically offered according to the Law.[250] Thus he adds above: "You have not asked for holocausts for sin; then I said: Behold, I come,"[251] that is: I come accepting the form of the servant after I judged that it would not be theft that I be equal to God; I come

245. Ps 50.16. Again, Ambrose's numbering follows the LXX.
246. Ps 51.15.
247. Cf. Col 4.3.
248. Cf. ibid.
249. Ps 45.1.
250. Cf. Ps 51.17; Lv 1.1–17; 5.1–26; Ps 40.7; Heb 10.1, 6.
251. Ps 40.6.

in the form of human adoption, in the truth of the Cross; I will show obedience by humility unto death, so that disobedience will be wiped out.[252]

17.81. Thus it is right that he says at this point: "Since if you had wished it, I would indeed have given sacrifice; but you will not delight in holocausts. The sacrifice to God is a contrite spirit; a heart contrite and humble God will not spurn."[253] And just as I said above, it is clear that it befits the mystery that the Lord Jesus himself seems to be speaking also from his own person here, who above had drawn out this point by the clear testimony of his own voice. For he is himself the true David, strong in his hand, truly humble and meek, first and last, first in eternity, last in humility, through whose obedience the sin of the human race has been wiped out and justice is restored.[254] He himself, I say, Jesus, as the end of the shadow and the law, came as teacher of humility to teach the proud, who were puffed up in their intellect and the swelling of their heart, that they should turn to humility and simplicity.[255] How can the sin be imputed in the figure of this mystery when the remission of sins is found in the mystery itself? Unless perhaps David confessed his iniquity and the sin of that crime, so that he himself would arrive at the remission of sin and the grace of the mystery.

17.82. For what does the man confessing his own sins desire for himself when he sings in regard to Zion and Jerusalem, proclaiming, "Do good, Lord, to Zion in your good will, and let the walls of Jerusalem be built"?[256] Does it not mean that it pleases him that the gathering of the Church be hastened by means of the call of the nations, who are not slaves to the daughters but rather the freewomen of Jerusalem, of the Jerusalem that is in heaven?[257] This city spreads the offspring of her faith throughout the whole world and establishes the fortification of spiritual walls by the proclamation of apostolic doctrine.[258]

252. Cf. Phil 2.6–8; Rom 5.19.
253. Cf. Ps 51.16–17.
254. Cf. Mt 11.29; Rv 1.17; Rom 5.19.
255. Cf. Rom 10.4; Heb 10.1; Mt 11.29.
256. Ps 51.18.
257. Cf. Gal 4.22, 26, 31; Heb 12.22.
258. Cf. Eph 2.20; Rv 21.24.

17.83. Thus the walls of Jerusalem are the ramparts of the faith, the defenses of the disputations, the bulwarks of the virtues; the walls of Jerusalem are the gatherings of the churches established throughout the whole world; for the Church says: "I am the wall, and my bosom is the tower."[259] And rightly the walls of Jerusalem are the assemblies of the churches, since everyone who enters the Church by good faith and good works becomes a citizen and an inhabitant of that city on high that comes down from heaven.[260] The arrangement of living stones builds these walls.[261]

17.84. Thus, seeing the true Jerusalem and Zion, he said: "When in your will you bless Jerusalem and Zion, then you will accept a sacrifice of justice,"[262] that is, the sacrifice of the body of Christ, who says, when he speaks about his own Passion: "Open the gates of justice to me, and having entered into them I will confess to the Lord."[263] And in the Gospel he says to John: "Allow it for now; for thus it is fitting for us to fulfill all justice," and later: "Blessed are those who suffer persecution on account of justice."[264] Justice is Christ; David asserts therefore that the sacrifice of Christ would be acceptable to the Father. And this is what he speaks about in a previous Psalm: "Sacrifice the sacrifice of justice, and hope in the Lord."[265] This is the offering of spiritual justice and the holocaust of fervent devotion and of the infusion of the Holy Spirit, which he says will take place when the souls of believers begin to move to that spiritual altar of the Lord; these are the souls that, so to speak, drag a plough through their bowels by renouncing pleasures and delights, so that they bear the fruits of reverent cultivation.

17.85. Or at least David means this: when you have blessed the Church gathered from the nations and the spiritual sacrifice of justice was beginning to be observed, then even the holy

259. Song 8.10.
260. Cf. Rv 21.2.
261. Cf. 1 Pt 2.5.
262. Ps 51.18–19.
263. Ps 118.19.
264. Mt 3.15; 5.10.
265. Ps 4.5.

martyrs, who offered their bodies to be furrowed[266] for Christ, will be offered like calves on holy altars, as we find it written in the Apocalypse of John that under the altar there were the souls of those who offered their bodies in witness for the name of the Lord Jesus, that they might purchase for themselves the grace of Christ.[267] To him is honor, glory, and eternal praise with God the Father and the Holy Spirit from the ages and now and always and unto ages of ages. Amen.

266. "furrowed": by flogging. Ambrose is continuing the metaphor of the plough.

267. Cf. Rv 6.9.

THE SECOND DEFENSE OF DAVID

PERHAPS THE title of the Psalm that you heard read out will have upset many, namely: "Nathan the prophet came to him, after he had gone in to Bathsheba."[1] At the same time, the reading from the Gospel that has been treated could stir the concern of the inexperienced in no small measure, for in it you note that the adulterous woman has been presented to Christ and that she is sent off without condemnation.[2] For indeed if anyone takes in these matters with idle ears, he comes upon an incentive for sin, since he reads of the adultery of a holy man and the exoneration of an adulterous woman, and he would be led to fall by following a model that was nearly both human and divine, because a human being would have thought adultery should be committed and God would have determined that adultery should not be condemned. Thus the path that leads to a fall is precarious, either through pardon or through lust.

1.2. The text adds that which seems to inflame the very torches of young lust: that David was not ashamed of his adultery, he did not conceal it, but rather he made it public by proclaiming it, as it were, in a divine poem. What then? Was the saintly David so impudent and rash that he would sing out his own wretchedness, which is especially noteworthy since he would himself say in another Psalm, which was proclaimed today: "How long will sinners, Lord, how long will sinners boast?"[3] How is it that he

1. Ambrose returns frequently to the inscription of Psalm 51 (50 in the LXX), which indicates the liturgical occasion and setting for the original composition; the other readings are most likely Jn 8.3–11, on the woman caught in adultery, and Psalm 94, treated in the next paragraphs.

2. Cf. Jn 8.35–36.

3. Ps 94.3.

prohibits others from boasting of their sin, and yet he himself boasts of his own in a sacred poem? How then can we distinguish those two actions?

1.3. Let it be, then, that David blundered imprudently: did Christ blunder as well, that we should think he did not have right judgment? Thus in today's Psalm David prophesied as though to those who think this way, when he said: "O you senseless, understand, and fools, be wise at last."[4] For how could Christ blunder? It is not permitted that this thought enter into our minds. "Does the one who has fashioned the ear not hear or the one who has formed the eye not see? Will the one who disciplines the nations not condemn them, the one who teaches man knowledge?"[5] Thus does Christ not know how to investigate a sin and to hear a just accusation? Could Christ approve imprudence? Did Christ, who disciplines the nations, not think adultery should be condemned? Could Christ, who knows the inmost workings of each one's heart, and teaches the knowledge of the law, either deceive by an error or judge contrary to the dictates of the law? And how did he himself say: "I have not come to abolish the Law but to fulfill it"?[6] Could Christ, who condemns what is hidden, neglect what is public? Can Christ, who made time to exist, not know the proper moment? Does he who knows the idle thoughts of men not know their criminal thoughts as well?

1.4. And this is enough of a reply to those who, even though they cannot deny that there is a Creator, still deny the power of the Creator, who, even when they confess his wisdom, assert his foolishness by attributing to him the ignorance of future things. I could speak about this at greater length, but it seems another matter has been proposed for our treatment. And although there has been a series of different readings proclaimed today, still they all lead to the same conclusion, especially the inscription of the Psalm and the Gospel reading.[7] But although one

4. Ps 94.8.

5. Ps 94.9–10.

6. Mt 5.17.

7. Ambrose is following the sequence of the liturgical readings; on the practice, see Luigi Pizzolato, *La doctrina esegetica di sant'Ambrogio* (Milan: Università Cattolica, 1978), 285.

conclusion fits them all, nevertheless one should proceed according to the order of the readings, and therefore it seems that first I should treat the title of the Psalm.

2.5. The account, which includes the adultery and the homicide, has been brought to our attention. For so we find it written in the book of Kingdoms that King David, while he was walking in his home, saw the wife of Uriah bathing; and at that moment he loved her, and he ordered her to be brought to him.[8] Then he ordered her innocent husband, as Scripture indicates, to be set opposite the fiercest warriors, so that he might be overrun by the enemy force. These things took place, and they are not denied. How then can they be excused? The Gospel reading indicates clearly that even when sin is obvious, still the judge's decision should be clear-headed and each should be mindful of his own circumstances and merit.[9] For often in judging itself there is a greater sin in the judgment than there is sin in the one about whom the judgment is made. For if it has been determined by some wise men of the world that one be cautious in judging lest the penalty be more severe than the crime, and that determination is preserved, how much more should we maintain that each who would pass judgment on another should first pass judgment about himself? Should he condemn lesser mistakes in another when he has committed more serious ones himself? Who, then, are you who judge the holy man David? I speak to the gentile, I speak to the Jew, I speak to the Christian. Thus, it seems to me, the treatise should be divided into three parts: one against the gentiles, another against the Jews, and the third for the Christians.

3.6. Thus first my discourse is directed against gentiles who are often accustomed to object: "See how Christians strive for innocence, how they esteem faith, honor religion, and teach chastity, while their rulers are shown to have committed murders and adulteries! David himself, from whose race—so you claim—Christ chose to be born, has repeatedly sung his own murders

8. Cf. 2 Sm 11.2–17. In Ambrose's biblical text the first two books of Samuel were identified as "Books of Kingdoms," and 1 and 2 Kings were called 3 and 4 Kingdoms.

9. Cf. Jn 8.11.

and adulteries. What sort of students can these be whose teachers are like this?"

3.7. What then? Shall we deny the deed or repudiate the teacher? Nothing of the sort: but let the one who objects to the individual consider the characteristics of what is common. For the individuality of the deed comes from the commonality of the nature. Thus there is nothing unusual if the individual case falls within the characteristics of the type. For I acknowledge that David was a man, and that is nothing unusual; I acknowledge that, generally, man sins. For this is not some new weakness of the human condition, and, indeed, it would be more surprising that a man lacks sin than that he falls into it. Thus holy David committed sin—I will accept your claim without any discussion—he committed adultery, he plotted a murder; he plotted it and accomplished it. He sinned as kings are accustomed to do, but he did penance and he wept, which kings are not accustomed to do. He asked pardon, not clinging to his power, but acknowledging his weakness; falling prostrate on the ground, he covered himself with sackcloth, forgetting his power and remembering his fault.

3.8. Can you find for me another man of this type, one who, while established in power, no longer loves his crimes, who proclaims his guilt, who rejects his own sins; who believes that what is indecent is forbidden to him; who limits himself by his own laws and knows whatever is not permitted by reason of justice is not otherwise permitted by means of authority? For power does not nullify justice but justice nullifies power; the king is not absolved from laws, but he undermines laws by his own [bad] example. Or could it happen that he who judges about others is exempt from his own judgment and that he permits for himself what he constrains in others?

3.9. Thus David is good and he who overcomes his power is much more admirable than he who overcomes his lust. For chastity sometimes defers to the body, often in error; power is subject to God, and one controls himself in lust more easily than he is temperate in power.[10] For this reason do you not forgive

10. The references to political power may relate to Ambrose's dealings with Theodosius.

the minor faults of the one in whom you marvel at greater attributes? Nature is precarious in all men and prone to sin, and the license granted by power and the allowances of authority are precarious even for the morally upright. For the anger of the king is not far from the anger of the lion;[11] but the one who provokes him or becomes mixed up with him sins against his own soul. Thus be alert not to provoke power, lest the soul be ensnared in corporeal nets and be left unable to set itself free from vice. It is therefore also no wonder if David fell because of the allure of power, but it is much more to be admired that he was recalled by the consideration of the faith.[12]

3.10. Thus you see that this secular power often profits nothing and, in fact, usually causes harm; for often the occasion for a sin is found in the advantages of power. Thus do not, you who are king, whoever you are, presume on your power and your ability, for "the heart of the king is in the hand of the Lord."[13] Do not be flattered because the people are subjected to you, for "the king will not be saved by the greatness of his power and the warrior will not be saved in the greatness of his strength."[14] For the good pleasure of the Lord is neither in the high summits of his dwellings nor in the exquisite heights of his roofs but is "upon those who fear him and those who hope on his mercy."[15]

3.11. Thus we see that power teeters in the direction of the vices, and yet I will not say that it is always perverted in this way, since we read that when David was exalted in his royal power he improved the divine ceremonies and that Solomon consecrated the Temple to the Lord.

3.12. Now let us assert what we have touched upon: the capacity for ruling is an incentive to sinning. And let us proceed according to the sequence of the account. David would not have committed adultery against the rights of another man's marriage and the vows of a settled union if he had not seen from his own inner house a naked woman bathing. And thus is it fittingly

11. Cf. Prv 19.12.
12. Cf. *Apol. Dau.* 10.51.
13. Prv 21.1.
14. Ps 33.16.
15. Ps 147.11.

written: "Do not fall headlong at the appearance of a woman, and do not lust after a woman,"[16] and elsewhere: "be wary of the eyes of every irreverent woman."[17] Do not at all be overconfident about your self-control and virtue. Indeed "a woman's fornication is recognized in the boldness of her eyes and in her eyelids."[18] Thus flee first the cause of the sin; for no one is strong for very long, and it is said not only to the weak man but to everyone: "Let not the lust for beauty conquer you"[19]—if you do not wish to be conquered, do not have company with sins, lest in your case vices be crowned—"and may you not be seized by eyes and snatched by eyelids." The woman seems a trifle to you as a prize, but she is a powerful force for vice, because the woman "snatches the precious souls of men."[20]

3.13. Thus it is difficult for any man bound by the snares of lust to escape unharmed. And not only in my estimation is this judged difficult, but it has been judged impossible in the Proverbs of holy Solomon, who draws on his own example and says: "Who will take fire into his bosom, and not burn his garments? Or who is there who will walk on fiery coals but will not scorch his feet?"[21] Thus be careful that you too do not inflame the fire of lust and passionate love within the bosom of your mind, lest the garment of the body along with the eternal resurrection be consumed by that blaze of the soul, or, at least, the vestige of your heart be inflamed, because you decided that you should walk through the torches of lusts; for whoever burns in his heart burns also in his body.

3.14. Thus in every way an encounter with a lascivious woman should be avoided. And therefore, "Acquire for yourself wisdom as a companion," he says, "that she may guard you from another's wife and fornication"[22]—lest she entrap you by the snares of her lips or tie you up with the tresses of her sin. Thus the prophet teaches you why you should avoid the harlot, that you

16. Sir 25.21.
17. Sir 26.11.
18. Sir 26.9.
19. Prv 6.25.
20. Prv 6.26.
21. Prv 6.27–28.
22. Prv 7.4–5.

remain wary lest she enter through the window.[23] For she enters by the window of her house, the window is her eye, and thus guard yourself from the eyes of every irreverent woman,[24] lest desire enter through the window, and lust penetrate. For in this way the promiscuous woman entices the lover with her gaze and unless you check the unruly gawking of the heart and the soul, death enters through the window. For the insolence of the adulteress is not idle, her wantonness is not in vain, for she makes the hearts of young men fly about so that they cannot maintain the constancy of their own hearts and they are tossed about here and there by fervent love. Thus beware of a woman of this sort, who does not rest on her feet, who wanders outside, who lurks in corners, who ensnares with her eyes, who binds with her words, who covers her couch with ruffles and the Egyptian tapestries.[25] For the one who acquires her adornment not from familiarity with the divine, but from worldly charm, accurately says that her husband is away, since there is no adulteress who can have Christ present.

3.15. Thus you see by how many traps even the hearts of saints are captured, and therefore do not wonder if even holy David was ensnared, a great man indeed and one who through his faith conquered a foreigner with a huge body who was spreading terror with fearful weapons.[26] But would that he had conquered himself; would that, just as he laid low that enemy, so too he could have laid low and conquered his interior adversary! The battle of the one who fights inwardly is fiercer than that of the one who fights outwardly.

3.16. But why do I speak about David alone? Let us also collect other examples for the same sort of treatment so that we do not conclude this frailty belonged only to David, that is, to one particular man, but rather that it is the frailty of the bodily condition. Samson the strong and hearty choked a lion,[27] but he

23. Cf. Jer 9.21.

24. Cf. Sir 26.11.

25. Cf. Prv 7.12–16; this section is an extended allusion to the wiles of the wicked woman depicted in Prv 7.

26. 1 Sm 17.32–49.

27. Cf. Jgs 14.6.

could not choke back his passionate love. He broke the chains of his enemies but he could not break the bonds of his own lusts.[28] He scorched foreign harvests, but, ignited by the spark of a single woman, he lost the harvest of his own strength.[29] Solomon built a temple to God; but would that he had preserved the temple of his own body!

But now let my speech return to where it left off. David triumphed against tens of thousands, but he failed in twenty and more thousands;[30] and, because he failed, he acknowledged that he was a man, he confessed his guilt, he beseeched pardon saying to the Lord: "Lord, do not rebuke me in your anger, and do not cast me down in your rage. Have mercy on me, Lord, since I am weak."[31] If David is weak, are you strong? If Solomon fell, do you remain steadfast? If Paul is the first of the sinners, can you be the first of the saints?[32] Thus if those men erred, they erred insofar as they were human beings, but they acknowledged their own sin insofar as they were just. If the just received a verdict of a harsher penalty, how could you imagine hope of exoneration for yourself, for Scripture says: "If the just is scarcely saved, when shall the ungodly and the sinner obey?"[33]

3.17. Thus you note, my sons, how very often the occasion of sinning undermines a good intention, and thus you should flee and avoid the occasions themselves. You do not want to be seized by passionate love: Do not look on the beauty of a woman, "because when your eyes see another woman, your mouth will then speak twisted things and you will be tossed as though on the heart of the sea just like a captain in a great storm."[34] For the multitudes of desires make a great storm, and they toss the sailor to and fro as though in a sort of strait of the body, so that the soul cannot be captain of itself, not knowing whether it is day or night in the murkiness of passionate love.

3.18. Thus lust is aroused by the eyes, but it is inflamed by

28. Cf. Jgs 15.14.
29. Cf. Jgs 15.5.
30. 1 Sm 18.7.
31. Ps 6.2–3; cf. 1 Sm 18.7 and 2 Sm 18.7.
32. Cf. 1 Tm 1.15.
33. Prv 11.31; 1 Pt 4.18.
34. Prv 23.33–34.

drunkenness; for every drunkard and fornicator will become a poor man. So do not delude yourself about the power of drinking. Noah was a drunk, and so he who was not drunk by the flood was drunk by wine.[35] But he did not know the nature of wine, for he had not drunk before; you have learned by his example what you should avoid. Lot was deceived through sleep, and if you do not wish to be deceived, shake the sleep from your mind, lest a son or a daughter abuse you while you are sleeping drunkenly.[36] In that passage it is not devotion but rather drunkenness that is ridiculed, and he is not deceived as a father but as one who falls asleep. You do not want to burn? Do not approach the fire. You do not wish to be cast down? Flee the areas that are tottering, avoid the cliffs, stay away from whatever staggers.

3.19. And so you see in those who have earned a place among the just that they did not have a different nature, but rather a different self-discipline. For after the fall of the first man and his just condemnation, although the appetite of the flesh was condemned in one man, the human condition took on vice, and sin infected human nature; but faith moderated the vice of this same nature, and the desire for devotion lightened the offense.

3.20. Therefore, nations, turn to God and "know that the Lord himself is God. He himself made us, and we did not make ourselves."[37] Know that we are flesh and dust. Thus let us abandon what we have done, and let us honor our Author himself, who has given life, has forgiven sins, who alone can say: "I am, I am, who wipe out your iniquities and who will not remember them."[38] Clearly God is great and merciful, who confers a benefit and does not make the gift of his benefit a reproach. Are you surprised that he made David king and the victor over many nations? So he is accustomed to elevate his lowly servants. He is not greedy for gifts nor sparing in his benefits nor stingy with his grace and his offering, but rich in generosity; he increases the reward of those whom he redeems from sin.

35. Cf. Gn 9.21.
36. Lot's daughters; cf. Gn 19.33–36.
37. Ps 100.3.
38. Is 43.25.

That is what I have to say against the objections of the gentiles.

4.21. But since we have promised that this treatise would be divided into three parts, one against the gentiles, another against the Jews, the third addressed to the Church, now it seems we should treat the section against the Jews.

Therefore, let us review what is proposed to us. The text says, "The title of the Psalm of understanding of David, when Nathan the prophet came to him, after he had gone in to Bathsheba."[39] Surely this account presents us with David the adulterer and the murderer, and you, Jews, say that this man is the Son of God! But God is the God of virtues, not of crimes, and about this God the Father says: "His throne is as the days of heaven."[40] Whoever has committed deceit has not conquered sins: and how is it written: "No one is without sin except God alone"?[41] But if he who is the son of God cannot not be God, the Son of God is the arbiter of justice, not guilty of a crime.

4.22. But by what logic do you determine David to be the Son of God, or do you think Solomon is he? Is it because it is written: "God, give your judgment to the king and your justice to the king's son," and because the title of that Psalm says that Psalm 71 [72] was composed for Solomon?[42] But consider whom he calls "Solomon." For Solomon is "the peaceful one," as the interpretation of his name indicates. The Psalm is spoken regarding him whom we know truly to be a lover of peace. But how was Solomon peaceful? The blood of Joab does not indicate that he had this quality—for he ordered Joab to be killed among the altars of the temple.[43] Neither does the penalty for Adonijah indicate this; he struck Adonijah down as guilty for pretending to the royal kinship, and he was not prevented from this indignity

39. Ambrose takes *intellectus* ("understanding") to characterize the Psalm, which probably derives from *psalmus sapientiae* or "psalm of wisdom." See Filippo Lucidi, *Opere esegetiche V: Le due apologie di David* (Milan: Biblioteca Ambrosiana, 1981), 161 n.1.

40. Ps 89.30.

41. Lk 18.19.

42. Ps 72.1 (according to the Hebrew numbering).

43. Cf. 1 Kgs 2.28–30.

even by his mother.[44] But how, then, do you determine that it applies to Solomon, the son of David, that it is written: "he will remain as long as the sun and before the moon unto ages of ages,"[45] since Solomon was granted the enjoyment of a short life and traversed his time of life within narrow limits? And how is it said about him: "He will reign from sea unto the sea"[46] when he was established within Syria, that is, the limits of the empire he possessed were circumscribed within the province of one region? But Christ alone is the one who expanded his empire to the borders of the entire world. For he alone is the one about whom the text of the Psalm properly prophesied: "The kings of the Arabah and of Saba will bring him gifts, and all the kings of the land will worship him, and all the nations will serve him."[47] For we know that he is ruling over all the nations and peoples with an unbounded empire, with unlimited power.

4.23. Thus Solomon is not the Son of God. But on what grounds did you think he was the Son of God? Because he was wise? But he begged for wisdom so that he might receive what he did not have.[48] By contrast, Christ himself is wisdom, having by nature in every matter what Solomon received by grace in human matters alone. And whatever is received at a certain time is possessed only for a certain time. For Solomon did not have wisdom in the beginning of his life, and he did not possess it at the end of his life. For he did not believe that he had what he was seeking; and afterwards he turned from the worship of God, and not like a wise man but like a fool he fell, so that he committed an offense. And Solomon so offended God that he lost even what he had earned. Why, then, do you think this is the Son of God? Because he built the Temple to God? But you should not believe him to be God and Lord for this reason, because it is written: "Unless the Lord will build the house for them, in vain do those who build it labor."[49] He labored in vain who built that

44. Cf. 1 Kgs 2.19–25.
45. Ps 72.5.
46. Ps 72.8.
47. Ps 72.10.
48. 1 Kgs 3.9.
49. Ps 127.1.

Temple, which burned up when it was subjected to the fire. Or perhaps you assert that it was said to Solomon's father David: "You will not build my house, but when you sleep, I will raise up your seed after you."[50] But in that statement the temple promised is not a bodily or material one; for God does not dwell in what is made by hand, but the temple is the holy Church, which in fact is constructed not by human but by heavenly strength.

4.24. For if we are marveling at works of power that are quite impressive, and yet still human, we find many men of this sort, whom we can compare with Solomon. And therefore where you find equality of achievement, there is no distinction in power. And we cannot say that there are many sons of God when we read that the Son of God is one; one should not insult the Son of God by misunderstanding the benefits that he conferred to our fathers. For there were many outstanding men, but through one alone, Joshua son of Nun, was it said, "Let the sun stand still over Gibeon."[51] You see that he exceeded the power of David; for David ruled the lands, but not the stars. You also see that the sun is Joshua's servant, and not his master, and even obeys a human voice. Yet the sun stood still, because in Joshua it recognized the type and the name of the one to come.[52] For Joshua son of Nun ordered the celestial luminaries not by his own power but by the mystery of Christ; for it was designated that the Son of God was to come into this world, who by his divine power would delay the setting of the earthly light that goes down and then turns to darkness; he would send forth light and introduce splendor.

Enoch was also snatched up to heaven;[53] but even though Christ was snatched up, he returned. Enoch was snatched up so that wickedness would not change his heart;[54] Christ abolished the wickedness of this world. Elijah ascended to heaven by chariot and horses, but Christ descended from heaven neither

50. 2 Sm 7.12.

51. Jos 10.12.

52. That is, Jesus, according to the understanding that the Hebrew (and Greek and Latin) name is the same for both men.

53. Cf. Gn 5.24.

54. Cf. Wis 5.11.

by chariot nor by horses.[55] Elijah ascended in this way because he could not have gone otherwise; Christ returned by his own power.

Elisha ordered the leper to wash in the Jordan in order to be cleansed from every infection;[56] Christ washed the whole world in the Jordan. Likewise Moses, to whom the crossing [of the Red Sea] by the Jewish people was entrusted, divided the water.[57] And he indeed divided the elements because he did not divide the power of the Trinity; he separated the mass of the waters because he did not separate the Father from the Son.

4.25. You see what great men they were and how great were the deeds to which they provide testimony. Then why indeed do you judge those whom you know to be equal to King David or to Solomon in their power to be unequal to them in status, such that you think Solomon the son of David sits at the right hand of God, especially since David himself made it clear to whom this statement refers? For he did not say about his son: "The Lord said to my lord: Sit at my right hand,"[58] for how could he name his son "the Lord"? The Law prohibits this, religion stands against it, faith abhors this, that you should place a mortal man at the right hand of God the almighty. There must be another one who sits at the right hand, one who has taken up a body, not one who began from a body, one who was born before the daystar, that is, who is before the splendor of all the stars, since he created the splendors of the various lights; for Solomon indeed came after the daystar and Solomon was not a priest; and thus it could not be spoken to him by the almighty God: "From the womb before the daystar I have begotten you";[59] it could not be said to him: "You are a priest forever according to the order of Melchizedek,"[60] especially since in the time when Solomon lived, priests were according to the order of Aaron and not "of Melchizedek." For at that time the priests were still offering

55. Cf. 2 Kgs 2.11.
56. Cf. 2 Kgs 5.14.
57. Cf. Ex 14.21.
58. Ps 110.1.
59. Ps 110.3.
60. Ps 110.4.

the blood of goats and bulls for the sins and transgressions of the people; but afterwards came the one who offered himself for the salvation of the world, and the blood of Christ purified those whom the blood of bulls could not wash, and priests began to offer themselves in place of their victims.

4.26. Thus with a single question our Lord Jesus Christ has bound up the mouths of all heretics; he has shut up all their impieties. For with this question he reproved not only Jews, but also Photinians and Arians and Sabellians.[61] And therefore, since we have already seen that the Jews have failed and their despicable perfidy has been reduced, we must now somehow examine in the treatment of this question the Arians, who do not differ much from Jews, and the Photinians and Sabellians. Thus let Photinus be silent, who says Christ is the son of David and not the Son of God, and let him be silent as he is condemned by the voice from heaven. For how does he say that Christ is the son of David, when "David himself said in the book of Psalms: 'The Lord said to my lord: Sit at my right hand, until your foes I will place beneath your feet.'[62] If David calls that man 'Lord,' how is he his son?"[63] And thus Christ is not the son of David, but the Son of God. Let the Sabellian be silent as well: when he reads that the Lord spoke to the lord, let him not interpret as one and the same the one who speaks and the one who is addressed—for the Father does not say to himself, "Sit at my right hand," and he does not say to himself, "I will place your foes"—and let all understand at some point that he is the Son who sits at the right hand, and let all observe this distinction between

61. The archetypal heresies included here promoted distinct views on the person and identity of Jesus Christ; Photinus may have been a follower of Marcellus of Ancyra (c.285–374), and was accused of Modalism; Arius (c.256–336) identified the Son of God with the created order; and Sabellius, who lived in the third century, was identified with the heresy of Modalism, which claimed that Christ the Son was simply one manner or "mode" in which the single God appeared. For an overview, see Lewis Ayres, *Nicaea and its Legacy: An Approach to Fourth-Century Trinitarian Theology* (Oxford: Oxford University Press, 2004), 41–130, and D. H. Williams, "Monarchianism and Photinus of Sirmium as the Persistent Heretical Face of the Fourth Century," *Harvard Theological Review* 99 (2006): 187–206.

62. Ps 110.1.

63. Lk 20.42–44.

the Father and the Son: that the distinction of the Father and the Son is thus, that one is the Father, and another is the Son, but because they sit in one seat, they enjoy one majesty and they are seated not according to some distinction in their dignity nor in the order of their power, but in a union of charity, and so let them understand that the power of Father and Son is one.

In this regard let Arius be quiet as well, who advances on the tracks of an error contrary to Sabellius. Let him hear the Lord speak to the lord, let him hear that the Son sits at the right hand of the Father, and let him leave off attempting an investigation into divinity according to the speech and logic of men. And let not it be argued that here the Father says "Sit" as a command; for we read elsewhere as well that the Son sits without the command of the Father, just as it is written: "And he sits at the right hand of God"[64] and elsewhere: "From now on, you will see the Son of Man seated at the right hand of God."[65] For the one who is named the Son of Man is the one to whom it is said, "Sit." He hears as a man, he sits as the Son of God. What can be said to be more supreme than this power, which places even the flesh of man at the right hand of God and joins to the eternal divinity the weakness of the human condition, after, that is, the Word became flesh?

4.27. But what is this? Even after Photinus went quiet, Arius fell silent, Sabellius lost his voice, yet still I observe heresy raising different voices against the Church. For see how the Manichean and the Valentinian and every progeny of the Manicheans depend on this weapon, by which others are killed: their preconception of the faith departs from the witness of the faith.[66] For the detestable heresy says: "Look, Christ denied that he was the son of David, and thus,"[67] it adds, "one should believe that he did not take up flesh." Scripture responds to them most directly in the very beginning of the Gospel: "The book of the genera-

64. Mk 16.19.

65. Mt 26.64.

66. On Manicheism and Valentinianism, see Samuel N. C. Lieu, *Manichaeism in Mesopotamia and the Roman East* (Leiden and Boston: Brill, 1994), and Einar Thomassen, *The Spiritual Seed: The Church of the "Valentinians"* (Leiden and Boston: Brill, 2006).

67. Cf. Lk 20.41–44.

tion of Jesus the Christ the son of David."[68] Why, then, is he at one point called "son of David" and elsewhere it is denied that he is "son of David" unless so that you see that it is one thing to be Son according to the divine essence and another to be son according to the assumption of the flesh? For according to the divine essence he is Son of God; according to the flesh he is the son of David. Thus when the generation of the Savior is described according to the flesh, he is named "son of David," but when the fullness of the confession is required, when the generation of the Savior is designated, the Son of God does not wish to be named the son of David; for the designation of his majesty indicates his [true] nature.

But now that the interpretations of the wicked are refuted, the account should be turned back to the Church.

5.28. And so, the fact that we often repeat the inscription of Psalm 50 is an example not of our stubbornness but of our infirmity. For either because of the limits of my talent or because of the weakness of my voice, I cannot complete the entire sequence of the treatise in a single day.[69] Hence, since our sermon yesterday was directed against the Jews, whom in fact the evidence of the faith has compelled to come to the conclusion that Christ is placed on the heavenly throne, which cannot be fitting for a man—for one cannot believe that anyone other than the Son of God should sit at the right hand of God—once all ambiguities are resolved, we must maintain that no one other than the Son of God sits at the right hand of God. Again, since Scripture indicates: "From the fruit of your womb I will place you on your throne,"[70] then certainly the Son of God must be believed to have taken flesh from Mary; in her is the fruit of the prophesied womb, so that you might rightly recognize the sequence from its origin and you would not doubt that the Son of God, afterward having become a son of man through that very assumption of the flesh, sits on the heavenly throne. For it is not the case that Christ had any sort of royal throne in this current age, so that you might think that another throne was promised

68. Mt 1.1.

69. Ambrose elsewhere refers to the weakness of his voice; see *Sacr.* 1.6.24.

70. Ps 132.11.

to the seed of David, especially since the Lord himself said: "My kingdom is not of this world."[71]

5.29. Thus hemmed in on all sides, they pour out the arguments for their own perfidy, and they assert that it is unbelievable that God assumed flesh, yet they cannot explain why he could not assume flesh. For I ask whether they believe that flesh could not be assumed by God because it was impossible or because it would be offensive to him. If it is a matter of impossibility, then is anything impossible for God? For there is nothing that he wants to do that he cannot do. Thus it only remains to be proven that he either wanted or did not want to assume flesh. But what can be a greater indication of his will than the fact that he himself says: "I have appeared to those who do not seek me. I stretched out my hands to a people that does not believe and speaks against me"?[72] Then if he wished and could do it, do we think that he refused because it would be offensive? And what offense does his divinity feel? For he has no experience of injury, and he is not subject to our passions; for flesh could impart neither decrease nor increase to the divinity.

5.30. Yet if they are gentiles who object on this ground, namely that the Son of God could not assume flesh, how do they assert that their gods were seen with a human appearance, since they cannot deny that they were men? If the king of their gods, whom they place above all their gods, could assume miraculous forms for the sake of lust, could not Christ assume the flesh of man, whom he made unto his own image, and who was his most outstanding work, for the salvation of the world? Or does it seem more fitting to them that the appearance of flesh was assumed for the sake of committing adultery in another's bed than for the redemption of all? But if the Jew objects to this, how does he interpret this passage: "Behold, the virgin will receive in her womb, and she will bear a son, and his name will be called Emmanuel, which means 'God with us'"?[73] How does he interpret: "See, it is I who said that"?[74] And how does he interpret the reading: "See,

71. Jn 18.36.
72. Rom 10.20–21; Is 65.1–2.
73. Mt 1.23; Is 7.14.
74. Is 52.6.

like a panther and a wounded bear I will pounce on them"?[75] Is it that the Son of God could not assume flesh for the redemption of all, even though the Jews themselves cannot deny that for the punishment of our sins God could feign to appear with an attitude of brutish cruelty, and that the one who is pious and merciful by nature, when he was upset by the atrocity of our crimes, assumed an apparent bestial viciousness against us?

5.31. But now that I think we have responded to the many Jews yesterday and today, for your sake, beloved brothers, I must demonstrate the reason for the prophetic deed. For when this title of the Psalm was first read, that "Nathan came to David, after he had gone in to Bathsheba," we said that many would be offended in the presentation of this account, and thus we undertook a threefold division for the treatise, and I thought the division of the treatise should be treated so that, for the gentiles, the fall of the human condition would not be denied and the correction of the error would be offered; for the Jews, that we might teach that the saintly David fell, so that the perfidy of the Jews would stumble along no further and that they would cease to believe that David is the Son of God, whom they would see as guilty in sin by reason of his shared human condition, and that Christians could recognize the mysteries of the rising Church. That threefold division has been made: first, according to nature; second, according to faith; and third, according to grace. And weakness does not exclude one from forgiveness, and faith does not excuse one from guilt, and the sacraments procure the grace that has now been long promised.

6.32. David sinned so that the whole world would not err; he sinned in respect to himself, to correct all of us; and, last, he sinned against his own body—for whoever fornicates "sins against his own body"[76]—he sinned against his own body, so that he might be redeemed in the body of Christ. See how the one we thought could hardly be defended now appears as one who should be proclaimed out loud. For who is there who refuses to proclaim the gifts that God has given to him rather than human works? For, according to the Apostle, "we judge that

75. Hos 13.7–8.
76. 1 Cor 16.18.

man is justified through faith without works of the Law."[77] Thus let David be justified by faith, who through the Law acknowledged his sin, but from his faith he believed in pardon for his sin; let David be justified because the mysteries of the Church that would arise have shone out in his sin.

6.33. Someone will say: why did the chosen progenitor of the Lord's people commit both adultery and murder? Yet I phrase it differently: such a man had to be chosen as the source for the Lord's body. For what is "embodiment" (*incorporatio*) if not the remission of sins? And thus he could not be free from sin, so that he might prefigure divine grace by both his example and his message. And so by following this design we see that Bathsheba and Tamar are reckoned among the sources of the Lord's ancestry, even though one of them committed adultery and the other committed incest.[78] By this design both Ahab and Jechoniah, as the Evangelist Matthew describes, are numbered among the ancestors of Christ,[79] so that the one who would come to redeem all people would lay the foundation of the benefit with his ancestors, while at the same time the one who would subject himself to the point of bodily suffering would not appear to have claimed the nobility of an undefiled ancestry; for it is a boast of men to seek another's glory rather than their own; and yet even by human reckoning the grace of virtue is greater than that of nobility. At the same time, the example had to be given so that all might understand that the failures of the ancestors could not be shameful to their descendants because each one could abolish the pollution that comes from his own ancestry through the merit of his own virtue. You see how many and how terribly criminal were those included in the line of the Lord's generation. Christ was not ashamed to be born from this source for you. And if you believe, these things are the gifts of divine mercy in you and the mark of heavenly power; for sin superabounded that grace might superabound.[80] Therefore, David was not exempt from guilt so that he might be chosen for grace.

77. Rom 3.28.
78. Cf. Mt 1.6 and 3; 2 Kgs 11.4 and Gn 38.18.
79. Cf. Mt 1.9, 11.
80. Cf. Rom 5.20.

6.34. But now let us review the mysteries of the account itself, and let us drink from the very sources of the Scriptures, and, so that we can investigate the entire sequence of the mysteries, let us repeat the text of the history itself. For surely in the book of Kingdoms we recall that it is stated that when David saw Bathsheba, the wife of Uriah, bathing, he fell in love with her, and then he ordered her to come to his home, at the time when the woman's husband would be away. Not long after, her husband returned as a messenger of the war; he was a very religious and devout man, who would not think of entering his home in a time of war, since he saw his companions intent on war and not sleeping in the domestic shelters but in the battle tents. Afterwards, by a decree of David, he was called back into war under the instruction that he be placed in the way of the enemy's warriors, so that by the husband's death the king would have free access to take advantage of his wife.[81] And here there is significant shame for the sin and embarrassment for the crime, because he sought to hide his error and he did not take responsibility for the unjust killing that rightly belonged to him through his royal power, but he avoided hostility. I admit his guilt, but it is more acceptable that his guilt be suppressed because of shame than that it be broadcast through arrogance. Thus Uriah was killed when he was placed in front of the warriors, and afterwards those who killed him were slaughtered by the decree of David once the city was stormed. This is the chronicle of the history in which it is still possible to observe deep mysteries.

7.35. And since we take it that David should not be defended—for he does not need my help—but excused or even proclaimed, so that I do not dawdle in such a depth of mysteries, it is right that I use the speech of the one whose account I am using. Thus I will use his prophetic response by saying: "Create a clean heart in me, God, and renew in my inmost parts an upright spirit."[82] For without the infusion of the Holy Spirit no one can gaze on such great depths of the divine mystery. But if even that great prophet begged that the gift of the Holy Spirit

81. Cf. 2 Sm 11.2–17.
82. Ps 51.10.

be infused in him, what should I who am weak do? Consider especially how even the holy Apostle also sought to be aided by the prayers of the people, that a gate might be opened for him to speak the mystery of the Word.[83] O that Christ would deign to open that gate for me! Let us simply knock; for he is accustomed to hearing those who knock, because he himself says: "Knock, and it will be opened to you."[84] O if he would open himself up to me, because Christ is the gate. He is inside, he is outside, he is the way that leads, he is the life that we strive to reach.

7.36. Come then, Lord Jesus, and open your fountains to us, so that we might drink water; whoever drinks this water will never [again] thirst eternally, or if we cannot yet drink from your fountain, deign to permit that we can at least drink from the well from which you promised a drink to that Samaritan woman who was still doubting.[85] And you indeed promise a drink from the fountain to all, but to those who doubt, as that Samaritan woman did, your fountain is the well that is still deep.[86] Let us also drink the water of the heavenly secrets and, since we deserve to come to your fountain, allow us to glimpse at least the image of the heavenly mysteries.

7.37. In this way, unless I am mistaken, through the prophet let us understand the Holy Spirit, and through the adulteress let us recognize the various fornications of the Synagogue. And thus we see what was revealed long ago from the Holy Spirit and from the family of the Jews, "whose are the fathers from whom Christ was according to the flesh," the Lord Jesus had to be begotten;[87] he indeed was born as a Jew as though from an adulterous family, but as a spotless child he was born from a virgin. For he was under the Law, just as the family of the Jews was under a man. The observance of the Law had to be abolished so that truth and grace might be substituted.

7.38. Here we have one mystery; receive another, that, as you

83. Cf. Col 4.3.
84. Lk 11.9.
85. Cf. Jn 4.6 and 4.14.
86. Cf. Jn 4.11.
87. Rom 9.5.

recall, the baby born from the first conception of Bathsheba died, and afterwards Solomon was born: the first child was from the illicit conception, but this one, Solomon, was from a legal marriage.[88] Thus it is clear that through the figure of David we understand the prophet, and through the prophet we understand a prophetic people; and from David the firstborn is the Synagogue. And since the nation of the Jews, formed through crimes and conceived through vices, degenerated from its elders, could not reach the age of the resurrection and could not grow into the perfect man, but in the puny insignificance of their thinking they failed in the infancy, as it were, of their virtue. And yet the one who was afterwards conceived by a legitimate union is the Christian people, "wise and peaceful"—for these meanings are revealed with the proper interpretation of "Solomon"—and arrives at the hoary old age of the long-awaited resurrection and at the heavenly kingdom. But through the Jewish people the Law is abolished; through the Christian people grace is refashioned.

7.39. Receive in addition a third mystery: the Hebrew term "David" is interpreted as *humiliatum* ("humiliated") in Latin. For who is truly humiliated if not the one who "did not judge it robbery that he be equal to God, but accepting the form of a servant he humiliated himself, becoming obedient unto death"?[89] Thus this man is the one who is meant by "David," for he is exalted by nature, but humiliated through mercy, sublime in his divinity, but meek in his body.[90] Thus when he is humiliated, then he is obedient. For from this man obedience is born, from him humility is born, and in him they end. For when he is described as "becoming obedient unto death," it is not indeed the death of the divinity but the death of the body; in fact, the obedience was not of the divinity but of the body, and the humility was not of the majesty but of the flesh. As concerns the assumption of a body, the reading from the Apostle declared in what the humility of Christ consists: but as concerns the nature of the

88. Cf. 2 Kgs 11.26; 12.18; 12.24.

89. Phil 2.6–8.

90. Ambrose's source for this etymology of "David," which differs from the one (borrowed from Origen) offered in *Apol. Dau.* 3.9, is unclear.

divinity, that has been disclosed in the Gospel reading, which you have followed with pious attention when you heard it read that the Son of God said: "I and the Father are one";[91] for the Son and the Father are one in divinity, but the sacrament of the body and the eternity of the divinity are not one. Yet it was not only the Apostle who said that the Lord was humbled, but the Lord himself stated that he was humble in saying: "Take my yoke because it is light, since I am meek and humble of heart."[92] And yet this is indicated not only by that interpretation but also by a clear identification, because it is written: "I found David my servant, in my holy oil I have anointed him,"[93] and further on: "He will say to me: 'You are my father,'"[94] and, "I will say to him: 'You are my son.'"[95] Thus the David whom we were seeking we found to be in fact a servant in appearance but the Lord in truth.

8.40. Thus this David was wandering about his home. And what is the house of Christ unless the one about which he says: "In my Father's house there are many dwelling places"?[96] Located, then, in that royal home, he saw the naked human condition and had mercy on it, loving it, for it was still stripped of virtues. Through the deceits of the serpent, it was stripped of the clothing of its nature with which it had been born. But this does not seem like the truth, that a woman was stripped in front of the house of the king, that a wife would wash herself before the house of the king, as though there could be no other place more appropriate for bathing: it does not square, it does not fit, and does not align with faith: it is far from the truth, it is repugnant to the senses. The king could not have loved, but rather despised someone so unwholesome and audacious. Could that woman possibly not have been ashamed before men's gaze or at least not have feared the king's gaze? Or could it be that her servants did not protect her before the king saw her?

8.41. Then, if this does not fit with faith, let us ask what this

91. Jn 10.30.
92. Mt 11.29.
93. Ps 89.21.
94. Ps 89.27.
95. Ps 2.7.
96. Jn 14.2.

naked woman means: clearly it refers to the human condition stripped of all coverings of its nature, lacking the clothing of immortality and stripped of the veil of innocence; for he is naked who is naked through sin and guilt. Thus that first sinner of our race and he alone, before he sinned, did not feel that he was naked; after he sinned, he saw that he was naked, and he thought he should be covered by leaves, because he knew he was naked. Thus he became naked to himself after he became guilty of sin. In him the entire human condition is naked; through the transmission of his nature it is subject not only to sin, but also to hardship. Thus he sensed and he saw that he was naked. So too our condition is like this: that whoever considered himself naked both sees it and senses it. And so whoever desires riches is naked, and he who disregards them is wealthy. Therefore, each one's sensitivity is a hardship, but each one's virtue has no part in wrongdoing. Thus Christ vindicated the human condition first through the Law (which he would later repudiate) by uniting it to himself in marriage.[97] Hence he also says: "What is the bill of your mother's divorce by which I sent her away?"[98] Therefore, by this account Christ saw his family naked and loved them; for Christ loves the holy soul. Thus Jesus loved Lazarus and Mary; Christ loved his Church although she was nude, although she was not yet clothed in the beauty of any virtues.[99]

8.42. Thus to know that the chronicle of the Scriptures fits with the proposed outline, let us learn that the Church is naked, let us learn that she is seeking, she is hastening and washing herself before the house of Christ, when John baptized in the Jordan, saying: "In fact I baptize you in water unto repentance, but the one coming after me is mightier than I, whose sandals I am not worthy to carry. He will baptize you in the Holy Spirit."[100] Thus when the people were baptized to repentance, they were now near to his house seeking Christ in order to come to grace. And therefore the Church was looking for Christ in the person

97. On the three stages of the "marriage" in Ambrose's account of God's union with Israel, see *Apol. Dau.* 9.11.

98. Is 50.1.

99. Cf. Jn 11.5.

100. Mt 3.11.

of John, saying: "Tell me whom my soul loves,"[101] recalling the very source of the desire, the very reason for her baptism, just as you have it written: "I am black and beautiful, daughters of Jerusalem, like the tent of Kedar, like the fleece of Solomon."[102] You have here the reason why she rejoices to wash herself, because she recalls that she is black. For it is as though she is speaking to John asking why the numerous people gather together and rejoice to be washed; she says: "I am black and beautiful, daughters of Jerusalem." Because she is black, she longs to be washed; because she is beautiful, she does not fear to be seen naked. "Do not look on me," she says, "because I am darkened, because the sun has not gazed on me."[103] Thus we are darkened when we are not seen by Christ, but when we are seen we are brilliant white. Thus he sees her; he is the one for whom all things are naked and the inmost parts of the breast cannot be hidden because he is an investigator of the heart and the inmost part;[104] nothing is hidden to him, nothing is covered over. He saw his Church naked, and, as he saw her, he loved her. He saw the beloved naked, and as though a son of charity he loved her.

8.43. See how he allures her, see how he beckons her. In this passage there is no charge of adultery, but only the mysteries of chastity. He says, "You are entirely beautiful, my darling, and there is no blame in you. Come here from Lebanon, my bride, come here from Lebanon; you will cross and cross over from the beginning of faith."[105] And rightly he says "from the beginning of faith." Thus, when you have faith, you should not fear adultery; for faith is characteristic of marriage, while deceit is characteristic of adultery. But that she can come from Lebanon, he established beforehand saying: "Rise, come, my darling, my lovely, my dove, my perfect one."[106] In fact she is his darling in

101. Song 1.7.

102. Song 1.6.

103. Ibid.

104. Cf. Ps. 7.9.

105. Song 4.7–9.

106. Song 2.10. Much of this section, until "my heart loves" in 8.44, was included in a twelfth-century compilation identified as Ambrose's "Commentary on Song of Songs"; William of Saint-Thierry, *Excerpta de libris beati Ambrosii super Cantica canticorum.*

her desire for the faith, lovely by the beauty of her virtue, and a dove by spiritual grace. For the phrase "the silvered feathers of the dove"[107] indicates her eternal power, and the flight of the dove has declared the presence of the Holy Spirit. Thus Christ calls her to himself so that she comes, since she came endowed with spiritual gifts, because "Behold," he says, "the winter has passed away, the rains have left and departed to themselves, the flowers have appeared on the earth."[108] See how the holy Church is invited. He says "the winter has departed to itself," lest the naked one fear the winter; I do not speak of the winter of a certain season, but of weakness, which despoils the fertile field of the soul of every flower. For the winter is not the one of the earthly sun; it is the winter of the soul, when the cold licks the spirit, when the warmth of the spirit vanishes, when the vigor of the senses dissipates, when too much fluid overflows and weighs down the mind, when the interior of one's vision goes cloudy.[109] And thus the Lord says: "See that your flight not happen in winter or on the Sabbath."[110] For it is good that the day of judgment or death may come at the time when the soothing balance of the soul flourishes, when the heavenly mystery shines out with a comforting light, when our hearts burn within us. For then Christ is present, just as in the Gospel Ammaon and Cleopas attest when they say:[111] "Was not our heart burning within us on the road, when he opened for us the Scriptures?"[112] Indeed, the soul thrives at the time when the blossom appears on the earth. Who is that sweet-smelling blossom if not the one who said: "I am the flower of the field and the lily of the valley"?[113] It is also written about him in Isaiah: "The branch will sprout from the root of Jesse, and the branch will reach up from the root, and

107. Ps 68.14.

108. Song 2.11.

109. Cf. Vergil, *Georgics* 1.88.

110. Mt 24.20.

111. See Hugh Connolly, "Some Disputed Works of St. Ambrose," *Downside Review* 65 (1947): 14–15, on the name Ammaon for the second of the two disciples on the way to Emmaus.

112. Lk 24.32.

113. Song 2.1.

the flower will go up from the branch."[114] In fact, the root is the people of the Jews, the branch is Mary, the blossom of Mary is Christ, and when he shines out in our land and spreads his perfume in the field of the soul or is verdant in his Church, we cannot fear the cold or be afraid of the rain, but we can await the day of judgment.

8.44. And thus when the Church sees this flower, she hastens with all eagerness, just as she herself attests, saying: "All night long on my bed I looked for the one my soul loves; I looked for him but did not find him. I called him, but he did not hear me. I will get up now and go into the house, into the city center and its squares; I will search for the one my heart loves. So I looked for him but did not find him. The watchmen found me as they made their rounds in the city; they struck me, and they took the covering from me."[115] You see in what sort of way she seeks the one she desires to find, so that she may not be afraid to be wounded. But these wounds should not be feared, but longed for, because they are the wounds of love, just as she herself said: "I have been wounded by love."[116] The wounds of love are good. Thus more valuable are wounds from a friend than kisses of desire from an enemy.[117]

9.45. Thus it is fitting that she is naked, because she lost her covering, or perhaps therefore naked because it is sometimes virtuous not to cover the chest, not to conceal the heart. Thus is that other woman concealed, namely the Synagogue, which was cloaked by a veil in the reading of the Old Testament, and therefore she is not unveiled—since the veil is taken away in Christ—for this reason I say that Christ despises and spurns the veiled Synagogue, and thus even today a veil is placed on the heart of the Jews.[118] But if a woman is converted to the Lord in her whole heart, she is naked and visible. For when anyone has been converted to the Lord, the veil is removed, so that as we gaze we might see the glory of God. Thus even elsewhere there

114. Is 11.1.
115. Song 3.1–3.
116. Song 5.7–8.
117. Cf. Prv 27.6.
118. Cf. 2 Cor 3.14.

is an indication that being naked is a mark of virtue, because it is written: "I have removed my tunic; how shall I place it on again? I have washed my feet; how will I soil them?"[119]

9.46. Let us find out from the Scriptures, then, which tunic she removed and how she did not find a way to put it on again, if we can. For it is a certain bodily tunic, which is somehow embroidered with coverings of desires, and thus sometimes it is better to be naked in body than veiled in heart. For Paul also cautions us that to be stripped is much better than to be clothed when he states at one point: "Strip off from yourselves the old man with his deeds, and put on the new one, the one who is renewed in knowledge according to the image of him who created him."[120] In this passage she has been stripped, and she has washed her feet and, because she is washing, she does not know how she can be soiled again; for she forgets through grace what she had imbibed through nature. This, then, is a great and just love, which characterizes the woman washing herself in front of the palace of David.

9.47. But she not only washed herself, but she also called to him, as we have it in the same book of Scripture, where the holy Church says: "Come, my brother, let us go out into the field; let us rest in the fortresses; let us rise at dawn to go to the vineyards; let us see if the vines are blossoming."[121] Thus she not only bathes, but she even beckons Christ to come to her and invites him, saying: "I will give my breasts to you."[122] And she promises not only what is her own but also the new and the old, as you read: "I have saved for you, my brother, the new and the old."[123] And as though she is impatient of any delay for her love, she seeks someone for support who might beg Christ to come. See her panting, see her desiring. "Who will give you," she says, "my brother, to nurse at the breasts of my mother?"[124] And the passage shows the reason she seeks and why she invites and in what way she can hold to him; it demonstrates how she waits out-

119. Song 5.3.
120. Col 3.9–10.
121. Song 7.12–13.
122. Song 7.12.
123. Song 7.13.
124. Song 8.1.

side as he delays and how she implores him to enter her house, when she says: "Finding you outside I will kiss you, I will take you and I will lead you into the home of my mother and into its hidden parts, where she conceived me."[125] You see how she is naked, as one who cannot keep covered the hidden parts of a nature that is entirely undefiled, the hidden parts of her inmost conscience that are not marked by any foolhardy vices. For this enclosed garden is the holy Church and immaculate is her virginity, which earns this grace from Christ because she sought the word of God and desired it and found it, holding vigil before the gates of wisdom, just as she herself says: "Blessed is the man who hears me, and the person who watches my ways, keeping vigil by my gates daily, guarding the fences of my entrance; for my gateways are the gateways of life."[126]

9.48. For Christ desired the beauty of his Church and prepared to acquire her as his wife. But because she was under the Law—for Peter, John, and the other apostles were under the Law—he first decided that we needed to be freed from the chains of bodily observance. For although the Law is religious, although the Law is just, it is like the person of Uriah, who was so religious and chaste that when he returned from war he did not acknowledge his wife and he did not enter into her presence. Yet when Uriah knew of the union of David [with Bathsheba], that is, when he knew that the union was with a humble man, he prepared a place for the future wedding rites of the Church by departing from union with the Synagogue.[127] Hence John the Baptist accepted the Law as a type, who, although he was from the patriarchs, announced that the ways of the Lord were to be prepared, and he prophesied a union of the Church; and for this reason John is presented as being killed so that he might show the end of the observance of the Law; for "the Law and the prophets lasted until John."[128] Thus Uriah was killed as a type of the Law to show that the Synagogue would be loosed from the tethers of the Law, since "the woman is bound by the

125. Song 8.1–2.
126. Prv 8.34–35.
127. An allegorical reading.
128. Lk 16.16.

Law under her husband while her husband is alive; but when the husband has died, she is freed from the law of her husband. Thus while her husband lives, the woman who couples with another man will be called an adulteress; but if her husband has died, she is freed from the law of her husband so that she is not an adulteress if she should be with another man."[129] Thus the human condition is not an adulteress; although it was under the Law, it was restored to grace when the observance of the Law was somehow abolished.

9.49. For Christ did not abolish the observance of the Law. In the same way David did not kill Uriah, but he allowed him to be killed by warriors; that is, Christ allowed the ritual observance that came from the Law to be profaned through the incursions of barbarians and through the captivity of the Jews. In fact, "Uri" means "my light."[130] For what is the light of Christ if not the Law and the Gospel: "For if you believed Moses you would also believe me; for that one wrote about me"[131]—because the light of Christ appeared earlier in the Law; and in the Gospel his grace afterward filled the entirety of the world as though in the *heptamyxos* (that is, septiform) Spirit. Thus he submitted his flesh to this Law and joined the Church to himself. A hostile people threatened the light of this Law when it violated the holy precepts of this Law. Thus the light of God was diminished in the people of the Jews, because partial blindness occurred in Israel, until the fullness of the nations entered in and so all of Israel was saved.[132]

10.50. Still remaining is the fourth mystery, which I ask that you listen to with tranquil ears, and I ask that you attend to our intention and not our words; for the kingdom of God is not in the word, but in the underlying force. There was an adultery, there was a murder. This is what was said to the prophet: "Take for yourself the branch of an almond tree."[133] And we read else-

129. Rom 7.2–3.

130. Throughout the treatise Ambrose uses the name "Uri," which I have translated "Uriah."

131. Jn 5.46.

132. Cf. Rom 11.25.

133. Jer 1.11.

where "branch of an almond tree,"[134] by which we understand a kind of law and a summary of prophecy; for in the manner of the almond, it is bitter in the skin that covers it, hard in the middle of its coating, but tender and fruitful within. And yet in the account [of David] you hear quite bitter things, in the prefiguration you recognize hard things, yet in the mystery take hope in fruitful things. I say that the adultery became a prefiguration of salvation; for not every adultery must be condemned. Thus it was said to the prophet: "Go and take to yourself a fornicator as a wife."[135] The Lord commands that the marriage take place with a woman who had been a fornicator; and from this marriage, as we said above, Christ is born. For the name Jezreel, which means "divine generation," has been imposed by the Lord on the son who was born from fornication.[136] Therefore, if that coupling in fornication was pious, then this coupling in adultery is also a pious companionship. But that concerns the Jews. While in divine matters I of course do not dare to call an adultery "pious," lest even the sound of the expression offend someone, still there is available a more respectable interpretation, which can be more carefully, if not more compellingly, stated: A holy cohabitation took place from unequal partners, when the Word became flesh.[137] For there is no lawful wedlock between divinity and the flesh, since their natures do not fit together by a distinctive bond, as the flesh does to the soul and the soul to the flesh; thus even the divinity and the flesh observe the law of a rightful marriage bed, in a certain sense. God assumed flesh, he took up a soul, he made there to be a lawful wedlock through an unprecedented and illegitimate Incarnation, so that God might be all things and in all.[138]

10.51. Therefore, interpret the individual words so that you might grasp the mystery. For you understand David as a type of Christ, and Bathsheba is understood to be the "daughter of the Sabbath" and "full daughter" and "the well of oath-taking." What, then, is clearer than that the "daughter of the Sabbath" is

134. Nm 17.23.
135. Hos 1.2.
136. Cf. Hos 1.4.
137. Jn 1.14.
138. Cf. Col 3.11.

the flesh of Christ because God sent his Son made from a woman, made under the Law?[139] The same thing for "full daughter," because in his Passion is the fullness of the Law or because he is full of the Holy Spirit; for Jesus returned from the Jordan full of the Holy Spirit.[140] But she is also "the well of oath-taking," that is, of religion and faith. And it is fitting that it is a well, because the streams of living water flow from his stomach.[141] Thus taking this woman to himself, God the Word made the union lawful. This mystery has also been indicated by those marriage rites that are in the Song of Songs, by which the Church weds Christ and the flesh weds the spirit. And thus she was running about and seeking where the word of God was, because she was wounded, because she was naked, because she was an adulteress in all things; even though she was immaculate in Christ, her wretched flesh was seeking a redeemer.

10.52. Christ joined this woman [that is, human nature] to himself, so that he might render her immaculate; he accompanied her, so that he might bear away her adultery. And because she was under the Law, death was necessary, so that she might be liberated from the Law, so that through her death, the marriage, as it were, between the Law and the flesh might be destroyed. Thus the flesh is dead in Christ, so that dead to the Law, as the Apostle said, through the body of Christ we might belong to the one who rose from the dead; and the passions and desires of the flesh and the thoughts of sins, which were in our members because of the Law, might die in his death, while we who are freed from the law of death might rise in the newness of the Spirit as though by a new union with Christ.[142]

10.53. And yet all those who have abolished the Law in the flesh of Christ and have thought the Law should be violated have been slain by soldiers at the command of David. By this sign—because they taught what was prefigured for later times—it shows that none of those who killed Christ escaped, and it is clearly revealed that those whom Christ took to himself before

139. Cf. Rom 13.10.
140. Cf. Lk 4.1.
141. Cf. Jn 6.38.
142. Cf. Rom 7.46.

his death perished like the Jews, small and poorly developed; but those whom he knew after his death have been preserved for the kingdom among the number of the sons. Hence according to this mystery it is fitting that the first birth, which was among the Jews, was weak, so that afterwards, there might be eternal fruit among the Christians.

11.54. But now let us move on to the messenger [Nathan]. For in the previous days we found that in the prophet David's despicable adultery and murder and in the mysteries proclaimed, there was not only nothing deserving condemnation but rather that there is something to be praised. Now the treatise begins to concern the messenger himself, who is indicated by the title of the Psalm we read, now often repeated. For it reads thus: "The Psalm of understanding of David, when the prophet Nathan came to him, when he had gone in to Bathsheba."[143]

11.55. One must review the part of the account that goes this way: It says, "'A rich man and a poor man were in a single city. The rich man had many flocks and many sheep; the poor man had one sheep, which was fed by the bread and wine of the poor man, and rested in his lap. A guest came to the rich man, and the rich man did not take anything from his own flock or from his cattle, but rather killed the one sheep of the poor man.' When David learned this, he said, 'That rich man must die and repay him fourfold.' Nathan replied to him: 'You are he.'"[144] Then Nathan revealed the heavenly commandment to David, saying that the Lord had sent many good things to him, that is, he gave royal wealth to one who had been raised up from a group of shepherds, and he had poured out his mercy on him; and therefore, since David had offended the Lord through his sin, all his possessions were to be taken from him, he was to be besieged by the enemy, and his house ruined. Then he said: "I have sinned," and Nathan responded: "Since you confess that you have sinned, the Lord will forgive your sin, but your son who was born from Bathsheba will die."[145] When this son grew sick, David wept, lay on the earth, covered himself in sackcloth,

143. Ps 51 (50), inscription.

144. A summary of 2 Sm 12.1–7.

145. Cf. 2 Sm 12.16–24.

and fasted. When he knew that he was dead, he got up, washed, dined, and he consoled others.

11.56. See how many points are here. First of all, note that God is kind and merciful and the adverse things that happen to us we accept as the cost for our fault. Thus we have learned that captivity is the cost for sin; for this appears as penalty for a crime. Then we note that the fall of kings is the punishment for their peoples. For just as we are preserved by their strength, so too are we imperiled by their error. Hence we should desire to have a glorious and perfect king. Thus do we who desire to have a perfect king refuse to have a perfect Lord? Or can those who do not want God to be perfect also want a man to be perfect? Even the text of the account moves through the events so briefly that we understand how quickly the hope of pardon followed. For it is no small fact that the one to denounce him was Nathan, that is, a lesser prophet; for it is a great embarrassment and shame that a sin be condemned by a lesser person. You see that sin diminishes grace. Nathan knew what David did not know: that the soul grows cloudy, overshadowed by the fog of vices. Hence this is Nathan, who prophesied earlier that David was accepted by the Lord,[146] so that David would be pained to have his sin pointed out by the same witness whose prophesying had proclaimed his worthiness.

11.57. But now let us consider the mystery. It says, "There were two men in one city, one rich and the other poor." Who is this rich man or the poor man if not perhaps the people of the Jews on the one hand and the Christian people on the other? One is the man rich in the Law, rich in the sayings of God entrusted to him, rich in prophecies, rich in oracles; but this other is the poor man. But do not flee from this poverty, which leads to the kingdom of heaven; for it is written: "Blessed are the poor in spirit, since theirs is the kingdom of heaven."[147] This is a noble poverty, which does not spend away what it has; this is a noble poverty, which, even if it does not have treasuries of money, still has treasuries of knowledge and wisdom. Sons, do not reject poverty as though it is paltry; "the poor man called

146. Cf. 2 Sm 7.4–17.
147. Mt 5.3.

out, and the Lord heard him."[148] Do not envy riches as though they are great: "The rich went hungry and thirsty."[149] But if you wish to have good things, seek the Lord; for "those who seek the Lord do not lack in any good."[150] Thus do not reject any poor man. Peter was poor, and he did not have a coin that he might give, but he gave salvation more precious than any sort of money.[151] That Lazarus of the Gospel was poor; but the rich man, while he was the one who was previously lying in opulence and in purple, after the end of his life was longing to be refreshed by the dripping finger of the poor man.[152] Although that rich man, who was proud in his royal purple and brilliant raiment, petulantly despised the wounds of the poor man, yet when he was placed in hell he longed to be in the place where Lazarus was. In this passage the reading does not seem to describe the one who is rich and poor in terms of money, but the one who is poor because he does not shrink before the wounds of the body in view of his faith and devotion; he endures hunger and fasting.

11.58. Although, therefore, the people of the Jews have many hordes of victims in their flocks, yet the one small lamb that the poor people had they snatched away and subjected to a glorious Passion. Do you want to know who the lamb is? "Like a lamb he was led to the slaughter,"[153] who is fed by the bread of the poor and takes the drink of the poor and sleeps in the lap of the poor. Indeed, he was nourished by our food, he rested in the bosom of our breast. For he recalled that he cannot rest in the lap of the Jews, saying: "The Son of Man has no place to lay his head."[154]

11.59. And next it says, "A guest came to that rich man." Who is that guest if not wretched sin? For indeed sin entered into this world like a guest, a foreigner and an outsider to our nature. Thus he did not offer a victim from his own flocks, but he took the lamb of the poor man and killed her. Although the lamb's suffering profits for the sacred saving act, yet it seems that for

148. Ps 34.7
149. Ps 34.10.
150. Ps 33.11.
151. Cf. Acts 3.6.
152. Cf. Lk 16.19–24.
153. Is 53.7.
154. Lk 9.58.

the rich man it was an increase in rage and the food of guilt and an incentive to sin. Thus Judas took bread from Christ and then was filled more by the devil, because he who was preparing to betray such a hospitable Lord did not receive the bread with faith.[155]

11.60. And "David was angry at that man."[156] We said that the prophet was shown to be the people of the Jews and thus under this appearance he condemns himself. "That man who did this deserves death, and he will repay for the lamb fourfold"; that is, the people of the Jews would die, but the Christian people would enjoy more abundant blessings, because the society that is indebted to the resurrection is more outstanding than the present one.

11.61. It was my intention, as you deem it worthwhile to recall, to respond in my sermon against those who condemn the saintly David's murder and adultery, and so, enjoying the support of your agreement, the course of our treatise has concluded that the man who we did not think could be defended should actually be proclaimed to all. But since the saintly man does not need our help, let him speak to you himself on his own behalf and let his own words defend his deed.

12.62. He says, "Have mercy on me, Lord, according to your great mercy."[157] Unless I am mistaken, dearest brothers, that is a new addition to the speech, that mercy would be called "great," and I do not easily recall reading this elsewhere. And thus we should consider what a "great" mercy is. For if we do not typically read that mercy is great, we still do read that the "power of God is great."[158] And thus, considering how power is great, we could conjecture what "great mercy" seeks to designate. For we read in holy Jeremiah: "Who are you, Lord? You made the heaven and the earth in your great power and with your outstretched arm."[159] Thus great power made the heaven. Which is the great power, that of the Father or of the Son? Indeed, great is the

155. Cf. Jn 13.27.
156. 2 Sm 12.5.
157. Ps 51.1.
158. Ps 147.5.
159. Jer 32.17.

power of the Father—for he himself made the heaven and the earth through the Son, as you have the text: "In the beginning God made the heaven and the earth"[160]— yet the Son also is a great power. For when you read that the Son is the "power of the Father," so you have the text that Christ is "the wisdom and the power of God";[161] indeed when the Son is the power of the Father, the Son is "great power." How is it denied that he is omnipotent, he whom we confess to be the great power of God? Thus the great power made heaven because the Son also made the heaven, since you have the text: "All things were made through him."[162] Thus if both the Father and the Son did this, then the unity of their act shows the unity of operation. Thus the operation of Father and Son does not differ. But if there is one operation, then one is the power of the operation, and the majesty of the deeds is one. This concerns the Father and the Son.

12.63. Why then are we silent about the Spirit, especially since the divine Scriptures do not allow us to be silent? For the passage gives a most fitting testimony for proving the unity of the Holy Spirit with the Father and the Son, so that we cannot separate the Spirit's operation from the work of the Father and the Son. For we read that the power of the Father is great, because he made heaven; that the Son is also the great power because he made heaven, and not only did he make it, but he also established it: for "the heavens are established by the word of the Lord."[163] Thus if both the making and the establishment of heaven are characteristics of great power, so too we cannot separate the Holy Spirit from the majesty of the great power, because it is written: "All their power is from the Spirit of his mouth."[164] For when heaven and earth were made, the Spirit was hovering over them, about whom in another place it is said through the prophet David: "Send forth your Spirit, and they will be created."[165] About the Spirit also elsewhere he says: "Since I will see

160. Gn 1.1.
161. 1 Cor 1.24.
162. Jn 1.3.
163. Ps 33.6.
164. Ibid.
165. Ps 103.30. Cf. Gn 1.2.

the heavens, the works of your fingers."[166] But God did not make heaven and earth with bodily fingers, but with the grace of the septiform Spirit, that is, by that finger about which you read in the Gospel: "But if I cast out demons by the finger of God."[167] For elsewhere it calls this finger the Spirit, as you read: "But if I cast out demons by the Spirit of God."[168] If, then, the Spirit is the finger of God, since the Son is the arm of God, then the Spirit working with the Father and the Son made the heaven and the earth through a unity of operation. For thus the Son named it "the finger," so that in this way he might express the unity of the divinity as though of one body. Indeed, if "great power" created heaven, then "great wisdom" created heaven, because it is written: "You made all things with wisdom."[169]

12.64. Thus we have learned what "great power" is: let us consider now what "great mercy" is. If great power made the heavens, great mercy should be from heaven and great justice should be from heaven; for "justice looked down from heaven," and mercy came from heaven.[170] Thus mercy became great because "the Word became flesh and dwelt among us."[171] Thus great power made the heaven, great power bowed down the heavens, as we read: "And he inclined the heavens and came down."[172] Here it is shown that the Son of God was never separated from his divinity, not even when he dwelt among men, since even when he assumed what he was not, he still did not abandon what he was. Thus when it says: "And he inclined the heavens and came down," it seems not so much that he descended from heaven as that he descended with heaven itself. For when the Father addressed the Son while he was located on earth, the angels ministered to him, so the Son of God does not seem so much to have changed his seat as to have borne it with him. Thus we have learned that his mercy is great.

166. Ps 8.4.
167. Lk 11.20.
168. Mt 12.28.
169. Ps 104.24; Christ is frequently identified as "Wisdom" in early Christian exegesis.
170. Ps 85.11.
171. Jn 1.14.
172. Ps 18.10.

12.65. Thus if it is a great mercy to have descended from heaven, we should distinguish and understand what "multitude of mercies" means. For the text continues in this way: "Wipe out my iniquity according to the multitude of your mercies."[173] For each verse does not signify the same thing, but one refers to the Incarnation, while the one that follows seems to refer to those injuries that the Son of God assumed in the flesh, because he fasted, he thirsted, he wept, he was beaten, he was crucified, he died, and he was buried; for these are marks of the flesh and not of divinity. And it was necessary that a multitude of mercies would expel the multitude of tribulations in the struggle of the Lord's Passion that was to be for our sake.

12.66. For he did not wipe out his own sins, because he committed no sins; but because he became sin,[174] our sins had to be wiped out, just as David says: "Wipe out my iniquity." What is "wipe out"? Let us look at that word: it is not random. Thus elsewhere it also says: "I am, I am, the one who wipes out your sins, and I do not remember them."[175] There are certain sores of our sins that have been indeed deeply impressed on our conscience, and there are welts on our hearts and souls, which are inflicted by the sores of our errors. Thus error has its own characters and features by which it stands out. We are not devising this by our own contrivance, but we confirm it through prophetic authority. Thus consider that it is inscribed and where it is inscribed. He says, "Upon the breast of your heart,"[176] that is: the chronicle of the error was written where the form of virtue is, not in stony tablets but in the fleshly tablets of the heart.[177]

But what is good is not inscribed with ink, but with the Spirit of the living God, while what is wicked is inscribed "with an iron stylus" and "a steel point."[178] The writing is such that it is almost a penalty for the sin. The writing will be inscribed by an iron stylus; it will be checked by an iron rod, just as it is written: "You will

173. Ps 51.1.
174. Cf. 2 Cor 5.21.
175. Is 43.25.
176. Jer 17.1.
177. Cf. 2 Cor 3.3.
178. Jer 17.1.

rule them with an iron rod."[179] Another is the "straight rod, the rod of your kingdom."[180] One rod checks harmful men through punishment; the other rod governs the innocent by its rule.

Thus the sin has been inscribed: let us consider where. Not outside, but within, in your heart and in your breast. For just as "the word is near, in your mouth and in your heart,"[181] so the figure of sin and the image of error are printed in the very heart of the unfaithful. Thus sin is within, and power is within. And thus the Lord says, "I feel power went out of me,"[182] to show that what is good proceeds from within, and, on the contrary, what is evil goes forth from within. For it is "not what enters his mouth that pollutes the man, but what goes forth from his mouth."[183] For thoughts proceed from your heart, and thus beware that evil thoughts do not go forth from your heart; they testify against you and accuse you at a later time. For God does not need witnesses and proofs to condemn you; your sin itself accuses you and betrays you.

12.67. Hence David speaks rightly in this Psalm when he says: "My sin is before me always."[184] Woe is me because I desire to hide and I cannot hide! For how will I hide when I carry the marks of my crimes written on my heart? On that day of judgment the breast of each one will be laid bare, and his conscience will offer testimony to everyone, and his thoughts will accuse and defend him in turn, on the day when God will judge the hidden things of men. Consider the shame, when what we thought was hidden will begin to be presented to everyone, when the image of each one's sin will begin to reveal itself, so that each one is convicted by the recounting of his crime. Consider the shame, when you will see brought forth that man whom you judged despicable in this age, that one who is your servant, the one whom you judged to be inept and incapable according to the ruses of this world, and you will recognize that he is honored by the rich-

179. Ps 2.9.
180. Ps 45.6.
181. Rom 10.8; Dt 30.14.
182. Lk 8.46.
183. Mt 15.11.
184. Ps 51.3.

es of his simplicity. Thus, while we live, let us flee to him who can wipe out sin. And do not fear that it is written with an iron stylus and a steel point—for this one shatters gates of iron and of steel—and do not fear to confess your sin.

12.68. David confessed, he recognized his iniquity, he knew his error, and thus he said: "Since I know my iniquity."[185] David recognized it, and do you not recognize it? David confesses, and do you deny? Paul calls himself a guilty man, and do you declare that you are innocent? For is this not the highest degree of shame, since we have mingled with so many sins—if only we would pursue a desire for correction . . .[186] Do not again be afraid that the confession of one's sin be considered a penalty. For the good and merciful God is not only accustomed to forgive those who confess their sins, but also to grant rewards to those who correct themselves, if only each would seek to be pardoned of what he knows is not hidden. Thus "speak your iniquities that you might be justified."[187] It is the voice of God who wants to forgive these things; it is the voice of God promising that he desires to wipe out your sin.

12.69. David says, "I have sinned against you, and I have done evil before you,"[188] that is: even if people do not see it, still you see it; even if people who are partakers of sin cannot judge me, still you who have no part in sins are the judge of individuals. To whatever extent guilty thoughts hide in the inmost heart, yet they are still present to you, so that you can say: "Why do you contrive evil in your hearts?"[189] Surely Christ says this. Thus he who knows what is written on the heart can wipe out whatever is inscribed there. To him the saintly David confesses that he sinned not only in himself alone, but even in the first man, whenever the divine precepts are dishonored.

12.70. Here, then, one is able to observe, my beloved brothers, how all heresies end up in the same place even while they attack each other. Thus the Arians, when they separate the pow-

185. Ps 51.3.
186. Schenkl indicates a lacuna in the text.
187. Is 43.26.
188. Ps 51.4.
189. Mt 9.4.

er of the Father and the Son, hasten madly to such a conclusion of the debate that their assertion concurs with the Manicheans. For the Manicheans say that there is one god of the Old Testament and another god of the New Testament. The holy Church condemns that profane assertion when she reads that there is one God: "There is one God, the Father, from whom all things come, and we are unto him, and there is one Lord Jesus Christ, through whom all things are and we ourselves are through him."[190] Indeed, the almighty power of both the Father and the Son is declared one, so that we cannot separate the Father from the grace of the New Testament and likewise we cannot separate the Son from the creation of the world.

12.71. Therefore, let us consider whether the same God is the founder of each testament. For surely we all have sinned in the first man, and through the succession of nature there is also a succession of guilt transmitted from one to all. Against whom, then, have I sinned: against the Father or against the Son? Indeed, against the one who entrusted to me that very command that I violated in not observing it. It was commanded to man that he might taste from all that was in paradise but that he not touch the tree of knowledge of good and evil.[191] Thus Adam is in each one of us. For in him the human condition sinned, because sin passed through one to all.[192] I see the high command entrusted to me, I see what debts I have contracted through dishonesty, when I gorge on the forbidden and impermissible. Hence I owe interest on the lot entrusted to me, because I could not preserve with an inviolate faith the profit entrusted to me, which was accrued from the heavenly commandments.

12.72. We have identified what was entrusted to us; let us identify as well the creditor. For surely it is the right of the creditor to demand payment and to remit his demand. And thus the one who has the right to payment is the same one who remits it. Thus when Christ told me in the Gospels: "Your sins are forgiven you,"[193] do I not recognize that the arbiter of the pardon is the

190. 1 Cor 8.6.
191. Cf. Gn 2.17.
192. Cf. Rom 5.12.
193. Lk 5.20.

same one I know to be the bestower of the loan? Or if it is the Father who lends and the Son who remits, not through unity of power, as we say, but as the Arians maintain, through a difference of power, then would one god lend, while another would remit? In this way the Arians fall in together so that they do not avoid the perfidy of the Manicheans. Hence in saying that there is one good God, let them note into which snares of their own senselessness they fall. If he who lends is good, how is he who has remitted the debt not good? Thus let the Arians belong to the same party as those whose opinions they share. And it is no surprise that the one who began to deviate from the truth entangled himself in the nets of another's error.

12.73. And thus there is one judgment that destroys the tricks of all the heretics, namely that we believe the Trinity to be of one power, majesty, and strength; thus let us not separate the Father from what the Son did, and let us not mark off the Son from what the Father commanded. For thus it will happen that we do not assert that there is one God of the Old and another of the New Testament, but through the unity of power the Son is understood to be in the Father, and the Father in the Son, and the Son grants loans in the Father, and the Father remits in the Son. For the Father also forgives sin; we said already that the Son forgave.

12.74. Understand that the Father forgives: [Scripture] says, "Forgive us our debts, just as we forgive our debtors."[194] Indeed, the Son says this to the Father on our behalf. And he does not say it in this way as though himself he cannot forgive, but he says it that you might understand the unity of their power.

12.75. So if you seek the authority in the Son, he says, "Now you are clean on account of my word, which I spoke to you."[195] He forgives by his speech, he forgives by his rule, but he forgives with an instruction, saying: "Go, see that after this you do not sin."[196] You have an indication of his authority because he forgave what was past; you have an indication of his judgment because he prescribed what was to come.

194. Mt 6.12.
195. Jn 15.3.
196. Jn 8.11.

INDICES

GENERAL INDEX

INDEX OF HOLY SCRIPTURE

Old Testament

New Testament

RECENT VOLUMES IN THE FATHERS OF THE CHURCH SERIES

RUFINUS OF AQUILEIA, *Inquiry about the Monks in Egypt*, translated by Andrew Cain, Volume 139 (2019)

ST. CYRIL OF ALEXANDRIA, *Glaphyra on the Pentateuch, Volume 2: Exodus through Deuteronomy*, translated by Nicholas P. Lunn, Volume 138 (2019)

ST. CYRIL OF ALEXANDRIA, *Glaphyra on the Pentateuch, Volume 1: Genesis*, translated by Nicholas P. Lunn, with introduction by Gregory K. Hillis, Volume 137 (2018)

ST. MAXIMOS THE CONFESSOR, *On Difficulties in Sacred Scripture: The Responses to Thalassios*, translated by Fr. Maximos Constas, Volume 136 (2018)

EUSEBIUS OF CAESAREA, *Against Marcellus and On Ecclesiastical Theology*, translated by Kelley McCarthy Spoerl and Markus Vinzent, Volume 135 (2017)

TYCONIUS, *Exposition of the Apocalypse*, translated by Francis X. Gumerlock, with introduction and notes by David C. Robinson, Volume 134 (2017)

RUFINUS OF AQUILEIA, *History of the Church*, translated by Philip R. Amidon, SJ, Volume 133 (2016)

DIDYMUS THE BLIND, *Commentary on Genesis*, translated by Robert C. Hill, Volume 132 (2016)

ST. GREGORY OF NYSSA, *Anti-Apollinarian Writings*, translated by Robin Orton, Volume 131 (2015)

WORKS OF ST. AMBROSE IN THIS SERIES

Treatises on Noah and David, translated by Brian P. Dunkle, SJ, Fathers of the Church 140 (2020)

Seven Exegetical Works, translated by Michael P. McHugh, Fathers of the Church 65 (1972)

Theological and Dogmatic Works, translated by Roy J. Deferrari, Fathers of the Church 44 (1963)

Hexameron, Paradise, and Cain and Abel, translated by John J. Savage, Fathers of the Church 42 (1961)

Letters 1–91, translated by Mary Melchior Beyenka, OP, Fathers of the Church 26 (1954; reprinted with corrections, 1967; reprinted 1987 and 2001)